THE HANDBOOK TO
Edinburgh

MERCAT PRESS

KEY TO MAP

GENERAL
1. Bus station
2. Edinburgh International Conference Centre
3. Post Office (St James Centre)
4. Royal Infirmary
5. St Mary's Cathedral (Episcopalian)
6. St Mary's Cathedral (RC)
7. Tourist Information Office

ART GALLERIES, HISTORIC BUILDINGS & MUSEUMS
8. City Art Centre
9. Fruitmarket Gallery
10. Georgian House
11. Gladstone's Land
12. Greyfriars Kirk
13. Huntly House Museum
14. John Knox House
15. Lady Stair's House/ The Writers' Museum
16. Museum of Childhood
17. Museum of Scotland
18. National Gallery of Scotland
19. National Library of Scotland
20. National Portrait Gallery
21. Old College
22. Palace of Holyroodhouse
23. Parliament Hall
24. People's Story Museum
25. Royal Museum of Scotland
26. Royal Scottish Academy
27. Scotch Whisky Heritage Centre
28. Scott Monument
29. St Giles Cathedral

CULTURE & ENTERTAINMENT
30. Assembly Rooms
31. Camera Obscura
32. Edinburgh Festival Theatre
33. Filmhouse
34. Fringe Office
35. King's Theatre
36. Netherbow Theatre
37. Playhouse Theatre
38. Queen's Hall
39. Royal Botanic Garden
40. Royal Commonwealth Pool
41. Royal Lyceum Theatre
42. Theatre Workshop
43. Traverse Theatre
44. University of Edinburgh
45. Usher Hall

First published 1981
Revised edition 1987
Second revised edition 1991
This edtion published 1998 by Mercat Press
at James Thin, 53-59 South Bridge, Edinburgh EH1 1YS

© Mercat Press

ISBN 1873644 736

Printed in Hong Kong through World Print Ltd

Acknowledgements

General Editor (1998 edition): Kate Blackadder

Authors
Myrtle Ashmole
Francis Bamford
Geoffrey Baskerville
Alice Beberman
Robin Bell
Joana Blythman
Patricia Brindle
Andrew Brown
Ann Charlish
Jane Collins
Patrick Conyngham
Ank Crees
George Dalgleish
Andrew Dalmayer
Danuta Doroszenko
Allan Edwards
Richard Emerson
Dr R A Fawcett
Gilly Gaskell
John Gifford
Gilly Glass
Veronica Gordon-Smith
Rory Knight-Bruce
Gordon Knott
Carolyn McAdam
Brian McAbe

Sheena McDonald
Janet McEwan
Ann McKim
Bill McLean
Julia Merrick
Glen Murray
Norman Orr
Alice Rugheimer
Ann Simpson
Anne Simpson
Betty Smith
Gill Summers
Kim Tweedie
Hilary Whyte
Andrew Williams
Conrad Wilson
Editors
Liv O'Hanlon
Hope Cohen
Ronald Thompson
Marilyn Bowering
Cartography
Cartografics (Edin) Ltd.
Mark Blackadder
Illustrators
Richard Blakely
Marilyn Bruce

Terry Burton
Bob Chapman
Chris Forsey
Sheila Hadley
Elaine Keenan
Edwina Keene
Sally Launder
Brian Sayers
Rosalind Taylor
Lorna Turpin
David Weeks
Photographers
Walter Bell
Stuart Linsley
Alan McCrone
Sean Hudson
Trevor Wood
John Wyand
Paul Zanre
White House Studios
Picture Research
Judy Garlick
Liz Ogilvy
Design Assistants
Andrew Fenton
Simon Borrough
Paul O'Connor

For their help with the compilation of this edition, the publishers would like to thank: Dawson International; Edinburgh Castle; Edinburgh Fringe Festival Society; Joanna Baker and Jackie Westbrook, Edinburgh International Festival Society; Edinburgh International Film Festival; Amanda Alabaster, Edinburgh Zoological Park; Mitchell Graphics, Glasgow; Deborah Hunter, National Galleries of Scotland; the Trustees of the National Museums of Scotland; Angela Kilday, Royal Botanic Garden; Scottish Tourist Board; Chris Tabraham, Historic Scotland; Unique Events Ltd.; John Macsween

Contents

Introduction

Scotland's capital is one of the most rewarding cities in the world. This guide book is purpose-planned to enable every reader to get the most out of everything Edinburgh has to offer.

Not only is Edinburgh one of the most historic cities of Europe; it is also one of the most attractive, with architectural glories, such as the New Town and Holyroodhouse, vying with treasures of the national heritage, such as the vast art collections of the Scottish National Gallery and the other great museums of the city.

Edinburgh, however, is much more than even this. Its Festival is world-famous. In addition, there is no city sprawl. Within a few minutes' walk of the city centre can be found the small village communities, oases of quiet calm that have existed in Edinburgh for many centuries.

This volume is the ultimate handbook to all this and to much more. Not only does it include an authoritative guide to all the city's major places of interest, lavishly illustrated with hundreds of specially commissioned colour photographs and drawings; it also covers such important areas as shopping, history, literature, folklore and statues and monuments. The book also has a list of useful addresses.

The Edinburgh handbook is an essential reference whether you are a visitor to Edinburgh or live in the city.

The Story of Edinburgh

A town born in trouble and beset by rebellion that has blossomed in maturity to become one of the most distinguished cities in the world.

*E*dinburgh, like Rome, is built on seven hills. But, in the words of Robert Louis Stevenson, 'Edinburgh pays cruelly for her high seat in one of the vilest climates under heaven. She is liable to be beaten upon by all the winds that blow, to be drenched with rain, to be buried in cold sea fogs out of the east, and powdered with the snow as it comes flying southward from the Highland hills. The weather is raw and boisterous in winter, shifty and ungenial in summer, and a downright meteorological purgatory in the spring.'

In this turbulent climate the city's history, too, has been tumultuous. It has been the site of endless warring and argument, fighting and rebellion. But now, after centuries of history—and prehistory—the city stands as one of the most ordered and classically beautiful in Europe.

The fighting began thousands of years ago. The first people to arrive were the stone-using hunters, about 5000 years ago. They were followed by primitive farmers 2000 years later and immigrant Beaker people who brought pottery and metal-working skills from the continent.

The Celts started arriving, too, driven north by successive invasions of England by tribes from lowland Europe, and they caused more warring and battling with the natives. The long brawl of Scottish history had begun.

The Romans came north in AD 78 and defeated Calgacus 'the Swordsman', who, according to Tacitus, said, 'They made a desert, and they called it peace.'

When the Romans left, in the second century, the people were faced with ceaseless invasions. There came Angles, Britons, Vikings and eventually the Scots from Western Ireland—after whom the country takes its name.

The Scots finally took possession of the Castle Rock in Edinburgh when the Northumbrians abandoned their northern border town. In 1018 Malcolm II managed to push the boundary further south and Edinburgh ceased to be a frontier stronghold.

Ironically the Southerners—or a few of them anyway—were welcomed back 50 years later after the Norman invasion of England in 1066. Among the refugees who went to the court of Malcolm III (Canmore) was Margaret, sister of Edgar Atheling, King-elect of England after Harold's death at Hastings.

Margaret and Malcolm married and produced six sons, four of whom in time were kings.

In the meantime Margaret spread her sophisticated Saxon culture and her profound religious thinking among her new people. She lived periodically at Castle Rock and died there. On the rock was built the small Norman chapel in her memory that is Edinburgh's oldest chapel and the oldest ecclesiastical building in use in Scotland.

David I founded the Abbey of Holyrood in 1128. Legend has it that after a miracle prevented his being killed by a stag, the wounded David heard voices telling him to found a house of canons devoted to the Cross. So the abbey was built—by 20 skilled men summoned from France.

In the foundation charter for the abbey, King David refers to 'my town', which suggests that Edwinesburgh was at least from that time regarded as a royal burgh. But, at least 600 years before, the town had been known as Dun Edin, hillfort of Edin.

Along with the abbey the Augustinian canons were given the right to build a burgh (later the Canongate) between the abbey and the royal burgh. Thus the future city began to grow. The burghers or 'burgesses' of this new village were given privileges to sell their wares and buy freely in the Edinburgh market.

David began establishing Anglo-Norman families in Scotland and over the next century they married into the Scottish nobility. Some, like Robert the Bruce (the elder), acquired, along with the earldoms, claims to the throne in these unions of families. The upshot was that by 1286 Scotland was under the rule of a succession of regents as there was total confusion about who was the rightful heir to the Scottish throne.

Edward I was asked to arbitrate for the regents who could come to no decision. It was a chance that the land-hungry Edward had been waiting for. He chose a puppet monarch, John Balliol, whose claim to the throne was through his mother Devorguilla, the foundress of Balliol College, Oxford, in 1250.

Balliol was summoned to Edward's court where he was told to supply money and men for the King's French war but the Scots would have none of it. Four Scottish bishops, four earls and four barons formed a council and in October 1295 concluded the first formal treaty with the French. The alliance was a constant feature of Scottish history over the next 500 years'—so much so that it became known as the 'Auld Alliance'.

Edward was furious and in 1296 sent north an invading army who put the leaderless Scots to the sword, deposed Balliol and looted the Castle. The Stone of Destiny on which Scottish monarchs were traditionally crowned was removed to London from Scone and formed part of the coronation chair in Westminster Abbey. In 1996, however, it was returned, with much ceremony, to Scotland and can now be seen in Edinburgh Castle.

The fighting of these continuing wars of independence with the English came to a pause in 1314 when Robert the Bruce succeeded in defeating the English at Bannockburn. But the English returned to Scotland in 1322, under

Edward II, and sacked Holyrood Abbey. Bruce prevailed and in 1329 gave his principal city its first recorded charter.

The charter gave the burgh and the Port of Leith (for 52 marks, about £34, a year) to the burgesses and recognition to the huddle of rough buildings sheltering by the castle.

After the death of Bruce, Edinburgh was once again in trouble. Edward III plundered the town and King Edward Balliol (who had no real claim to the throne) was forced to surrender his crown and in 1334 gave land in the southern counties to the English Crown.

The Scots were in despair and sent their boy king, David II, to France where he stayed until 1341. He was able to return only when Edward's attention was centred on the French throne and the Hundred Years' War between England and France.

Scotland, impoverished by war and disorder, needed peace and good government. David II gave neither. In fact he brought more war with the English and ended up lodged in the Tower of London. He was liberated by the promise to pay a 100,000 marks ransom to the English.

He returned to Scotland in 1357 and found the country wasted by constant war and the Black Death. There followed an uneasy truce with England and experiments in taxation which gave the burghs of Scotland more power. Edinburgh's port at Leith developed and the burgesses shook off the direct control of the financial officers of the Crown. The town, at last, began to prosper.

---

*R*ecords show that in 1376 the population of Edinburgh was about 2000 with 400 houses. The inhabitants must have been a hardy bunch, well used to adversity. Richard II wrought more havoc in the. city in 1385, and Henry IV laid siege in 1400.

In 1424, James I landed at Leith with his Queen and succeeded to the Scottish throne after 19 years as captive of the English.

The couple received a welcome and as they rode through the town James must have noted the tremendous changes. The houses of the Royal Mile were rising higher. Timber was giving way to stone and thatch was being replaced by sturdier roofing. But thatch had had its advantages. During the endless firings of the town by the English, the Edinburgh townsfolk would load all their goods and chattels on wagons and 'take to the heather'—and they took their highly inflammable roofing with them.

James I made Scotland a place fit to live in again. His legislation was aimed at keeping 'firm and sure peace' throughout the country and building a firm foundation for the economy. He also instituted a system for 'a poor man's advocate' whose services went to 'any poor creature who could not pay for his own defence'.

But James was not without enemies and in 1437 two of his lords, eager to put the Earl of Atholl on the throne, had him stabbed to death at Perth, where he was spending Christmas.

James II became King of the Scots at the age of six. He had been smuggled from the Castle in 1438 in his mother's trunk and it was he who, some years later, gave a charter for a city wall starting below the northeastern rock of the Castle. The King also ordered that his pleasure garden should be swept away to create the Nor' Loch directly below the Castle as a defence.

But he too was killed—by one of his own cannon bursting at a siege of Roxburgh Castle near Kelso in 1460. He was followed by James III who fell foul of his power-grasping lords and was murdered in 1488.

James III had, though, in 1482, rewarded the loyalty of the Edinburgh burgesses by granting the provost and bailies (magistrates) important privileges including the almost complete control over the dispensing of justice—an independence they maintained until the Union of Parliaments in 1707.

At the beginning of the fifteenth century the King, his court, Parliament and courts of justice were itinerant. But by 1483 Edinburgh was the undisputed capital of Scotland: it was the permanent seat of government, and had the principal Royal residence—Holyrood—the central administration and the law courts.

Peace, prosperity and a new enlightenment reigned with James IV. 'There is as great a difference between the Scotland of the old time and the Scotland of today as there is between good and bad', wrote a Spanish diplomat in 1498.

The King had an intelligent and questing mind. He was a patron of the arts and a great promoter of learning: he granted in 1506 a royal charter to the college of surgeons in Edinburgh and founded, among other institutions, the nation's third university at Aberdeen. He also granted a charter to two burgesses of Edinburgh, Andrew Myllar and Walter Chapman, to set up the first Scottish printing press for the purpose of producing books of laws, Acts of Parliament, chronicles, and Mass books 'after our Scottish use'.

This era of renaissance and chivalry—when jousting tourneys were held at the King's Stables area, west of the Grassmarket—came to an end with the tragedy of Flodden.

James had left his Queen and baby to lead his army against the English at Flodden Field in September 1513. The Scottish army was annihilated on the nation's blackest day and many Edinburgh men, including all the bailies, died with their King. When news reached the town lamentation was mingled with fear of immediate invasion by the English.

A town guard was formed and a new wall speedily thrown up, within which plague soon spread through the streets. Not for the next 250 years did the citizens dare build outside this Flodden Wall in case of invasion. Instead they built upwards, as the population increased, storey upon storey to a height of eight or ten floors—unmatched elsewhere in Europe.

James's body was found on the field at Flodden and taken to London where Henry VIII designed a splendid funeral. It did not take place. The royal corpse lay in its lead coffin at Sheen until the house was ruined after the Reformation. Eventually the embalmed head was hacked off by Queen Elizabeth I's master-glazier who used it as a sort of pot until he tired of it!

James's infant son of 13 months became King James V and yet another bloody power struggle between the leading nobles ensued for control of the kingdom. The fight between English and French interests ended with a coup d'état, led by the Earl of Angus, which put James in nominal control at the age of 14.

The King grew to be greedy and brutal and succeeded in making himself the most disliked of the Stuart kings of Scotland.

It was during his reign that the first voices spoke out against Roman Catholicism.

The Roman Church had reigned supreme from the time of Malcolm II until 1559 when, a little behind the rest of Europe, Scotland was overturned by the Reformation. And as in the Reformations elsewhere it was more than a change in the Church system—it was also a political and economic revolt.

The Church in Scotland during the fifteenth and early sixteenth centuries had enormous political influence. It was far richer than the state—the revenue was 15 times that of the Crown—and the taxes it demanded of each commoner nurtured bitterness among the people.

Bishoprics were allocated by favouritism; bastardy, in a church that supposedly practised celibacy, was common among all ranks of the

---

The speech of Edinburgh reflects the city's history as vividly as does its architecture. The stylized Morningside accent can be traced back precisely to 1761, when a group of citizens eager to ditch their Scottish accents engaged as their elocution teacher Thomas Sheridan, father of the playwright-actor and Irishman.

This would not have happened in Glasgow which never shared Edinburgh's Anglophilia or literary aspirations. The everyday speech of the rival cities, only a 45-minute train ride apart, differs widely. A naked child in Edinburgh is 'a bairn in his bare buff' and in Glasgow 'a wean in his bare scuddie'. Truant children in Edinburgh 'plunk or kip school' and in Glasgow they 'dog the school'.

The Scottish language, still in use, is mainly based on an Anglo-Saxon dialect and supplanted the historic language of Gaelic, still spoken in the Highlands and Islands.

Language

Scots was the national language until the Union of the Parliaments in 1707 and has been revived in literature over the past 60 years.

Naturally many common words were carried over from Gaelic, including *loch, glen, bog, cairn* and *caber*, as in 'tossing the caber'. But other words as distinctively Scottish as these are corruptions of continental languages introduced by settlers or traders. The famous Edinburgh cry to warn passers-by that rubbish and slops are about to fall on them from tenement windows above is 'gardyloo' from the eighteenth-century French, 'gare de l'eau', look out for water. The Auld Alliance between Scotland and France, lasting from 1295 until the Reformation, and the presence of numerous Norman settlers accounts for many Scots words of French origin—tartan from *tiretaine*, petticoat tails from *petit gateau* and hogmanay from *aguillaneuf*.

Viking settlers bequeathed Norse words: *flit*, (move), as in 'moonlicht flit'; *lug*, (ear), as in 'lug-hole'; and the various 'k'-ending words, *kirk* for church, and *dike* for ditch.

In its turn the Scots language has given many words to the English-speaking world, including blackmail, canny, uncanny, cosy, eerie, flunkey, fogie, heckle, pony, and spate.

Scottish languages and dialects have survived four centuries of erosion by the English—erosion which can be traced back to the introduction of the English bible in the 1500s. In Edinburgh literary figures faced a particular dilemma: how to preserve their heritage and excel as Britons. The philosopher David Hume and novelist Robert Louis Stevenson solved it by speaking Scots but writing English and Walter Scott combined dialect and Standard English.

priesthood; and priests failed in their pastoral duties.

The records of the Edinburgh Town Council in 1501 show that the civil bailies had to take legal action against the prebendaries of St. Giles to force them to say masses.

Pockets of reform, however, were emerging and found support among the less corrupt clergy and the nobility and merchant classes who controlled the council. The time was ripe for revolution.

Had the next monarch, Mary, been more far-sighted perhaps some of the ferocity of the coming years would have been avoided.

Mary, Queen of Scots, was proclaimed Queen as a seven-day-old child on the death of her father James V in 1542. Two years later Edinburgh was laid waste by Henry VIII's army, the houses put to fire and the countryside for seven miles around was ravaged—Holyrood Palace, the castles of Craigmillar and Rosslyn, the town of Leith and its pier, all were destroyed—simply because the Scots revoked an earlier agreement that Henry's son should be married to the young Queen. It was the beginning of Henry's 'rough wooing'.

The Queen's mother, Mary of Guise-Lorraine, appealed to her native France for help which came. But in return the Scots had to send their little Queen to Paris where she was betrothed, and later married, to the Dauphin. The English, knowing they were out-manoeuvred, left Scotland.

With the English gone, the French stayed on to protect Catholic interests, but all that they achieved was the antagonism of the many Scots who already supported the new doctrines of Calvin and the reformed Church.

The new religious movement was also allowed its leader back—a tactical mistake on the part of Mary of Guise who had been made Regent in 1554. He was John Knox who had fled Scotland in 1547. The teachings of George Wishart had formed the basis for Knox's views on religion and politics. Wishart had set out the first principles of the reformed faith in his writings, stating that the only sources of truth were the Holy Scriptures; that the Pope's role was invalid; and that there were only two sacraments—Baptism and Holy Communion. He was burnt at the stake for heresy.

Knox spent most of his exile in Geneva at the church of John Calvin which Knox described as 'the most perfect school of Christ that ever was on earth since the days of the Apostles'.

The news of his return to Edinburgh on May 2, 1559, spread like wildfire through the streets: 'John Knox is come, John Knox is come' was the message and soon, by way of merchants, travellers, fishermen and shepherds, much of the country knew it too.

John Knox

Knox's powers of oratory stirred first of all the crowds in Perth to violent action—they sacked the town's monasteries, pillaged, burned and looted every friary in the city. Mary of Guise sent her troops into action but underestimated the support the new Church had. She was forced to retire.

Knox and his followers moved on to St. Andrews where Knox preached—lambasting the Church of Rome as the 'synagogue of Satan'; the Pope as that 'man of sin of whom the Apostle speaks'; the Virgin Mary as 'that Roman harlot'; and said the Roman Church was 'polluted with all kinds of spiritual fornication'. Once more the incited crowds ransacked all the religious establishments, burning 'idols' and sharing out the spoils of the friaries.

At the end of June they marched to Edinburgh and the Queen Regent retired to Dunbar. On July 1, 1559, Knox preached his first sermon from the pulpit of St. Giles. It seemed as if, in the space of two months, the Reformation had been achieved, but it was in fact only the start of a battle that continued for 130 years from the establishment of the reformed Church. Knox never witnessed a secure Kirk.

In 1559 a Protestant league known as the Lords of the Congregation turned to the new Queen in England, Elizabeth I, for help in their armed struggle against Mary of Guise. The French, who had heavily fortified Leith, were besieged. Mary, who had left Holyrood and had a sumptuous mansion at Leith, tried to arrange a truce but died of dropsy in June 1560 before it was achieved. The following month, in the Treaty of Edinburgh, it was agreed that all French troops should leave Scotland.

Shortly afterwards the city's council ordered that the Leith fortifications which faced Edinburgh should be demolished 'in caiss strangearis sall at ony time hereafter intruse thameselfs thairin'.

At a meeting in August, Parliament rejected the supremacy of the Pope. /continued on page 18

Folklore

Headless phantoms, body snatchers, witches . . . and a faithful terrier

Edinburgh is a city of ghosts and goblins, horrors and hauntings, with a blood-steeped folklore handed down through the centuries and undoubtedly often embellished in the taverns of the town. There are tales of phantom squadrons of soldiers, a sword-wielding White Lady, a death coach drawn by headless horses, an evil major who rises from the grave, and a 'Street of Sorrow' where the spirits of plague victims roam in anguish.

In a chronicle laden with terror, witchcraft and bloodlust, one of the few folk characters remembered with fondness is Greyfriars Bobby, a Skye terrier who kept a 14-year vigil by his master's grave. He belonged to a shepherd named Jock Gray who died in 1858, and from then until his own death in 1872 Bobby maintained night-and-day watch over the grave in Greyfriars Churchyard. The faithful terrier became a legend in his own lifetime when he was granted virtual freedom of the city in 1867. In 1981 a new memorial was erected to Greyfriars Bobby and a pop song was written about him.

But villainy and nightmarish events predominate in Edinburgh folklore, none more than the story of Major Thomas Weir, Captain of the Town Guard and among the most respected of preachers. In a city-shaking scandal, the major suddenly confessed publicly in 1670 that he had dedicated much of his life to fornication, bestiality and incest with his sister. Outrage succeeded disbelief among his followers, and Weir and his sister were burned at the stake for making a compact with the devil. Long after his death the major was said to ride furiously through Leith— the district of his death—on a

Right Murderers Hare and Burke.
Below right William Burke's execution.
Below Deacon Brodie— the original Jekyll and Hyde.

black horse and then vanish in a burst of flames while lights blazed miraculously in his empty house. Another character with two lives was Deacon Brodie, a city councillor and thriving business-man thought to be the inspiration of Robert Louis Stevenson's famous novel *Dr. Jekyll and Mr. Hyde.* His fortune dissipated by gambling, the Deacon went in for a night-time career of burglary and mayhem which led him to the hangman at the Tolbooth on October 1, 1788, watched by 40,000 people. His moaning apparition is said to linger at the site of the gallows, which he mounted three times before the gibbet worked.

The visitor who might happen to hear midnight drums and the tramping of feet on the Castle Esplanade can take some comfort from the fact that a ghostly squadron of troops has been on the move there since the days of Oliver Cromwell. The mystery column was first seen in 1650, according to legend, by sentries guarding the Castle against a threatened attack by Cromwell's army. Ancient documents also record that in the same area a 'death coach' pulled by fire-flashing steeds races headlong from Holyrood to the Castle to warn of impending disaster.

The White Lady of Corstophine was Christian Nimmo. the wife of a prosperous merchant. who used to meet her lover under a sycamore tree and finally killed him with a sword for being drunk. She was beheaded in 1679, but the story goes that she still appears near the sycamore, wearing a stark white robe and carrying a bloody sword. The Street of Sorrow is Mary King's Close, whose residents were totally wiped out in the bubonic plague of 1645. The street, reputed to be the haunt of headless phantoms, still survives below ground. It can be seen from Cockburn Street, its entrance barred by a gate.

Stories of witchcraft abound in the lore of Edinburgh, where hundreds of women were burned at Castle Hill during a Scottish national frenzy that took 17,000 lives between the years 1479 and 1722. Most were tortured and put to death for allegedly possessing magical powers, including in one instance the supposed ability to sink a royal ship.

But inevitably to the forefront of Edinburgh truthlegend is the case of the murderers William Burke and William Hare, Irish labourers who strangled at least 16 paupers in 1827 and sold the bodies to surgeons for medical research. Hare testified against his companion during a sensational trial and escaped the gallows, but Burke was hanged on January 28, 1829. The story still grips the imagination of Edinburgh people more than the city's most supernatural tales.

Below The grave of Bobby's master 'Auld Jock' is in Greyfriars Churchyard, **Left**. **Above** Nearby is the pub named after Bobby.

The Church

Centuries of bitter struggle established Scotland's spiritual capital

The hundreds of church buildings in Edinburgh give the visitor an immediate impression of a city in which religion has played a vital role—a role which at various times has brought both turbulence and reassurance.

From the year AD 563, when St. Columba established his monastery on the small island of Iona, Scotland was known as Christian, although it took three centuries to convert the native tribes. By the middle of the ninth century Scotland was ruled by a Roman Catholic monarchy, and it remained a Catholic nation until the The

medieval cathedrals, abbeys and parish churches were taken over for Protestant worship or allowed to fall into ruin.

Knox's dream was not only to create a reformed Church in Scotland, and banish 'popery' from her shores, but also to strengthen democracy and to set up a system of comprehensive education. But it was to take almost 130 years of bitter struggle to achieve the religious transition.

Between 1559 and 1689 various monarchs attempted to re-establish the Catholic Church, but the seeds of

reform had been deeply sown, and the Covenanters, as they came to be called, fought steadfastly and determinedly for Knox's principles.

James I and VI and his son Charles I sought to make Scotland's ministers bring their Church more in line with the English Church. In 1637 Charles I attempted to introduce Archbishop Laud's new Service Book, based on the English Book of Common Prayer. As soon as the Dean of Edinburgh began to read from it he was bombarded with folding stools, Bibles and anything else the congregation

Reformation in 1559.

In sixteenth-century Scotland as in other countries, Church reform was urgently needed. Scotland forsook its traditional friendship with Catholic France, allied itself with England instead and accepted a Protestant Reformation. It was a radical reform but carried through without much violence. The

Right Central to the city's religious turmoil, St.Giles' Cathedral is over a thousand years old. **Above** 1787, a meeting of the General Assembly.

could lay hands on. Jenny Geddes, who made her living selling cabbages outside St. Giles, ensured herself a place in history by throwing the first stool and screaming 'Daur ye say mass in my lug!'

The heirs of Knox's reforms were determined that their religious freedom should not be jeopardized by a London monarch. In 1638 they gathered in the small churchyard of Greyfriars that was to become so closely associated with their fight and signed the National Covenant, swearing loyalty to the King but rejecting his rulings on the Church. And in 1643 the Solemn League and Covenant was signed, pledging its subscribers not only to preserve the reformed religion, but also to advance it in England and Ireland.

Meanwhile in England Cromwell deposed and executed Charles I and defeated the exhausted Scottish army. The Restoration of Charles II in 1660 again meant the reformed Church was threatened. It was not until the Dutch Calvinist William of Orange took the English throne in 1688 that Protestantism was assured of its survival. When in 1707 the two crowns were joined by the Act of Union, Scotland was granted its independent legal system, judicature and Church—the Church of Scotland.

But the Church was to suffer yet another blow to its confidence. At the 1843 meeting of the General Assembly nearly 500 ministers walked out to form the Free Church of Scotland, an action which became known as the Disruption.

In 1900 most of the Free Church and other Presbyterian groups joined to become the United Free Church and in 1929 the United Free Church reunited with the Church of Scotland, which had

Left Near the church where he so often preached is John Knox's House, reputed to be the oldest dwelling place in Edinburgh.

Above In the room where he died on November 24, 1572 is a stained-glass window of the fiery reformer.

agreed to abolish patronage by influential landowners. However, there was still a small minority who remained outside the union.

Catholicism had survived, however, chiefly in the northeast and the Highlands. The Relief Act of 1793 gave freedom to worship and own property, and Emancipation in 1829 restored other rights.

During the nineteenth century, great numbers of Irish settled in Scotland, so that now the Roman Catholic Church is strongest in the central belt, especially Clydeside.

But for the Reformed Churches, to which 80 percent of the people belong, Edinburgh has always remained the spiritual capital of the country.

The beautiful 18-year-old Catholic widow of the King of France, Mary, returned to Scotland in August 1561 to this civil and religious upheaval. She was given a tremendous welcome by the people while John Knox protested.

The sad catalogue of trouble with her nobles and her people; her confrontation with Knox and his followers on religion; her marriage to Darnley—by whom she bore James VI and I—and her husband's subsequent murder in an explosion at Kirk o' Field in 1567; her unpopular marriage to Bothwell (who was suspected of Darnley's murder)—were some of the ingredients in the period of turmoil that finally saw Mary imprisoned in Loch Leven Castle. She escaped to England, only to be imprisoned by her cousin Elizabeth, on whose orders she was beheaded.

After Mary's flight a group of nobles formed a coalition known as the Queen's Lords who resented the power of Regent Morton who ruled on behalf of the infant James. Civil war ensued: the governor of Edinburgh Castle, Sir William Kirkcaldy, allied himself with the Queen's men against the Regent. As a result the city suffered badly—the castle was under siege for five years.

It was finally defeated by the guns of the Earl of Morton. Five batteries of English guns opened simultaneously and the David Tower crashed down with men and guns to the rocks beneath, the debris choking the draw-wells of the Castle. Even so 13 hours of hand-to-hand fighting followed before Kirkcaldy surrendered the Castle and was hanged.

So, with the support of Elizabeth I of England, Morton had taken Edinburgh. But the Castle was destroyed and the city was thus undefended. Never knowing who might attack he had the Half Moon Battery built on the foundations of the ruined tower.

Morton was coerced into resignation in 1578 by a group of hostile nobles and James VI took the throne at the age of 17. But his mother, Mary, was still alive, although imprisoned.

The situation in Scotland was attracting international interest. Both Spain and France were uncertain whether to deal with Mary or James. Mary did not want to give up her part as champion of the Catholics but equally her staunchly Protestant son was the one with the power.

Fearing that France was deserting her she promised in 1580 to put herself and her son and the realm under the protection of the Spanish King Philip II—none of which endeared Mary to her English cousin who feared Mary's claim to the English throne. The result was that no one viewed Mary's death in 1587 with any great sorrow—apart from her diminishing band of Scots supporters.

James, well-educated and intelligent, very aware of his position, tried to bring peace to his nation by encouraging his feuding nobles to join forces. But he was also determined to cast himself in the Elizabethan mould and have power over Kirk as well as government.

He was soon in deep trouble with Knox's successor Andrew Melville who declared that there were two kingdoms in Scotland and that James was a subject of the realm of Christ.

The royal argument with the Kirk about power, political and religious, lasted until 1603 by which time James had determined to make the Scots Kirk conform more closely with the English pattern, with the monarch as head of the Church.

Despite his erudition and intelligence, James had a firm belief in sorcery and it is claimed that more witches were burned and strangled on Castle Hill than in any other area of Scotland.

The story of Elsie Peat, in 1589, was not an unusual one. She was an elderly woman who was often seen muttering to herself and so it was suspected that she was in league with the Devil and conversed with him. A 'dookin' was demanded.

It involved the suspected witch being thrown into the Nor' Loch with her thumbs and toes tied. Her innocence would be assured if she sank and drowned but if she floated it would be proof that she was bedevilled. Poor Elsie's voluminous skirts filled with air and she floated—which gave the crowd the excuse they wanted to drag her to Castle Hill to her death.

---

*D*ucking in the Nor' Loch was the punishment for fornication in these times. The tongues of perjurers were bored; drowning followed conviction for theft and when the Loch was drained in 1820 workmen found a large coffin containing the skeletons of a man and a woman, thought to be a brother and sister who were drowned in 1623 for incest.

Although punishments were hard on transgressors, measures were taken to help the poor. The problem of what to do with them came about with the dissolution of the monasteries which had provided alms and hospitals. The town council, carefully distinguishing between the 'deserving and the undeserving', issued badges to the former, authorizing them to beg, and banished the latter from the burgh.

James's capital also had the unsavoury distinction of being the filthiest city in Europe. The houses were crowded closely together round the Castle for protection and because of the terrain which restricted building on the eastern slope.

Streets were narrow, dunghills piled up and, as swine were kept by many householders in pens under the outside stairs, it was little wonder that the plague was rife.

And yet this century saw a new building for

George Heriot's School

the twelfth-century high school and the foundation of the university in 1583; the Scottish Mint was moved from Holyrood and erected in the Cowgate; in lighter vein, James licensed comedians.

It also saw the rise of an Edinburgh goldsmith and friend to the King, George Heriot. He was symbolic of an age of building and of business. The war-torn capital was settling down and fear of invasion was a thing of the past. Foreign trade was increased enormously and goods coming into Edinburgh included fine woollens from England; luxury dress materials from France, Flanders and Italy; wine from Bordeaux and La Rochelle; fruit, vegetables, spices and salt.

Heriot, meanwhile, was making his fortune too. He lent money to the impoverished King and his Danish Queen. 'Jingling Geordie', as he was called, was appointed goldsmith to the Queen in 1597.

When the childless Heriot died in 1612 he left his fortune to the municipality and clergy of Edinburgh to found and endow a hospital for the maintenance and education of fatherless boys and sons of freemen and burgesses in the town.

The school was started in 1628, completed in 1659, and is still one of the most striking buildings in the city, now the co-educational George Heriot's School. His example in founding the hospital for scholars was to be followed by many other prosperous citizens—notably George Watson, James Gillespie, William Fettes, Daniel Stewart, John Watson and Mary Erskine.

In 1603, a dramatic event changed the course of Scottish history. Elizabeth I of England died and James succeeded as her nearest heir. He took the road south and Scotland's capital lost its permanent royal presence and its court. He had promised to return every three years but involvements in England meant that he came back only once, in 1617. His departure meant loss of prosperity to many in the city.

There followed, however, a period of comparative peace until the accession of Charles I in 1625. Charles celebrated his Scottish coronation in Holyrood in 1633, welcomed lavishly by the town council.

But the few following quiet years ended at a service in St. Giles after Charles, who had learned little about the Scots during his visit, had insisted on the use of the English Episcopal service book in the fiercely Presbyterian country.

On July 23, 1637, a crowded congregation in the cathedral—a title Charles had imposed which was to hold officially for only 50 years despite which it is still popularly called that—heard the new Dean of Edinburgh start to use the revised prayer book of the Anglican Church.

Uproar followed. And in the following year the National Covenant, calling on its supporters to renounce popery and resist all religious innovation, was drawn up and signed in Greyfriars Churchyard.

The city and the nation faced more civil war. In England Oliver Cromwell was stirring his forces to war. In 1642 the Scots joined the English parliamentarians in a league and covenant against the King.

The opposition of the Covenanters to the King had been a reaction to his hated religious policies but they were horrified at his execution. Six days after Charles was beheaded his son was proclaimed King in Scotland.

Before his barbarous execution in 1650, organized by the Earl of Argyll, the Marquis of Montrose had kept the royal banner flying in Scotland. He was hanged for three hours at the Mercat Cross in the capital, then his head was cut off and displayed on the Tolbooth; his legs and arms were removed to go on display in other towns, and the remnants of his body were finally buried.

In 1650 Cromwell invaded Edinburgh. The town's defensive wall was no match for Cromwell's military genius and the town council surrendered without a fight after the battle of Dunbar. Cromwell's troops, some of whom were billeted in the half-finished Heriot's Hospital, treated the city and its citizens with severity. But finally a working relationship between the city fathers and the Cromwellian regime emerged.

Despite cooperation with Cromwell there was a general rejoicing when Charles II was restored to the throne in 1660. However, when the celebrations were over the Scots found themselves facing a government committed to Episcopalianism with its structure of government-appointed bishops. The Scots Kirk wanted to elect its own leaders.

In 1662 an edict was issued ordering the use of Episcopal services and ministers were deposed for not doing so.

The Covenanters rose again only to be crushed by General Tam Dalyell and then by James Graham of Claverhouse. Martyrs faced death defiantly at the Grassmarket where their memorial stands, and the Covenanters were finally defeated at Bothwell Bridge in 1679.

About 1000 Covenanters were held in atrocious conditions for five months in what is now Greyfriars Churchyard. The man who led much of the prosecution against them was Lord Advocate Sir George Mackenzie, whose zeal won him the title of 'Bluidy Mackenzie', the man who wrote a standard work on Scottish criminal law and founded the Faculty of Advocates' Library.

Life in the city was not entirely bound up with religious disruption: the Edinburgh Gazette, the city's first newspaper, started publication in 1679; two years later the Merchant Company was founded; in 1681 the Royal College of Physicians was chartered.

---

*I*n August 1686 James granted freedom of worship to Catholics in private houses and the following year Catholics and Quakers were allowed to worship more openly. In an attempt to counteract the unpopularity of these measures he granted the same rights to Presbyterians in June 1687.

But the proclamation failed to reduce anti-Catholic feeling; rather it increased mistrust and suspicion. It also made the Episcopalians feel that their royal support had weakened.

In the meantime, James's elder daughter Mary had married William of Orange who was himself a grandson of Charles I and, more to the point, a Protestant. Here was an alternative heir to those who hated Catholicism.

James's fate was sealed when his wife, Mary of Modena, produced a son—a Catholic heir— in June 1688. The 'Glorious Revolution' began. William's English anti-Catholic supporters encouraged him to come to Britain. James fled to France a month later.

In Edinburgh the mob showed its anti-Catholic feeling by sacking the Catholic Chapel Royal and driving the Jesuits from their school at Holyrood; they also desecrated the tombs of the Stuart monarchs buried there.

Popular feeling and the arrival of Protestant William brought about the reinstatement of the Presbyterian Church government in Scotland.

The Stuarts and their Catholic cause seemed at an end. The rightful heir, James Francis Edward, was denied the Crown—the usurpers William and Mary sat firmly on the throne. This led, in 1715 and 1745, to two uprisings by supporters in Scotland but neither achieved the return of the Stuarts.

By then the nations of Scotland and England had been joined under one parliament.

The union was partly due to a huge financial disaster in Scotland that brought the people to a psychological and monetary misery.

A company was formed in 1695 for trading with Africa and the Indies—an attempt to break the monopoly of the English East India Company. It was a cause that excited the Edinburgh imagination and in which William Paterson, who conceived the idea of the Bank of England, was a driving force. Eager subscribers put up 400,000 Scottish pounds.

A group of Scots colonists were landed on the coast of Darien, possibly the unhealthiest part of the Isthmus of Panama, and after a few years of unprofitable struggle were finally driven out by the Spanish in 1700.

The venture was the worst commercial undertaking in Scotland's history. There was no glory and the loss of pride and money were enormous. Scotland's exchequer and store-houses were empty and the challenge to English mercantilism was a mockery. Nine ships that the company had bought or chartered were lost; the huge capital had disappeared without profit and 2000 men, women and children had died in Darien, been abandoned in Spanish prison, or become indentured servants to English colonies.

When news of the Darien Scheme reached Edinburgh the mobs took to the streets to vent their fury at their lost hopes and fortunes and their wrath against the English who had failed to help the colonists in favour of keeping on good terms with the Spanish who had claimed Darien. The disastrous scheme so impoverished Scotland that many concluded the nation would only be successful financially if it had equal trading rights with England. In 1707 the Scottish Parliament cut its own throat by passing the Act of Union.

It was finally ratified in the Edinburgh Parliament by 110 votes to 67 and when the treaty passed through Westminster without opposition the Parliaments of Scotland and England ceased to exist. In their places was one Parliament of Great Britain with 513 English representatives and 45 Scottish in the House of Commons. In the Lords 16 elected Scottish peers would sit.

Some independence remained: Scotland kept the Kirk, the system of education, the courts and legal code, and the royal burghs with their special privileges. However, the administration did move south and with it Scotland's political, cultural and economic force.

'Bought and sold for English gold' sang the Jacobite ballad of the day and, indeed, Queen Anne paid £20,000 to reduce the arrears of the Scottish government; bribes and inducements had no doubt passed hands during the long arguments. But without the union and the financial benefits it brought it is possible that Scotland would not have survived.

The General Assembly and the Court of Session stayed in Edinburgh, but the men of influence and talent moved to England. Streets like the Canongate, where the nobility had lived, declined.

But the city did not die: horse racing was still popular, cock fighting at Leith Links and other venues was a public obsession and concerts were held at Bailie Fyfe's Close every Saturday during the winter. Gentlemen exercised themselves playing golf, tennis and shooting bows and arrows.

The Jacobites revived Catholic hopes in 1715 and 1745 but their efforts never achieved return of the Stuarts and a Catholic monarchy. In 1715 they tried to put James, the 'Old Pretender', on the throne. A raid on the Castle was beaten off and the uprising, with little support in southern Scotland, died in spite of French backing.

It had never been easy to maintain order in Edinburgh and over the years various attempts were made to control crime and riot. At the end of the seventeenth century the city had appointed a city corps of guards, nicknamed by the people as the 'Toun Rats'.

Their reputation was never good but it sank to an all-time low, along with the name of the town's magistrates, when the Edinburgh mob took to the streets once more in April 1736.

It was then that the Grassmarket became the scene of a virtual lynching which has gone down in the history books as the Porteous Riot. Captain John Porteous was a Captain of the town guard who had the unsavoury reputation of relishing public executions. On April 14, a demonstration broke out when he presided over the hanging of a popular smuggler named Andrew Wilson. Wilson was highly regarded for having accepted full personal responsibility for robbing an excise officer, and thus allowing an equally guilty colleague to go free. Members of the town guard opened fire on the crowd, killing nine people and wounding many others. In the outcry that followed, Porteous was put on trial for murder and was condemned to death by the High Court. But on September 7 word spread through the city that he was about to be reprieved by royal decree. An angry mob broke into the Tolbooth jail, dragged Porteous out in his nightgown and hanged him from a pole which marked a dyer's premises, close to the scene of the shooting. The pole, symbolizing perhaps the most dramatic example of Grassmarket law and legend, stood in front of Hunter's Close on the south side of the rectangle. Porteous's body was laid to rest in nearby Greyfriars Churchyard. Except for a post inscribed P. 1736, his grave remained unmarked for 237 years. Then, in 1973, a headstone replaced the post, providing the extra information: 'John Porteous, a Captain of Edinburgh City Guard, murdered 7 September 1736. All passion spent.'

Rebellion and violence came again to Scotland with the second Jacobite uprising of 1745 which sought to place Bonnie Prince Charlie, the 'Young Pretender', on the throne. When news of his arrival from France reached the city a band of 1000 men was raised to defend the town. The 'Young Pretender's' army of Highlanders camped in Holyrood Park and a large crowd went out to meet the Catholic Prince, whose official recognition lay with the Pope.

The Highlanders easily entered the city and subsequently the Lord Provost Archibald Stewart had to face trial for failing to offer stiff enough resistance to the Jacobites. Their cause, though, died on the moors of Culloden the following year and the Prince fled into humiliating exile.

His supporters paid heavily for their loyalty. Apart from the blockades of the navy and revenge of the English army which hounded Culloden's survivors, about 120 of the prisoners were executed—peers by the axe and the others by the rope. A further 1150 were banished or transported and the fate of another 700 is still unknown.

Politically Scotland was also repressed. The office of Secretary of State was abolished and the post of Lord Advocate came to represent royal power in Scotland under the direction of the Secretary of the Northern Department.

Rigorous laws were passed against Episcopalians; the wearing of kilts and playing of bagpipes were banned. Some lands were annexed to the Crown.

Trustees were appointed to run the forfeited estates of Jacobite supporters and order was restored; schools were established; land tenure for crofters was improved; cottage industries were introduced and the Scottish economy began to flourish. /continued on page 26

The Law

A unique tradition marries the two great schools of European law

*N*ot Proven—it's a court verdict you will not hear in any other part of the world. But it symbolizes a tradition of fiercely independent Scottish law born out of repeated wars with England and the Auld Alliance with France. Often quirky, sometimes at variance with the legal system in other areas of the United Kingdom, the law of Scotland stands proudly alone.

In no other part of Britain can a jury declare that the case against a defendant has not been proved. Such a verdict means simply that there was insufficient evidence to establish that the accused person was guilty or not. He or she leaves court without penalty but not without suspicion. It is a unique finding, in that few people who stand in the dock elsewhere ever walk away without being declared guilty or innocent.

'Not Proven' undoubtedly carries a kind of stigma—the notion that someone has been clever enough to get away with something—but the Scots regard it as merely a sign of commonsense. Perhaps there were genuine doubts back in June 1852, when a truly sensational trial took place in Edinburgh. High-born Madeleine Smith, her story re-enacted a hundred times in books and films, stood accused of murdering her French lover with liberal doses of arsenic. The verdict was 'Not Proven'—and Madeleine went on to live to a ripe old age in the United States.

Between its close ties to France and proximity to England, Scotland has created its own coherent legal system incorporating Roman law, feudal law, canon law, special customs and local practices. A wealth of experience went into the Scottish law first defined in the seventeenth century by Sir James

Dalrymple, later Viscount Stair. His formula persisted through the 1707 Act of Union with England to remain the basis of the law of the land. But that was also when Parliament in London began infusing its own flavour.

Critics still feel that acts of Parliament do not always take account of Scottish precedent, one of the mainstays of the system practised north of the border. The courts will always pay high regard to judicial opinions passed down in similar cases decided many years earlier.

Until 1820 the bulk of Scottish law owed its origin to those Roman regulations, feudal laws and ancient customs—in common with France and Germany and most of the then developed world, but distinct from the great common law systems of England, the United States and the majority of Commonwealth countries. Since then, Scottish law has moved away from its Roman base and taken a middle ground between the continental system and the common law of England.

In modern times Scotland has administered its own criminal law since 1926, although civil law ultimately comes under the jurisdiction of the House of Lords at Westminster. The London government appoints a Lord Advocate, usually a lawyer-politician, who represents the state in all criminal proceed-ings. These range from Scotland's supreme criminal tribunal, the High Court of Justiciary, to local hearings in Sheriff's and District courts. Most High Court cases are heard by a judge sitting not with 12 but 15 jurors—another unique aspect of Scottish law.

The Edinburgh Sheriff's Court is now in Chambers Street.

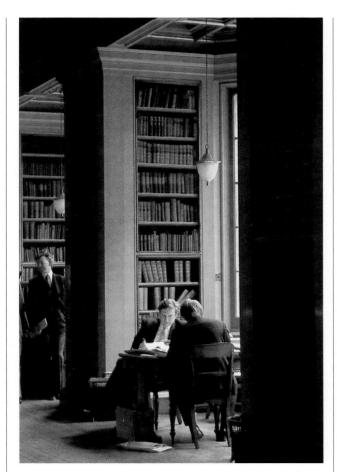

Far left The Great Hall of Parliament Hall, home of the Scottish Parliament until 1707 and now a meeting place for lawyers from the adjacent courts. The great stained glass window dates from 1532 and shows James V, one of the great protectors of Scottish law, together with Abbot Mylne, first Lord President of the Court of Session.
Above The Advocates' Library, founded in 1682. It now houses the legal collection of the National Library. **Right** Examples from the library's valuable collection of books and documents.

Literature

Great men of letters rose from the tradition of ancient Celtic bards

*E*dinburgh remembers its writers and poets. And is remembered by them. Its first poet, the sixteenth-century William Dunbar, described the city as 'nobill toun'; Burns as 'Edina! Scotia's darling seat'; Scott as 'mine own romantic town' and for Stevenson, far away in Samoa, it was 'a precipitous city' whose gusty winds could make it 'scowling'.

Its characters, too, are recalled. The merchants of Dunbar's days were castigated by him for their wares which cluttered the streets and fouled the air with the 'stink of haddockis and of scattis' (skate). Allan Ramsay portrayed Lucky Spence, the madame who kept a brothel in the Canongate of the eighteenth century; Stevenson found inspiration for Dr. Jekyll and Mr. Hyde in Deacon Brodie, a respectable city councillor by day and burglar by night; Conan Doyle modelled Sherlock Holmes on the Edinburgh surgeon Dr. Joseph Bell.

The Celts have a long and revered literary heritage in their myths, legends and bardic poetry but an international seal of approval was set on the capital in the late eighteenth and early nineteenth centuries.

It was, as Smollett said, 'a hotbed of genius', when the brilliant circle of literati lived and met under the acknowledged leadership of David Hume (1711-1776), historian, philosopher, religious sceptic and humanitarian. With him were the likes of Adam Smith (1723-1790), economist and author of *The Wealth of Nations*; Adam Ferguson (1723-1816), philosopher and historian; William Robertson (1721-1793), historian and principal of Edinburgh University and Dugald Stewart (1753-1828), philosopher.

They started the popularity of literary clubs such as the Easy Club, The Cape Club and the Speculative Society, which met at the taverns tucked away in the wynds and lanes of the Old Town. They frequented the booksellers like William Creech, Burns' Edinburgh publisher, and Blackwood's 'great lounging book-shop'.

Sir Walter Scott's signature and the small statue of the author reading which marks the house in Castle Street where he moved in 1801. The printing press below is the one James Ballantyne used to print the first editions of Scott's Waverley Novels.

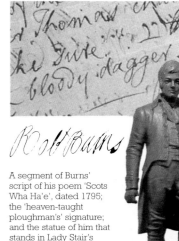

A segment of Burns' script of his poem 'Scots Wha Ha'e', dated 1795; the 'heaven-taught ploughman's' signature; and the statue of him that stands in Lady Stair's House, a museum dedicated to three great Scottish men of letters.

There was Robert Fergusson, born in 1750, who died of drink and madness in an asylum at 24, hailed by Burns as 'my elder brother in the Muse' and by others for his part in the revival of Scottish poetry.

Burns spent time in the city, lionized by the literati as 'the heaven-taught ploughman', amused by his landlady's complaints about the prostitutes in the flat above.

Edinburgh also attracted, over the centuries, many other writers: Daniel Defoe was here in 1710 as a government spy sent to report on Scottish attitudes to the recent Act of Union and later wrote about the 'stench and nastiness' of the Old Town; Oliver Goldsmith studied medicine here but was more interested in the social life and beauty of Scots women; Dr. Johnson visited on his way to the Hebrides with his biographer James Boswell and gave the Scots an opportunity to get their own back on him after all his insults about them.

Wordsworth, an admirer of Walter Scott, stayed as Scott's guest after a tour of the Highlands; Thomas Carlyle attended the university and trained for the ministry; Thomas de Quincey contributed to *Blackwood's Magazine* and Blackwood published his *Confessions of an English Opium Eater* in 1822; J. M. Barrie was at the university; and John Buchan became Lord Chancellor of the university.

Of all native Scots writers Sir Walter Scott and Robert Louis Stevenson are probably best known. Scott was born in 1771 and as a sickly child read poetry and romances when confined to bed. He was a prolific writer and while he wrote his old tomcat and his favourite dog, Maida, kept him company. He wrote long into the night, by hand, page after page and, in one period of three weeks, completed the last two volumes of *Waverley*.

Stevenson was another invalid child and his physical weakness drove him from Edinburgh to the sunnier shores of the South Pacific. But childhood memories remained with him and led to his collection of poems, *A Child's Garden of Verses*, with the much-loved Leerie the Lamplighter.

The city still inspires its authors: Muriel Spark, born in 1918, was educated in Edinburgh and her novel *The Prime of Miss Jean Brodie* might well have been based on her own school—James Gillespie's School for Girls. The Scottish Renaissance Movement of the 1920s and 1930s injected new life into poetry with the appearance of writers like Hugh MacDiarmid. The Abbotsford Bar in Rose Street, the Cafe Royal near Register House and Milne's Bar in Hanover Street became meeting places for the new literati—men like Sydney Goodsir Smith (1915-1975), Robert Garioch (1909-1981) and Norman MacCaig (1910-1996), who have all written about their lives in the capital. Irvine Welsh is the figurehead of a dynamic new group of Scottish writers. His first novel *Trainspotting* (1993) 'defines the chemical generation' and has become a cult bestseller and film. Ian Rankin and Quintin Jardine have each set a series of detective novels in and around Edinburgh.

This statue of Robert Louis Stevenson stands in his boyhood home at 17 Heriot Row, and the handsome brass plaque that marks the spot is inscribed with a verse from his children's poem 'The Lamplighter'. The author died at the age of 44 in Samoa where he lived for three years presiding like a native chief in his adopted land.

Edinburgh was now beginning to burst at the seams. Around the time of 'the forty-five', conditions for the 51,000 citizens were very mixed. One estimate shows that ten percent lived in houses in the streets, 60 percent in the tight closes, 20 percent in dugouts or sheds and the remaining ten percent straggled homeless through the streets, seeking shelter wherever they could.

The city buildings of Edinburgh were still concentrated around the spine of the High Street and down the slopes of the Grassmarket and Cowgate. By the middle of the seventeenth century high tenements were standard, pushing upward, restricted from spreading outwards by the ancient city walls.

Flats of six or seven rooms were common— with a great mixture of tenants in any one building. Merchants and bankers lived in this sort of building on higher floors and the poorer people took the dark ground floors.

As a result of this gross overcrowding—one story tells of 11 adults crammed into one room— small developments were starting to open outside the walls—like Nicholson and George Squares to the south.

*T*he push came from an extraordinary visionary, George Drummond, six times Lord Provost of Edinburgh.

In 1752 he was largely responsible for drawing up 'Proposals for carrying out certain public works in the City of Edinburgh' which in 7500 words outlined the overcrowded conditions of the city and suggested an extension of the town.

He then, in September 1753, as Grand Master of the Scottish Freemasons, laid the foundation stone of the Royal Exchange in the High Street (the building later became the City Chambers). He had also been instrumental in launching in 1729 an appeal fund for an infirmary which grew into one of the world's greatest teaching hospitals, the Royal Infirmary, now standing in Lauriston Place.

Ten years after the 'Proposals' were published, Drummond managed to persuade the town council to hold a competition for a plan of a new town on the far side of Nor' Loch.

It brought in six plans and the winner, announced in 1766, was 23-year-old James Craig, son of an Edinburgh merchant, who won a gold medal and the freedom of the city—as well as overnight fame.

His plan was symmetrical; a gridiron of three main streets balanced at either end by a square. Today its shape is basically unaltered from Princes Street to George Street and Queen Street, although the houses which once lined Princes Street have all but vanished.

St Giles and the Old Town

On the original plan Princes Street was named St. Giles Street but the name was altered. In the end the whole plan was dedicated to the House of Hanover and claimed to represent the new union between England and Scotland.

The first houses of the New Town were built in Thistle Court—where they still stand—and by 1774 the foundation stone of the magnificent Register House was laid. The designs for the building were drawn by the distinguished and fashionable Adam brothers.

Robert Adam was commissioned to provide a plan and complete elevations for Charlotte Square and, in doing so, one of the world's gems of Georgian architecture was started in 1792.

The New Town was largely built of grey Craigleith stone in a neo-classical style, influenced by the Greek revival then holding the interest of the nation's intellectuals.

It gave enormous opportunities to the architects of the time—like the Adam brothers, William Playfair, William Sibbald and Robert Reid and James Gillespie Graham—whose fame spread throughout Britain.

Reid, Sibbald and Playfair made their mark on the second phase of the New Town where the grand terraces of Royal and Regent Terraces were built and the monuments on Calton Hill sprang up.

'Forty years saw the Old Town changed as respects population', wrote Robert Chambers the publisher. 'One after another its nobles and gentry, its men of the robe, its writers, and even its substantial burghers, had during that time deserted their mansions in the High Street and Canongate, till few were left.'

The Lord Justice Clerk's house was occupied by a woman who sold furniture, the Lord President's by a French teacher, a duke's house taken over by a wheelwright—changed days indeed.

It was the town where James Boswell practised as an advocate; where Robert Fergusson died in Edinburgh's Bedlam at the age of 24 leaving some remarkable poetry and leaving another poet, Robert Burns, to appreciate its excellence and arrange for a headstone on Fergusson's grave in Canongate Kirkyard.

It was said you could stand at the Mercat Cross and take 'fifty men of genius and learning by the hand'. And yet it was a town where the household slops (and worse) were hurled from upper windows into the open gutters below.

Figures of genius were many and varied in this, Scotland's golden age, when Edinburgh earned a reputation as a brilliant intellectual and artistic centre, prompting even the cynical Voltaire to write: 'It is from Scotland we receive rules of taste in all the arts from the epic poem to gardening'.

There was the judge Lord Kames, a philosopher and jurist; William Creech, bookseller and publisher and one-time Lord Provost; David Hume, the philosopher, who went to university at the age of 12; Adam Smith, author of *The Wealth of Nations*; Henry Raeburn, the painter; Francis Jeffrey, founder of *The Edinburgh Review*, Walter Scott and Burns among the writers.

It was the time when Scotland, with a population a quarter of England's, had four universities to England's two; schools, hospitals and technical colleges were founded and produced brilliance in every direction; James Watt with his steam engine; Simpson and his discovery of chloroform —inventions and discoveries seemingly endless.

In 1790 the First Statistical Account of Scotland was under way and the publisher Creech was given his say in a comparison of Edinburgh in 1763 and in 1783.

Although he might be accused of a little exaggeration, he reported that in 1763 'five or six brothels and a very few of the lowest and most ignorant order of females skulked about the streets at night' but 20 years later 'brothels increased twenty-fold and women of the Town more than a hundred-fold'.

'Housebreaking was extremely rare' in 1763 but 1783 saw that 'housebreaking theft and robbery were frequent. Many of the crimes were committed by boys whose ages prevented them from being objects of capital punishment.'

Although bookselling was his trade, Creech was interested in all sorts of shops. 'Perfumers have splendid shops in every street. Some of them advertise they keep bears, to kill occasionally for greasing ladies' and gentlemen's hair, as superior to any other animal fat.'

Yet amid all the brilliance of the golden age which also brought a revival of pride in things Scottish and in the Gaelic language, there was still a shortage of grain in the city markets in 1800 and talk of famine among the poorer citizens as the population steadily increased. By 1811 it was 103,143 and, although the city increased in size

George Street

from its original site of 138 acres (55 ha) to several thousand acres, the Old Town was still grossly crowded and those who could not afford to move to the New Town suffered gruesome conditions.

The new century was not a peaceful one in the early years. New Year riots broke out at the end of 1811 and a policeman and clerk were killed: three youths hanged in consequence.

In 1824 one of the most disastrous fires ever to hit the city broke out. On November 15 smoke and flames burst from a house in Assembly Close off the High Street and spread rapidly to engulf the whole tenement. And before the fire was out, the entire area from the High Street below St. Giles to near the Tron Kirk and down the hill to the Cowgate was devastated. Shortly afterwards, the first municipal fire brigade in the world was founded under the direction of James Braidwood.

The city was rocked by public scandal in the late 1820s, with the Burke and Hare murders. William Burke faced trial for murdering to provide bodies for the anatomy classes run by Dr. Robert Knox. Burke and partner first supplied the body of a tenant from Hare's lodging house who had died of natural causes but soon turned to murder to provide the anatomy subjects.

Hare turned King's Evidence and, after Burke's execution in 1829, a crowd of 24,000 went to see his body on the dissecting table at Surgeon's Hall. His skeleton is still preserved in Edinburgh University's Medical School.

The mob reacted with their customary speed and violence to the scandal and gathered to throw stones and sticks at Dr. Knox's house. They also coined a ditty:

Down the close and up the stair
But an' ben wi' Burke and Hare
Burke's the butcher, Hare's the thief,
Knox the man that buys the beef.

Through pioneers like Dr. Knox, however, Edinburgh had a huge reputation for medicine and hospitals. But balanced against this is a sorry tale of disease and neglect.

The scourge through the years was smallpox. Inoculation was practised as far back as 1745 in the city but between 1740 and 1742 a smallpox outbreak claimed 17 percent of all deaths in Edinburgh. Typhus fever also struck, and cholera outbreaks in 1831-1832 and 1838-1840 increased public concern about the squalor in the dark insanitary houses in the Old Town.

There was pressure for the appointment of a public health officer but it was only after the collapse of a tenement in the High Street in 1861, which killed 35 inhabitants, that the town council were forced to act.

Dr. Henry Littlejohn took the post, which he

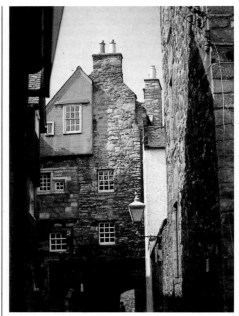

Bakehouse Close

held for the next 46 years, in 1862. Three years later he produced his first report in which he proved that Edinburgh's high death rate, for adults and babies, and all the disease was due to the insanitary and appallingly cramped conditions.

His recommendations for action were to pave and drain the closes; improve accommodation by introducing water and gas, cleaning common stairs and repairing houses; limit the number of people in each apartment; remove tenements that were in danger of collapse; and open up the worst of the narrow closes.

His ideas were backed by the Lord Provost William Chambers who did much to implement them and, by degrees, conditions improved.

The greatest impact the Industrial Revolution had on Edinburgh was probably in transport. The efforts of Thomas Telford, the engineer, and John Macadam, who invented his road surfacing, improved travel on the roads and the building of canals made transport speedier.

But it was the railways that were the most effective innovation. Edinburgh's first line was planned by Robert Stevenson to connect the coalfields of Midlothian with Edinburgh and the sea. It opened in 1831 and by 1834 passenger services were running.

Traffic on the Glasgow–Edinburgh line started moving in 1842 when the Edinburgh–Newhaven route also opened. Edinburgh and Berwick were connected to London in 1846. 'Railway mania' had begun. The Granton to Burntisland line saw the world's first train ferry—over the Forth.

Horse tramcars arrived in the city in 1871 and the system spread until, by 1891, there were 300 cars and more than 1000 horses in operation.

Cable cars were introduced in 1888 and ran down Hanover Street and Dundas Street to Canonmills and Goldenacre. Another opened two years later along the Stockbridge route. They were pulled by cables driven by a power station in Henderson Row.

Eventually the system, the fourth largest of its kind in the world, extended throughout the city with four power stations driving 52 miles (84 km) of cables through a 26-mile (42 km) network of routes.

Edinburgh had prospered with the Victorian industrial expansion: there was brewing, distilling, printing, baking and confectionary, the manufacture of glass and chemicals.

The city also took to the morality and formality of the Victorians which appealed to the ethics of Knox's followers. But there was still dissension in the Kirk. In 1843 four hundred minis-ters took about a third of the Kirk's members to establish the Free Church because they felt that the Church of Scotland had become too liberal, And again in 1892 a group split away—this time from the Free Church to set up the Free Presbyterian Church on the grounds that the Free Church had become insufferably liberal!

Morality was also the basis for the enormous support that William Ewart Gladstone found in his father's native Scotland. He conducted his Midlothian campaign in the city in 1879, and paid for the return of the Old Mercat Cross to its present site.

Gladstone also toyed with the idea of all-round devolution for Britain and, although his energies were devoted to Irish Home Rule, the Scots responded with enthusiasm. Nationalism had already been inflamed by the vast numbers of English troops which virtually occupied Scotland after the uprisings of 1715 and 1745 and it was helped along by the intellectual interest in Scottish language and history of writers like Burns and Scott.

In the 1880s a demand was made—and met—for a Scottish Secretary to deal exclusively with Scottish affairs, and a Scottish Home Rule Association sprang up.

From 1906 onwards there was an almost annual

Pier at Newhaven

Government of Scotland Bill but it was never successful because the parties in power failed to push it through Parliament. Had World War I not intervened it is possible that the government would have been forced to honour its pledge.

The Scots started a New Home Rule Association in 1917 and by 1928 the National Party of Scotland was formed. But it did not meet with quite the popular enthusiasm its leaders had hoped for, perhaps because it was too left wing and wanted total separation from England.

The agitation over the years did lead to the move of the Scottish administration to Edinburgh from Whitehall in 1939 and gradually, after World War II, the administrative powers were widened.

The Scottish National Party won its first by-election in 1945, only to lose the seat in the subsequent general election a few weeks later. It had to wait another 20 years or so before another Nationalist sat in Westminster. In 1974 there were seven SNP members in London and it seemed that the time was ripe for a referendum on devolution. It was taken in 1979 and the feeling was such that Edinburgh spent £3 million on converting the old Royal High School, built in 1825 on Calton Hill, for the Scottish Assembly. The vote was indecisive and the school remains empty. However, devolution remains a major political issue.

While Scottish nationalism flowered, literature and the arts blossomed too. Between the two World Wars, Edinburgh was still a great city for bookshop browsing and artists and writers were busy in the city—busy enough to start a 'Scottish

Universities

*E*stablished under royal charter by James VI in 1583, Edinburgh University is the sixth oldest in Britain. Beginning with ninety freshmen, it now has over 15,000 full-time students, and over 50,000 members of its General Council (living former students), Its size is obvious: it is spread throughout the city, making it the largest private owner of buildings in Scotland.

The university's founding principles were based on the firm doctrines of Calvinism and students were encouraged to attend the university to gain 'the manners of morality and virtue'. This was to be achieved by study within the college but residence 'in the presence of their friends'. Thus it was not until 1887 that Edinburgh's— and Scotland's—first hall of residence was established. This hall, Patrick Geddes (at number 2 Mound Place) is occupied by students today.

The university has always been non-collegiate (there is no system of colleges) and offers no multitude of lawns, chapels and stairways. Rather, it is the buildings in which the students were taught, the austere Georgian proportions of the Old College (on the corner of Chambers Street and South Bridge) and the Medical School (in Teviot Place), that provided the architectural and educational heart of the university.

In 1582, the Town Council purchased the Kirk o' Fields on which the Old College now stands. From the outset the Council financed building and teaching alike, beginning a long involvement with the university. In 1789, the university was granted an independent coat of arms but it was not until 1858 that autonomy from the Council was achieved.

From the beginning, university students took a four-year MA degree in the General Arts. Only then could they enter the Divinity School—the only other faculty. It was only later that Medicine (1705) and Law (1722) were established.

Originally, Edinburgh adopted the regent system of teaching, taken from the great university of Leyden. Each student was assigned a regent (or tutor) who taught him throughout his degree. This system was replaced in 1708 by the professorial system of today.

The demands upon the students were exacting. There were no set examinations; the regent or professor who did not examine his students daily was failing in his duty. 'Dictates' (given at dictation speed) began at five am (six am in midwinter) and continued until evening. The only break was two hours of compulsory exercise— the regent's parade—in mid-afternoon. The students were forbidden to attend the public hangings in the Grassmarket. Even funerals—except those of eminent councillors—were deemed too frivolous for attendance. Only the month of August was permitted for vacation. Calvin-ism reigned supreme.

This rigorous system of education did not, however, subdue all students. In 1680, Robert Brown, an Englishman, publicly burnt an effigy of the Pope in the Kirk o' Fields. This protest was directed at the Catholic heir-presumptive Duke of York who was in residence at the Palace of Holyroodhouse. The Old College and Town Guards could not prevent a student revolt from supporting Brown. The Privy Council charged the college with treason and closed it down. Brown was expelled. From this incident arose a pledge, which students must sign today upon matriculation, agreeing to accept expulsion if

Renaissance' in the 1930s with poets like Hugh McDiarmid and Albert Mackie bringing pride back to things Scottish. And while writers wrote through the 1930s and 1940s a new idea in cultural expression came to the capital in the form of the International Festival of the arts.

It was launched in 1947 under the leadership of the Lord Provost Sir John Falconer and was an act of inspiration and faith after the gloomy days of World War II. It brought, as intended, international stars and companies to the city. Now the Festival attracts about 100, 000 visitors each year and, in turn, the visitors support the town's tourism, restaurants, shops and hotels.

Dr. Johnson once wrote that the best sight for a Scotsman was the road to England. It is now a road that takes the financial and trading talents of the Scots all over the world.

Traders like Jardine Mathieson, of Hong Kong fame, had their beginnings in the city. Edinburgh is now a major centre for financial institutions to have their headquarters, some housed in impressive new buildings in Lothian Road. A newly-built conference centre in nearby Morrison Street has also transformed the look of the area.

The capital is flourishing and still has great beauty. And it retains an impression of mystery and magic of which Robert Louis Stevenson wrote: 'There is no Edinburgh emigrant, far or near, from China to Peru, but he or she carries some lively pictures of the mind, some sunset beneath the Castle cliffs, some snow scene, some maze of city lamps, indelible in the memory and delightful to study in the intervals of toil.'

---

they break the university laws or bring it into disrepute.

Throughout the nineteenth century the university continued to expand. The Divinity School, now the largest in Britain, was rehoused in the New College, where the assembly of the University meets annually each May.

The nineteenth century Prime Ministers Lord Palmerston and Lord John Russell (son of the Duke of Bedford) studied here. Other students included Mungo Park, James Boswell, Thomas Carlyle, Oliver Goldsmith, Charles Darwin, Sir Arthur Conan Doyle, Sir Walter Scott and Robert Louis Stevenson. David Hume was refused a professorship for publicly professing disbelief in God. From 1920-1929, successive Rectors of the University were David Lloyd George, Stanley Baldwin, Sir John Gilmour and Winston Churchill. Churchill had failed in his first Rectorial election in 1905. Their predecessors included the Liberal Prime Ministers Gladstone and Lord Rosebery. University Chancellors have included the literary figures Sir James Barrie, Bt., and Lord Tweedsmuir (John Buchan). HRH the Duke of Edinburgh is the present Chancellor.

Today, Edinburgh University's reputation in the fields of medicine and science remain pre-eminent. The modern science complex at Kings Buildings undertakes far-reaching and invaluable research, whilst many an advocate has studied within the traditional grandeur of the Old College. If the university offers no immediately recognizable identity perhaps the answer lies in its size. For character, humour, endeavour and achievement abound here—even if the university chooses to keep quiet about it.

The main part of Heriot-Watt University stands in the woodlands of Riccarton estate on the western side of the city. Founded in 1821 as a school providing evening classes in basic science for young artisans, it later took the name of the Watt Institution and School of Arts in memory of James Watt, developer of the steam engine. From a rented hall in long–demolished Adam Square, it moved to premises in Chambers Street where, in 1885, it became the Heriot-Watt College as a result of an amalgamation with George Heriot's hospital. The college achieved university status in 1966.

Edinburgh's third university started life as Napier College of Science and Technology (called after the mathematician John Napier). It became a polytechnic and then got university status in 1992. It now has campuses and halls of residence all over Edinburgh.

Thomas Shepherd's nineteenth-century view of Edinburgh University.

Medicine

From the horrors of plague rose a city renowned for medical research

For centuries Edinburgh has had the reputation of being a great centre of medical progress—but it was once one of the unhealthiest, dirtiest cities in Europe. From the earliest times disease was rife and the streets were clogged with refuse and sewage tossed at night from high tenement windows to the cry of 'gardyloo'.

In 1504, despite attempts at quarantine, bubonic plague hit the city badly. Victims were removed forcibly from the city, mass graves were excavated in areas like Bruntsfield Links. For the first time efforts were made to clean the city and King James IV, who was a keen amateur dentist founded the Incorporation of Barber-Surgeons, later to become the world famous Royal College of Surgeons of Edinburgh.

But another major plague devastated the city in 1645. Ten years later Oliver Cromwell was so concerned at the filth that he appointed a Town Scavenger to clear the main streets.

By this time, though, ideas from Europe were filtering through to Edinburgh. Robert Sibbald set up a practice with Andrew Balfour and in 1670 established a Physic Garden which had more than 1800 plants in it to supply the town's 20 or so physicians with their prescription ingredients. The garden formed the basis of the Royal Botanic Garden, the second oldest of its kind in the British Isles.

In 1681 Sibbald founded the Royal College of Physicians under a patent from Charles II. Sixteen years later Edinburgh surgeons opened their first fully equipped anatomy theatre giving the public a chance to view dissection. Only hanged criminals could be used for such purposes but body-snatching soon provided plenty of corpses and became so widespread that in 1725 the enraged townsfolk rioted. The snatching went on, however, and 100 years later Robert Knox, whose dissections were well-attended social occasions, found his career in ruins when the news spread of his use of bodies brought in by the murderers Burke and Hare.

Progress in medicine speeded up in the eighteenth century: the first dispensary for the poor was opened at its start; in 1729 Lord Provost George Drummond helped physicians open a hospital which later grew into the largest voluntary hospital in the British Isles—the Royal Infirmary; and in 1737 Andrew Duncan founded a medical students' club which

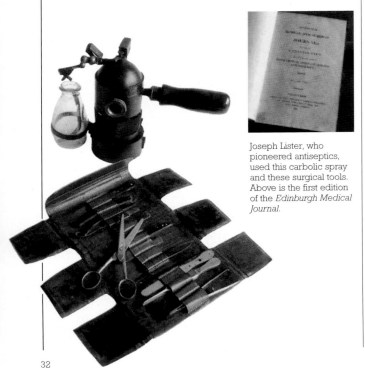

Joseph Lister, who pioneered antiseptics, used this carbolic spray and these surgical tools. Above is the first edition of the *Edinburgh Medical Journal.*

The death mask of William Burke who, with his partner William Hare, committed between 16 and 30 murders to provide bodies for dissection. The pocket book was made from Burke's own skin.

Buike

later the new Nightingale system of nursing was introduced to the city's hospitals. At last patients could expect care more or less in accordance with Lister's instruction to the medical profession to 'put yourself in the patient's place'.

'James' Barry, the city's first woman doctor, was awarded a medical degree in 1812. Throughout her life she had assumed the male identity necessary to achieve her goal. It was only at the autopsy that her sex was revealed.

In the early twentieth century medicine became more specialized, with the opening of the first post-graduate courses for specialists at the Royal Colleges and the University.

Today the city's reputation for medical research is still high.

The fine buildings of the Royal College of Surgeons and Physicians with their libraries and museums are evidence of their distinguished history, and the research units in the University Clinical Departments and in Edinburgh's hospitals ensure that these high traditions are carried on into the future.

later became the Royal Society of Medicine.

The teaching of medicine also forged ahead as William Cullen taught the classification of diseases by symptoms for the first time and started lecturing in English rather than Latin.

In 1805 the *Edinburgh Medical and Surgical Journal*—the first of its kind—was published with articles by the two great surgeons Robert Liston and James Syme. Syme's assistant was Joseph Lister who pioneered the use of carbolic acid in surgery to prevent wounds going septic and later was the first medical peer.

James Young Simpson discovered the anaesthetic properties of chloroform. Legend has it that his first 'guinea pigs' were guests at a dinner party at his home. His wife came in to find the assembled group literally 'under the table'.

In 1807 Andrew Duncan set up a hospital for the treatment of the insane and 50 years or so

Anaesthetics pioneer James Young Simpson owned this medicine chest, pill box and primitive stethoscope.

Cooking

From Bawd Bree to Bubblyjock—a distinctive culinary repertoire

The visitor to Edinburgh who associates Scottish cooking with such deadly sounding dishes as haggis and black bun is in for a pleasant surprise. Blessed with a wealth of natural produce from its rich land and teeming waters, Scotland has developed a culinary repertoire of exceptional quality and variety. Partridge, grouse and pheasant from the rolling moorlands, venison from the red deer running wild in the mountains, salmon and trout from Highland rivers, succulent beef from the Aberdeen Angus herds, shellfish of all kinds—with ingredients like these, only a truly lamentable cook could fail to come up with a feast.

Edinburgh folk tend to look back to bygone days when the streets of the capital rang to the cries of 'oyster wives' and vendors of everything from hot peas to Het Pints—a brew of ale, eggs and whisky flavoured with nutmeg and sold from a steaming copper kettle. Those were the times when a fish dinner, including ale and perhaps a dozen oysters, cost little more than one cigarette does now. As far back as the thirteenth century, salmon was so plentiful that it was pickled for export to London to be fed to the poor, and only a hundred years ago servants in big houses had contracts stipulating that it was to be served to them no more than three times a week.

But those are bygone days indeed. The allure of traditional Scottish fare, however, has carried through to modern times in all but price. Breakfast and tea have a special place in Scottish cooking, and the visitor who might think of these meals as something light has another think coming. It was Dr. Samuel Johnson who wrote: 'If an epicure could remove by a wish in quest of sensual gratification, he would breakfast in Scotland.' Oatmeal is still a staple of the national diet, and certainly most of the older people start the day with a bowl of porridge —flavoured with salt, not sugar, please. Then come the soft warm rolls known as baps, kippered herring from Loch Fyne or smoked haddock ('smokies') from Aberdeen and Arbroath, scones and oatcakes with heather honey, jams, jellies and marmalade, claimed by Scots as their own invention. Tea is the occasion for another mammoth spread of cold meats and eggs, potato scones, crunchy shortbread and such delicacies as Dundee cake, a fruity concoction strewn with almonds.

An elaborate dinner or late supper will bring out the matchless smoked salmon, rich dark venison or feathered game, roast beef or tender mutton, perhaps lobster from the Firth of Forth. Auld Alliance, a savoury of creamed cheese laced with whisky and served with hot buttered toast, can be a superb climax to the meal.

The visitor who comes across haggis or black bun should not be put off by the unappetizing names. Haggis consists of the heart, liver and lights of a sheep, cooked with oatmeal and onions inside its stomach bag. Hard to believe, but it's delicious. Black bun, also known as Scotch bun, is a tasty cake made with raisins,

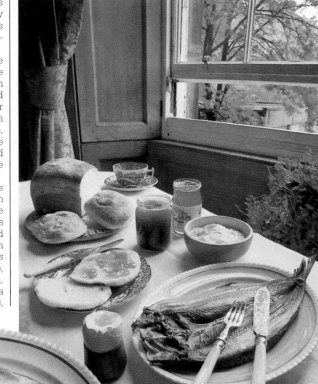

currants, almonds, ginger, cinnamon and brandy.

The names of many Scottish delicacies are nothing if not colourful. A few examples: Bawd Bree (hare soup), Bubbly-jock (roast turkey), Cock-a-Leekie (chicken and leek soup), Inky-Pinky (beef and carrot stew), Stovies (sliced potatoes cooked with onions and lamb) and Melting Moments (biscuits in rolled oats).

Scottish food at its best— the supreme high tea with the delights of bannocks and baps; Finnan haddie topped with poached egg for breakfast; and a fine brew from an ancient house to ease the evening.

Edinburgh Castle

The impenetrable fortress of Edinburgh Castle Rock has been be-seiged and attacked numerous times in its 3000 year history but it has rarely been overwhelmed. It stands today as a memorial to the turbulent history of a nation.

This drawing of Edinburgh Castle, perched high above the Grassmarket, is by the artist Thomas H. Shepard and was published in 1829.

𝓔dinburgh Castle dominates the city below. This is no accident but a deliberate strategy of its many military designers and part of the secret of its success as a fortress. For nearly 500 years the stone edifices topping Castle Rock were regularly under siege and, though famine and maybe even betrayal led their garrisons to surrender, the Castle was seldom successfully stormed. It was last besieged during the 1745-6 Jacobite Rising.

Twentieth-century visitors can pass freely through these once impregnable defences but can only penetrate the castles mysteries by understanding its history. It has served as a fort, palace, prison, garrison, arsenal, armoury and as a repository for the State regalia.

Castle Rock is the basalt core of one of the five extinct volcanos in the Edinburgh area. It rises 435 feet (133 m) above sea level and Ice Age glaciers made the north and south sides almost vertical. The summit can only be easily approached from the ridge on the east, and the west side, steep enough to be defended, providing grazing for animals, These factors, plus the presence of springs of good water, made it a natural stronghold.

Excavations in 1989 found evidence for a settlement of round houses on the Rock dating to the late Bronze Age (about 900 BC). This makes the Rock the longest occupied place of continued strength in the UK and the Castle has been there for about a third of that time. After a period of greatly reduced activity the hill-top settlement blossomed during the first and second centuries AD. By AD 142–3 the Roman Empire had established its most northerly frontier, the Antonine Wall, a little to the west of Edinburgh. Archaeologists have found a wealth of Roman material, suggesting close contact between the native Votadini tribe and the Roman military in the region. A Welsh poem, *Gododdin*, records a sixth-century king of the region feasting in his fortification of 'Din Eidyn' before setting out to attack the Angles. This probably refers to what we now know as the Castle Rock. The Rock was besieged by the Angles in AD 638. The place seems then to have received the English name—Edinburgh—which it has kept ever since.

It was Queen Margaret, wife of Malcolm III, who can be held partly responsible for Edinburgh's development in the eleventh century. In the Middle Ages the capital moved around the kingdom with the court. Malcolm Canmore, son of Shakespeare's Duncan and a successor to Macbeth had his capital in Dunfermline but his wife thought civilization lay further south. The crude fortress on the hill was converted to a royal residence and the name Castle of the Maidens originates from this period. Margaret's own chamber there was said to have been furnished more luxuriously than any in Scotland at that time. She was living there when the news of her husband's and eldest son's deaths in England reached her in 1093 and she died on the rock the same year.

Her death was followed by events to be repeated frequently in the nation's history— a disputed succession and siege of the Castle. The attempts failed. Her youngest son was crowned Scotland's king in 1124. David I built the summit's only surviving twelfth-century structure, a chapel dedicated to his mother's memory. But he also shaped the first real settlement around the Castle which stretched as far as the present intersection of High Street and South Bridge. David I was the first to use the Castle for the assembly of earls, barons and churchmen which later became the Parliament of Scotland

The pattern of alternating occupation of the fortress by Scots and English started in the late twelfth century. It was held by an English garrison between 1174 and 1186 but was safely back in Scots hands when their first official parliament was convened there by Alexander II in 1215. His son, Alexander III, made it a repository for the kingdom's records and regalia. On his death the succession to the throne was disputed and the English king, Edward I, called in as umpire, settled this by burning the town and seizing the castle in 1296 after a three-day siege. The Scots virtually razed the Castle in 1314 to prevent further domination by their foes from this stronghold. Only St. Margaret's Chapel was left standing.

The Castle began to take on more of its present form in the late fourteenth century. King David II, son of Robert the Bruce, returned from captivity in England in 1356 and built a 60-foot-high tower on the site of the present Half-Moon Battery. This royal residence, known as David's Tower, was so strong it withstood a major attack by Henry IV and succumbed only to the massive bombardment of cannon in 1573.

King Robert II, the first Stewart monarch, strengthened David's fortifications along the east, extending them to end in the Constable's Tower. In the 1430s James I moved the royal accommodation out of David's Tower to the site of the present palace block. This move did not prove as fatal for James I as his choice of Perth as a centre for his court and parliament. His assassination there in 1437 increased the importance of Edinburgh as its Castle was considered the safest in the land.

Perhaps it was safe for the nation's rulers but not for others with any claim to the throne. In 1440 when the boy King James II lived there, his regents Crichton and Livingstone lured two rivals, the young Douglas brothers, to a feast in the Castle's hall. When the food was brought to the table, the main course was a black bull's head, a symbol of death. The boys were taken from this meal, since known as the Black Dinner, to a mock trial, after which they were beheaded.

James III was so suspicious of his own brothers claiming his crown that he kept them imprisoned, holding the Duke of Albany in David's Tower in 1479 while he lived in the adjacent royal apartments. But Albany escaped after luring his guards into his chamber to drink wine before a blazing fire, killing them when they became drowsy and roasting

them in full armour on the fire. Ironically, before long James III was imprisoned for two months in David's Tower, to be released by the intervention of his former captive brother, Albany. Under James III, Edinburgh was finally declared the chief town in the kingdom and the permanent seat for the Scottish Parliament.

After the crowning of James IV in 1489, life took on a brighter look at the Castle and its tournaments brought it fame throughout Europe. His building programme included the splendid Great Hall which still stands, mounted on a vaulted structure over the southern rockface. Though the Palace was also improved, the Castle was no longer used as the Royal household's main residence. This era of success ended on Flodden Field in 1513 when James IV and his army of more than 100,000 suffered, at the hands of the English, the worst military disaster in Scottish history.

James V is thought to have taken little interest in the Castle except as an arsenal. The Flodden Wall was begun as a defence against the expected invasion of the English. But when the army arrived a full 31 years later it was still unfinished and drawings made by an English agent in 1544 show the eastern defences still dominated by David's Tower. The castle was not seriously harmed in this attack but an Italian engineer was nevertheless engaged to build an artillery bastion before the cross-wall.

By the time Mary, Queen of Scots began her reign, Edinburgh Castle was the nation's main armoury, making and storing gunpowder and artillery. In 1566 the armaments included at least 25 cast bronze guns, many of which were used in sieges around the country. Although Holyrood Palace was

The huge vaults, built to create a level surface for the Great Hall above them, are best known for holding foreign prisoners-of-war. The Hall was built in James IV's time for communal living. It became a barracks in 1650 and later a hospital. The restoration, rather too romantic, was done between 1887 and 1891.

1 Esplanade
2 Statue of Robert the Bruce
3 Statue of William Wallace
4 Gatehouse
5 Inner Barrier
6 Portcullis Gate
7 Castle Shop
8 Forewall Battery
9 Lang Stairs
10 St. Margaret's Chapel
11 Old water tanks
12 Foog's Gate

13 Queen Anne Barracks
14 Dury's Battery
15 Vaults/French Prisons
16 Mons Meg
17 Great Hall
18 Palace, including Crown Jewels, Stone of Destiny and Birth Chamber
19 Half Moon Battery
20 Public toilets
21 Seventeenth-century ditch
22 Crown Square
23 Scottish National War Memorial
24 The Fore Well

The inset, on the right, shows the whole Castle, with the major buildings, in the shaded area, detailed below.

A side door, or sallyport, led to the moat that used to front the Castle in the seventeenth century. A guard house and stables were built over them in the nineteenth century.

The remnants of the tower house built by David II are here visible beneath the walls of Half Moon Battery. The tower, dating from about 1370, was knocked down in the 1573 siege. The battery, an artillery platform, was built on the rubble, overlooking the main entrance.

St. Magaret's Chapel

The Constable's Tower

David's Tower

circa 1450

The Castle walls, built on the orders of David II, were passive defences. The occupants relied heavily on the natural advantage of Castle Rock and the thickness of the walls rather than on their military skills for protection of the King's Edinburgh residence.

Kitchens
Great Hall

Portcullis Gate
The Palace

Half Moon Battery

circa 1647

The Sp

New Barracks
Magazine and Armoury
Governor's House

Queen Anne Barracks
St. Margaret's Chapel extended

circa 1

preferred to the Castle as a residence, Mary was persuaded to give birth to the future king of Scotland and England, James VI and I, in the Castle, so long a symbol of the Scottish crown. The Castle was the last place to uphold Mary's cause in the most destructive siege in its history.

Sir William Kirkcaldy of Grange held the Castle against incredible odds for three years for the exiled Queen. There is a suspicion that he finally turned traitor as the attackers sent suddenly for help from Queen Elizabeth I. These reinforcements included 30 cannon sent by sea and by May 1573 five batteries were set up surrounding the Castle. David's Tower eventually collapsed, blocking the Castle's main well and within days there was no food, water or provisions. The Castle surrendered but contrary to the agreement made, Kirkcaldy and other leaders were hanged, beheaded and their heads displayed.

The Castle was put in the hands of Regent Morton and he

Edinburgh was, by now, the capital of Scotland. More active defences, like the artillery platforms of the Half Moon Battery and the earthworks at the entrance, were needed because the Castle was a repository for state records, the Royal Mint, the armoury and the Royal Household.

rebuilt the eastern defences much in their present form. Records show the massive Half Moon Battery cost £743 6s 6d and the expense led Morton to devalue the Scots currency. The Castle became a fortress seldom visited by kings, although huge sums were spent to extend and redecorate the Palace for the homecoming of James VI in 1617.

The Castle came under serious siege three times within 50 years during the seventeenth century, though no assault breached the walls. Most impact on the defences was made by the Covenanters Army, Presbyterian loyalists, besieging a company of

English soldiers. They held out for three months and were allowed to leave with honour.

In 1649 and 1650 the Castle was made even more impregnable when the citizens of Edinburgh were used as forced labour to demolish the spur in front of it. Though the Castle, ammunition and provisions all seemed to be holding up against Cromwell's attack in 1650, General Dundas surrendered to him. The Castle's reputation was redeemed by the Duke of Gordon, holding the Castle for the exiled Old Pretender in 1689 against the forces of William and Mary. In three months the brave and steadfast Duke cost his attackers 500 lives before famine and disease forced him to give in.

The guns of the Castle fired in March 1707 when the Act of Union was passed by the last Scottish Parliament; the Scottish Honours, the Crown jewels, were taken to the Palace building and immured. Sir Walter Scott, who played a major part in their rediscovery, said this was because 'these emblems, connected with so many galling and hostile recollections of past events, could be no safe spectacle for the public eye, while Men's minds were agitated by the supposed degradation of Scotland beneath her ancient enemy.'

The Castle came under attack only twice more, both attempts made by Jacobite forces and neither coming near to success. The first was in 1715 when a bold plan was formulated to scale the Castle's wall by night and prepare it for the Highland armies en route to England. But a combination of betrayal and bad planning turned this assault into a fiasco. Bonnie Prince Charlie fared no better in 1745. He was reluctantly accepted by the citizens of Edinburgh but the Castle troops fired first on Holyroodhouse, then on the houses nearby. The Stuart colours finally reached the Castle, displayed as spoils of war after the Young Pretender's defeat at Culloden.

A regular army, an innovation introduced in the mid-seventeenth century, kept a permanent garrison at the Castle from that time. Now the fortress's main military function was as a barracks and prison, especially during the Seven Years' War, the American War of Independence and the Napoleonic Wars with France. At the beginning of the nineteenth century as many as 1000 prisoners of war were kept in the Castle. Most were lodged in the vaults under the Great Hall, since known as the French Prisons. Their skill in carving can be seen in graffiti on the vault walls and handiwork made for sale, now on

The Unions of Crowns in 1603 and of Parliaments in 1707 had taken the Royal Court and administration south so the Castle was no longer needed for defence. The Scottish Army used the Great Hall as a barracks and Napoleonic War prisoners were kept in the vaults.

The War Memorial was built and restoration work, begun by an Army officer, Gore Booth, in the late nineteenth century, was continued. Statues of the national heroes, Wallace and Bruce, were also erected and the Castle's popularity as a tourist attraction grew.

Outworks

Parade Ground

Military Hospital

Military Prison

Scottish United Services Museum

St. Magaret's Chapel restored

War Memorial   circa 1930

Esplanade

view in the Castle's military museum. But they also carved mutton bones to make watermarks on forged banknotes. So skilful were these forgeries that advertisements appeared in the press offering rewards for information on the prisoners' lucrative sideline.

The prisoners were said to be kept in humane conditions but soldiers stationed at the Castle did not enjoy a much higher standard of accommodation. Up to 1000 could be lodged in barracks there at once and a 1791 census includes 159 women and 131 children. A mid-nineteenth century report described the married quarters as the worst in the United Kingdom, with no privacy and so insanitary that epidemics were rife. Even the New Barracks completed in 1799 are very austere. Troops were stationed at the Castle before serving overseas in India, North America or the Continent. The Castle was a major barracks until 1923 when the Redford Barracks south of the city were opened.

The process of restoration of Edinburgh Castle, begun in the nineteenth century, owes much to Sir Walter Scott's interest in it. He was named on a royal warrant, along with the Scottish Officers of State, allowing them to break open the oak chest in the Crown Room which was thought to contain the Scottish Honours. The Crown, Sceptre and Sword of Scotland were found inside, intact but dusty, and have only been hidden from public view twice since— during the two World Wars.

St. Margaret's Chapel was discovered by accident, as was the true nature of the Great Hall. Restoration work on the latter deviated rather a long way from its original state, but with far less damage to the Castle than would have occured if other grandiose Victorian schemes for 'improvements' had been allowed.

The age-old connection between Edinburgh Castle and military life still continues. It is the site of the National War Memorial and houses the Scottish United Services Museum. It is the headquarters for the Lowlands and the Scottish Division and the Regimental Headquarters of the Royal Scots and Royal Scots Dragoon Guards. It also has the only Army School of Piping in the country. Since 1947 the Castle has achieved international fame through its annual Military Tattoo, held on the Esplanade. But today the only invaders besieging Edinburgh Castle are tourists.

Castle Rock

Visitors to Castle Rock today need an active imagination to see why the site was an obvious choice for a defensible stronghold. The buildings of the Old Town nestle snugly up towards the defences and the North Loch has been filled in and turned into Princes Street Gardens and the railway station. But throughout most of its history Castle Rock had a far more cragged appearance and the broad terraces and sweeping approach roads are products of extensive levelling in the eighteenth and nineteenth centuries, when the fortress' working life was almost over.

The Esplanade

The Esplanade did not exist when the Castle was under siege. It was built as a parade ground in 1753 using earth from the foundations of the Royal Exchange (now the City Chambers in the Royal Mile) to level and widen the ridge formed by glacial action. The ornamental walls were added

Surmounted by the Royal Arms of Scotland and flanked by statues of Robert the Bruce and William Wallace, this Victorian gatehouse was built as an entrance worthy of the Castle rather than as a true fortification.

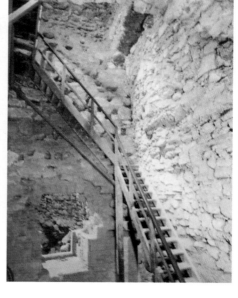

Above The cannon standing on the Half Moon Battery are 18-pounders made at the Carron Iron works near Falkirk.

Right This staircase links the remnants of the vaults in David's Tower with the battery platform above.

in 1812 and 1820. The Esplanade, with its magnificent views of the city and its surroundings, has a blaze of glory each year when it is used for the Military Tattoo, but otherwise serves as the Castle car park.

The Gatehouse

The Gatehouse is not part of the real defences of the Castle but a symbolic entrance way built in 1887; its statues of Robert the Bruce and William Wallace were added in 1929. However, the ditch in front of it was started by Cromwell in the mid-seventeenth century, and only completed a century later. Its unusual shape allowed coverage from the walls and this three-sided form is echoed in the design of the later gatehouse.

Eastern Defences

The rounded Half Moon Battery facing East is built over two storeys of the fourteenth century David's Tower, all but demolished in the great siege of 1573. Its artillery platform is at the same level as the principal buildings of the summit and the vaults were long used as a cistern to hold the Castle's water supply. The Forewall Battery extends northwards, incorporating a wall built in the 1540s. It ends in the Portcullis Gate, built over the gate-tower erected by Robert II. This had a residence for his constable on top and so was called the Constable's Tower.

The Portcullis Gate is also known as Argyle's Tower because the 9th Earl was thought to have been imprisoned there before being beheaded. The upper part is an architectural oddity as it was added in Victorian times; it has openings for archers but artillery was the weaponry in use when the lower part was erected. Renaissance decoration on the original part of the gateway includes the arms of Regent Morton who rebuilt the Eastern defences in their present form, mainly in the late 1570s. Their commanding position can best be appreciated by surveying from above the field of fire their guns command and then examining their invulnerability from the area below. Nevertheless, they did not survive the Civil War intact and needed to be repaired after Cromwell laid siege to the Castle in 1650.

Northern Defences

The Argyle or Six Gun Battery was constructed in the 1730s for Major General Wade. He had been called to Scotland to control the Jacobite insurgence and suggested also strengthening the northwestern and northeastern approaches to Edinburgh Castle. Wade is well known in Scotland as many of the military roads and bridges he instigated were named after him. Mill's Mount Battery also looks north, giving fine views of Princes Street Gardens and the New Town, although when it was built these did not exist. The one o'clock gun is fired from its artillery platform every day except Sunday. Below these batteries is the Low Defence, artillery outworks first built in the mid sixteenth century but rebuilt in the seventeenth and eighteenth. This terrace was once used as the Governor's garden.

Cart-shed
The mid-eighteenth century cart-shed with its double pitched roofs has been frequently modified to serve different purposes. Formerly a barrack and an ammunition store it now serves as the Castle's tea room.

Governor's House
Several of the buildings inside the walls of the Castle are in styles predating the era in which they were erected. In the case of the Governor's House with its crow-stepped gables the result is a happy one. Built in 1742 with wings to house the Master Gunner and Storekeeper, it is still in active use as an Officer's Mess while the right wing is the Governor's official residence.

Military Hospital
A side road leads to the Hospital, a series of buildings built as armouries in the eighteenth century but extensively remodelled as a hospital in the 'improvements' era of the late nineteenth century. The north block was then reconstructed in an early seventeenth century style but the south block retains many of its earlier features. The complex is now open as the Scottish United Services Museum.

Western Defences
Surrounding this range of buildings are the Western Defences built on two separate levels. The lower walls follow the natural line of the rock and mostly originate in the 1730s, although a walkway existed along this level in the mid-seventeenth century. This terrace has two sentry boxes and the northern one is named the Queen's Post. The upper terrace on the north and west sides of the Hospital dates from the 1850s. The two levels are joined by a stair inside a turret at the southern junction of these defences.

Southern Defences
The Southern Defences were built to prepare the Castle for a Jacobite attack in the early eighteenth century. They were the work of Scotland's military engineer, Theodore Dury and the highest battery bears his name. The other, Butts Battery, is so-called because the bow butts used for archery practice were nearby. These two batteries were five-gun emplacements connected to the Old Back Parade by steps. The defences were completed by 1713 and withstood the Jacobite assault two years later.

The Military Prison
The Military Prison was built about 1842 for offenders from all over Scotland. The exterior is carefully designed to fit into its historic setting and the interior to allow all prisoners to be kept in solitary confinement. The cells are grouped around a central stairway and all can be centrally heated.

The French Prisons
When James IV wanted to build his Great Hall he obtained sufficient level ground for it by constructing a vaulted substructure on the rock face. These vaults extend under the hall and further west and have had many uses, including an arsenal, barracks, bakehouse and stores. But they are now known as the French Prisons, commemorating their use for prisoners of war in the eighteenth and nineteenth centuries. At the main entrance opening on Dury's Battery is graffiti carved in the stonework. They also put their carving skills to more practical use and an impressive ship model is currently displayed in the Scottish United Services Museum.

The vaults now contain 'Mons Meg', a huge siege gun which is one of the pair given to James II by his uncle in marriage, Phillip, Duke of Burgundy, in 1457. It consists of wrought-iron bars welded into a cylinder over a wooden core and bound with iron hoops. It was probably used as a muzzle loader and could fire a 300-pound stone nearly two miles. It was moved to sieges around the country, its wheels greased with Orkney butter and tended by more than 100 men. 'Mons Meg' burst

Left Eighteenth-century graffiti. The name of *Proyol Prisonnier nee Natiffe de Bourbourg* is engraved for ever in the stonework of the French Prison's west entrance.

Right Mons Meg, an iron siege-gun, was forged in Flanders in 1449. It took 100 men, five carpenters and a large number of oxen to move the five-ton Meg.

Below Foog's Gate is the only archway leading to the upper enclosure. After many names, including 'foggy' and 'fogo', the mysterious 'foog' has stuck.

while firing a birthday salute in 1681.

Hawk Hill

Hawk Hill is the second highest point in the Castle enclosure and came into especially heavy use in the eighteenth century. The New Barracks, which Sir Walter Scott likened to a vulgar cotton mill, was built in 1798. Earlier structures on the site included a guardhouse and artillery battery.

Foog's Gate

The road leading from Hawk Hill to the upper enclosure of the Castle passes through the protective wall by a small opening, Foog's Gate, placed so that it could be easily covered by fire from the nearby wall. This name is of unknown origin.

Crown Square

Crown Square is the centre of the later medieval citadel but only two of its flanking buildings date from this period.

The Great Hall

The Great Hall was built by James IV and completed in the early years of the sixteenth century, but its interior has been over-imaginatively restored to the Victorian image of a medieval hall. Nonetheless it is remarkable so much survived as the building was crudely subdivided and used as a barracks and hospital for two centuries before its historic importance was realised. Earlier halls serving as communal living for the Castle household are mentioned in records but no traces survive. James IV used his hall for state ceremonial occasions and banquets. The King and his courtiers sat at the east end while the door at the west end was screened by draught-excluding timber screens. One of the hall's finest features is the hammer-beam roof, lost to view for two centuries. The restoration work done in 1887 to 1891 was financed by the publisher William Nelson.

There are many ancient and decorative features in the Great Hall.

Above The elaborate open-timbered roof.

Left A stone carving of a combined rose and thistle motif celebrating the marriage of James IV to Margaret Tudor of England.

Below The hall has a fine display of arms and armour.

Right The Scottish Crown was remodelled in 1540 by order of James V. Together with the Sword of State and the Sceptre it is part of the Scottish Regalia. Also included is the Stone of Destiny, or Stone of Scone, restored to Scotland after a 700-year exile.

Below In Queen Mary's Room the Old Pretender, father of Bonnie Prince Charlie, looks down from the oak panelling .

Below Right The Royal Palace dates from the fourteenth century. The stair turret was turned into the Castle's main flag-staff in the early nineteenth century.

The Palace

The exterior of the Palace Block fronting Crown Square shows a compilation of styles due to the huge number of modifications made by monarchs through the ages.

Royal residences have been built on this site since James I but the basis of the present building was shaped by James IV. Two storeys and the classical windows were added between 1615 and 1617 for James VI's homecoming. The rather overbearing extension of the central turret for a flag staff was built in the early nineteenth century.

One of the most fascinating rooms inside the royal residence is the tiny bed chamber where Mary Queen of Scots gave birth to James VI of Scotland, later crowned James I of England. The entwined initials

of Mary and Henry Darnley, MAH, are engraved outside thedoor with the birthdate— 1566. For the birth it was hung with blue velvet and taffeta but the present decorations mostly stem from the preparations for James VI's homecoming. Also of great interest is the Crown Room where the Scottish Re-

galia, including the Sceptre and Sword and the Crown made for James V are on display. These were walled up inside the roomfor over a century after the Union of the Parliaments. The Stone of Destiny is now on display with them, having been returned in 1996 after a 700-year exile in England.

The Scottish National War Memorial

The Scottish National War Memorial was created after the First World War in honour of the 150,000 Scots who died. The basic structure is an eighteenth century barracks standing on the site of the medieval church of St. Mary's which had been put to use as a munitions store. Sir Robert Lorimer transformed the interior of the barracks into a vaulted hall with the casket holding the names of the dead at the hall's focal point. The elaborate interior includes fine stained-glass windows by Douglas Strachan. The exterior was kept simple, with most decorative detail by the entrance. The memorial was opened by the Prince of Wales in 1927 and aroused such public interest that for some months queues of visitors stretched down to the Esplanade.

The Queen Anne Building

This building, originally officers' quarters, was erected during Queen Anne's reign in 1708 over a vaulted substructure.

St. Margaret's Chapel

St. Margaret's Chapel is the oldest building in the Castle and in Edinburgh. Its Romanesque architecture dates it as early twelfth century and it was probably built by David I in memory of his mother, Queen Margaret, who was canonized in the thirteenth century. It was a royal chapel until after Mary Queen of Scots' reign but then was linked up with other buildings and put to secular use, ending up as a powder magazine. In 1845, the garrison chaplain noticed a font-like piece of stonework which turned out to be the socket of a pillar for a chancel arch. Queen Victoria urged its restoration but the chapel became, before long, little more than a souvenir kiosk. It was completely refurbished and

The oldest structure on Castle Rock, St. Margaret's Chapel was the only building to survive when the Castle was captured by the Earl of Moray who razed it to the ground in 1314.
Above The simple interior of the Chapel. After three centuries as a gunners' storehouse the Chapel was rediscovered in 1845 and rededicated in 1934.

finally rededicated in 1934. Though unremarkable on the outside, the interior features an arch with exquisite zig-zag ornamentation.

The Lang Stairs

The main medieval approach to the Castle's upper enclosure was a steep winding staircase which has been continued to form the Lang Stairs.

Finally, no visitor to the Castle should fail to spend time admiring the magnificent view of Princes Street Gardens, the New Town and the Firth of Forth. On a clear day Fife can be seen in the distance.

The Royal Mile

The Royal Mile, a sequence of four connecting streets running roughly west to east from Edinburgh Castle to Holyrood Abbey, is the area of the city that is most steeped in history. Crossing the Esplanade below the Castle, you enter into Castle Hill, the oldest street in Edinburgh. Here you can see the development of a city from its medieval beginnings. Clustered at the start of Castle Hill and continuing along the ridge that comprises the Royal Mile are some of the most enticing sights and monuments of the city. Recent traffic-calming measures have made 'the Mile' more pedestrian-friendly and it is a popular shopping area for both tourists and locals.

Castle Hill

The first building on the south side of Castle Hill is Cannonball House, built c. 1630. It derives its name from the cannonball lodged in the west wall, which tradition claims was fired from the Castle during the siege of 1745. Another explanation is that the ball marked the level to which water could rise by gravitation from the city's first piped water system. The water was piped from Comiston Springs into the Castle Hill Reservoir, completed in 1851. The building is now the Edinburgh Old Town Weaving Company, a working mill producing tartan.

To the north is Ramsay Garden, built on the site of the poet Allan Ramsay's house, which was referred to by local wits as 'Goose-pie'. Ramsay Garden is a shrine for town planners worldwide. Built in 1893 by Sir Patrick Geddes, it is the earliest example of organized town planning as we know it.

Back on Castle Hill is the Outlook Tower or Camera Obscura. Built in the seventeenth century, it was extensively altered in the 1850s by an optician who installed a camera obscura—a lens system which on a clear day projects an image of Edinburgh onto a concave white table. The lens and mirror were replaced in 1945 with a much improved system. Sir Patrick Geddes owned the house from 1892 and created one of the first museums designed to teach people about other parts of the world. Much like an old-fashioned encyclopedia, there were rooms on geography, history and natural science, among others.

Opposite is Boswell's Court, a seventeenth-century tenement which is named after the uncle of James Boswell, Dr. Johnson's biographer. Just to the east of Boswell's Court is the Highland Church of Tolbooth St. John's, completed in 1844. Designed by James Gillespie Graham and Augustus W. N. Pugin, this Gothic Revival pile is topped by the highest spire in the city (240 feet/73 metres). The church is being renovated for use by the Edinburgh International Festival.

Crossing the street once again, you come to Semple's Close. The mansion at the foot of the close, dated 1638, was the home of Grissel, Lady Semple, widow of the 8th Lord Semple. Once a garden enclosure, these 'closes' were gradually filled in as land became scarce in the walled city. The narrow lane leading from the street took on the name close.

To the east is the site of the 'Palace' of Mary of Guise, demolished in 1861 to make way for the Church of Scotland General Assembly Hall, whilst across the road at the junction of Castle Hill, Lawnmarket and Johnston Terrace is the site of the Weigh House (demolished in 1822) and commemorated by a circle of 'setts' or rectangular stone blocks. This was the place for the weighing of butter and cheese for the use of the city.

Opposite is Milne's Court, an early attempt to create some open space in the Old Town. It was created by James Mylne, master mason to Charles II in 1690. Further down and set back from the street is James' Court. Built in 1725-1727, it was once a fashionable area, with a roster of distinguished tenants, including the philosopher David Hume.

Continuing down the same side is Gladstone's Land. The original building dated from 1550, but in 1617, Thomas Gledstanes acquired the property and rebuilt it into a six-storey tenement. The only block of flats in Edinburgh with the original arcaded front, original painted interior decorations of the early seventeenth century still survive. Part of the National Trust of Scotland since 1935, it has recently been furnished much as it might have appeared in the last quarter of the seventeenth century.

Lawnmarket

You are now actually in The Lawnmarket (land market), originally the *agora* or marketplace of the Old Town. Here produce, butter, cheese, milk, meat and other edibles were displayed in stalls, with the exception of Wednesdays, when a special sale of linen and woollen cloth was conducted.

The close at the side of Gladstone's Land leads to Lady Stair's House, constructed in 1622 by Sir William Gray of Pittendrum. Owned in the early eighteenth century by Elizabeth, Countess Dowager of Stair, widow of the 1st Earl of Stair, it now houses memorabilia and manuscripts of three great Scottish men of letters: Robert Burns, Sir Walter Scott and Robert Louis Stevenson.

Across the Lawnmarket will be found Riddle's Close and Court, rebuilt by Captain George Riddle after 1726. David Hume lived here before moving to James' Court. In the inner court is the late sixteenth-century mansion of Bailie John McMorran, shot to death by one of the students of the High School. The Bailie's house was nevertheless of high repute, and was borrowed in 1598 (three years after his death) by the Town Council for a banquet in honour of James VI and his Queen.

Next to Riddle's Close is Brodie's Close. One of the more colourful characters in the history of Edinburgh, Deacon William Brodie (son of Francis, after whom the Close is named) was a respected cabinetmaker and member of the town council by day and a burglar by night. His success was not without hazard however. On October 1, 1788, along with an accomplice, he was hanged at the Tolbooth on a scaffold of his own design. Robert Louis Stevenson used Deacon Brodie as the model for *Dr. Jekyll and Mr. Hyde*.

Just past the George IV Bridge, you will find one of the last remaining wells in the Old City. At one time ten public wells existed in different locations.

In front of St. Giles' Cathedral is the site of the Edinburgh Tolbooth, marked by a brass plaque in the roadway and a heart-shaped design of setts. The Tolbooth may well have dated from the last years of the fourteenth century. Since then it has accommodated the Scottish Parliament, Edinburgh Town Council and the Courts of Law, as well as being used for executions and as a prison. As a jail, it was immortalized by Sir Walter Scott in *The Heart of Midlothian*.

Though a church has existed on the site of St. Giles' Cathedral since AD 854, the present structure dates, in this form, from 1829, when the exterior was clad in ashlar. However, the four central pillars date from about 1120 and the crown spire was completed in 1495. Actually, it is more appropriate to refer to the Church as the High Kirk of Edinburgh since it was a cathedral proper only for the five years following the introduction of bishops to the Presbyterian Church of Scotland by Charles I. After the Revolution of 1688, the title remained. The rather gaudy Chapel of the Order of the Thistle was added in 1911. The name St. Giles derives from a Greek hermit who settled in Provence in the sixth century.

Commemorated in the interior, amongst others, are the Regent Moray, who was assassinated, and two implacable enemies, the 1st Marquis of Argyll and the 1st Marquis of Montrose, both of whom were executed.

Behind the cathedral are located the Signet Library and Parliament Hall. The Library is reached by passing through the narrow passage to the top half of Parliament Square. The Upper Hall is perhaps one of the finest examples of Georgian interior design in all of Edinburgh. The buildings themselves were finished in 1815 and are still in use by the Writers to HM Signet, now the principal body of solicitors in Scotland.

Parliament Hall was built at the behest of Charles I. It was the home of the Scots Parliament from 1639 to 1707 and the Treaty of Union. Since that time it has been the seat of Scotland's supreme courts.

Two statues beside Parliament Hall are worth your attention. To the west is a figure of John Knox by Pittendrigh McGillivray, erected in 1906 not far from Knox's grave; whilst to the east is the oldest lead equestrian statue in Britain, erected in 1688, of Charles II. Due east of the facade of Parliament Hall is the Mercat Cross. This marks the spot where merchants gathered to conduct business. Also the scene of assorted executions and other public celebrations, the Cross was the place from which Royal Proclamations were read. The Cross itself is nineteenth century with only a small section of the shaft left from the original sixteenth century erection.

High Street
The stretch of the Royal Mile from the Cathedral to opposite John Knox's House is known as the High Street.

The most imposing building on the High Street is the City Chambers, erected in 1761 as the Royal Exchange. It is now the meeting place of the City of Edinburgh Council. The City Chambers, with its Italian facade, has in front a quadrangle, the south side of which—facing the street—consists of seven arches. Within these arches are war memorials of 1914-1918 and 1939-1945.

Mary King's Close, a narrow street of shops, houses and taverns, abandoned in the middle of the seventeenth century after an epidemic of the plague, forms part of the foundation structure of the City Chambers building. Guided tours of the reputedly haunted close are available.

Tron Church (Kirk) founded in 1637 and opened for worship in 1641, was meant for the part of the congregation for whom there was not room in St. Giles. Named after the 'trone' or salt-weighing machine standing to the north, the great fire of 1824 destroyed the spire and did other extensive damage. The present steeple was erected in 1828. It was closed as a church in 1952. For many years it was the congregation point on Hogmanay, Old Year's Night, but this has been superseded by 'Edinburgh's Hogmanay', a six-day festival, now the biggest gathering of its kind in the world.

Further down the hill at the bottom of the High Street, next to John Knox's House, is Moubray House, with traces of the structure going back to 1477.

John Knox's House is the last house on the street to retain its top storey wooden gallery, saved by the supposed connection with the great religious reformer when plans for widening the street were proposed in 1849. Inside are displays on his life, and the architecture is a classic example of domestic structures of the time of Mary, Queen of Scots.

Down Chalmer's Close, in an old church building, is the Brass Rubbing Centre where visitors (including children) can make rubbings of moulded replicas of medieval brasses and Pictish inscriptions.

On the other side of the street is the Museum of Childhood, the first museum in the world devoted solely to childhood history, which contains one of the world's finest collections of toys, model dolls, hobby items and memorabilia of children.

The Canongate
The Canongate derives its name from the time when King David I gave the Augustinian canons of Holyrood permission to build on either side of their path or 'gait' between the abbey and the Royal Burgh of Edinburgh. In fact, it was a separate town, so to

speak, until 1636 and did not come under the aegis of the Edinburgh Town Council until 1856. Unlike Edinburgh proper, the Canongate was never a walled town and suffered accordingly. However, after James IV began building the Palace of Holyroodhouse, the area became increasingly fashionable as a residential sector for members of the court. After 1800, with the move to the more chic New Town, Canongate degenerated into a slum. After World War II, Robert Hurd led a crusade to save the Canongate houses, and the area has been restored and given a new lease of life. Once again it has become a fashionable residential district.

Chessel's Court, built in 1748 by Archibald Chessel, was advertised as 'neatly finished and fit to accommodate a genteel family'. In turn the building housed the Scottish Excise Office. A burglary here in 1788 led to the arrest of Deacon Brodie. Almost opposite is the Effigy of Moor, a remembrance of the tenement once here known as Morocco's Land. The legend has it that in the early seventeenth century, Andrew Gray, the younger son of a noble family, was sentenced to death for leading a riot. Escaping to sea, he made a fortune in Morocco, returned to Edinburgh in the disguise of a Moor and threatened to sack the city. Instead, he cured the Lord Provost's daughter (his cousin) of the plague, married her and set up house on the spot where the cure had been effected.

Old Playhouse Close is named after the theatre opened here in 1747. The scene of several riots from passionate audiences, the theatre was closed in 1767. At its peak, the box office draw was reputedly as much as £70 per night. Box seats cost half a crown and the pit cost one and sixpence. The theatre succeeded in spite of clerical opposition and Sarah Siddons played here.

Smack in the middle of the Canongate outside Old Playhouse Close is the site of St. John's Cross, indicated by a circle of setts in the roadway. Charles I, making his ceremonial entrance into Edinburgh in 1633, was greeted by the provost, whom he knighted in the time-honoured fashion on the spot.

Moray House, constructed about the time of Charles I's accession to the throne, remained in the possession of the Moray family until the middle of the nineteenth century. Cromwell stayed here twice. The seventeenth-century plaster ceilings are in a remarkable state of preservation. In that same century the gardens were particularly famed. Now part of a teacher-training college, Moray House stands as one of the monuments to a more gracious age.

Across the street is Bible Land. Built in 1677 by the Incorporation of Cordiners (shoemakers) of the Canongate, the tenement is named after the sculpture above the stair entrance, quoting the first verse of Psalm 133. Also upon the shield are to be found the crown and rounding knife of St. Crispin, the patron saint of the shoemakers, who practised their craft within these walls. Note particularly the gables and termination of the stair tower.

Canongate Tolbooth, built in 1591 in the Franco -Scottish style, was the centre for the collection of public dues, the courthouse, the prison and the municipal affairs centre for the independent borough of the Canongate. The motto of the armorial bearing of the Canongate is *Sic itur ad astra* (This is the path to the stars). It is now the People's Story museum, tracing the lives, work and pastimes of the city's ordinary people from the late 1700s to the present day.

Canongate Church was built in 1688 with funds willed by Thomas Moodie of Edinburgh for the purpose of providing an alternative place of worship for parishioners displaced from the old parish church in the Abbey of Holyrood. The churchyard contains the remains of many famous Scots including the economist Adam Smith, the poet Robert Ferguson (the stone paid for by Robert Burns), and Mrs. Agnes McLehose, Burns' Clarinda. The Fergusson marker contains a verse by Burns:

No sculptured Marble here nor pompous lay
No Storied Urn nor animated bust
This simple Stone directs Pale Scotia's way
To pour her Sorrows o'er her Poet's Dust.

The original Canongate Mercat Cross is now located in the churchyard.

Across Canongate are located the Huntly and Acheson Houses. Built in 1570 for John Acheson, Huntly House was originally three separate houses as can be seen from the gables above. Restored in 1932, it is now the museum of the local history of the city. Located within are a splendid collection of silver and glass and the National Covenant of 1638, signed by citizens as a protest against Charles I's attempt to establish Episcopacy in Scotland and introduce a new service into the Church. Huntly House is also known as the 'speaking house', because of the inscriptions displayed on sixteenth-century plaques on the front of the building, supposed to have been placed there to answer criticisms as to the magnificence of the structure.

Acheson House, to the east, dates from 1633 and was built for Sir Archibald Acheson, a councillor to Charles I. Since 1952 it has been the headquarters of the Scottish Craft Centre. In a rear courtyard is a doorway topped with Sir Archibald's crest—a cock surmounting a trumpet—and the motto *'Vigilantibus'* with the date, 1633.

On the north side of the Canongate, extending east from Canongate Church, are a number of interesting sites. The seventeenth-century garden, reached through Dunbar's Close, is a reconstruction of the formal gardens of the time. Panmure House, reached by way of Little Lochen Close, and once the town house of the Earls of Panmure, was the home of Adam Smith, author of *The Wealth of Nations*.

Reid's Court, named after an eighteenth-century coachmaker, was built c. 1690 and was the Manse of the Canongate until 1832 and again from 1958. The Site of Golfers' Land was supposedly erected by a shoemaker, John Paterson, with his share of the winnings from a golf match, The game took place on the Leith Links and his partner was the Duke of York, later James VII and II. Whitefoord House, now a home for veterans, was built in 1766, but stands on the site of 'Seton Palace' where Lord Darnley stayed on his first visit to Edinburgh.

Across from Whitefoord House stands Queensberry House, erected in 1681 by Lord Hatton. Now a hospital for the elderly, Queensberry House was bought a few years later by William, Ist Duke of Queensberry. His son, James, was the principal promoter of the Treaty of Union of 1707, a part played to the displeasure of nearly everyone in Scotland. Supposedly, when he was out gathering signatures for the treaty his eldest son, Lord Drumlanrig, who was thoroughly mad, roasted a Canongate kitchen boy and was found devouring his flesh.

Just before the Canongate runs off into Abbeyhill stands the site of Girth Cross, marked by a circle of setts in the roadway. Known to exist until 1750, the Cross was the scene of many executions and marked the sanctuary area (western boundary) that surrounded the Abbey and Palace.

White Horse Close was named after the White Horse Inn, which occupied the building (1623) at the rear of the close. Now restored, this was the main coaching house for travellers to and from London.

Finally, before entering the precincts of the abbey and Palace you come to the Abbey Strand and Sanctuary, once the residence of aristocratic debtors. The 'Abbey Lairds', as they were known, were safe from arrest within these precincts, including Holyrood Park and Arthur's Seat. Only on Sundays could they venture safely forth. The sanctuary was in effect from around 1128 until 1880 when imprisonment for debt was abolished.

And so, after a leisurely journey through the history of a city, you now stand at the gates of Holyroodhouse.

▲ 1 Ramsay Lodge
This row of remodelled
Georgian houses in a
highly romantic late
Victorian style was built
on the site of the gardens
of Ramsay Lodge.

▶ 2 Ramsay Gardens

Castle

Esplanade

◀ 6 Castle Gatehouse
The gatehouse was built
in 1887 to create a fitting
entrance to the Castle,
without much heed to any
military logic. The
drawbridge was the last
built in Scotland.

▶ ▲ 7 Canonball House
Legend says the ball,
lodged in the bricks, was
fired from the Castle in
the 1745 rebellion but
another theory claims it
marks the gravitation
height of the first water
supply

▲ 3 Witches Well

The iron fountain marks the spot where hundreds of witches, 'some evil, some misunderstood' were burned to death between 1479-1722.

◄ 4 Outlook Tower

An optician. Maria Theresa Short, installed a camera obscura here in the 1850s. A new lens and mirror were added in 1945 and the camera still gives a fine panoramic view of the city.

▼ Tolbooth Kirk

The kirk was built in 1842-1844 for the General Assembly of the Church of Scotland and the Tolbooth congregation. It has the tallest spire in the city—240 feet (73m).

▼ 2 Riddle's Close

King James VI and his Queen attended a banquet here in 1593, not long after it was built by burgess George Riddell.

◀▲ 1 Wardrop's Court

In 1790 a burgess and wright of the city, John Wardrop, built a tenement here. Four dragon figures guard the entrance and Lady Stair's house rises from within.

THE
ROYAL
MILE

Lawnmarket

Castlehill

◀ 4 Gladstone's Land

This six-storey tenement, completed in 1620, housed burgess Thomas Gledstanes. The main rooms now show a typical seventeenth-century home and the original shopbooths display period goods.

▶ 5 Milne's Court

This reconstruction of the city's first open square was named after the 'Master Mason to King Charles II, James Mylne, who designed the extensions to Holyroodhouse and the Castle.

◄▼ 3 Lady Stair's House
Relics of the writers Scott, Burns and Stevenson are on show in this 1622 house. The latter's possessions include the riding boots, crop, spurs and cap that he wore in Samoa.

3

1

Bank Street

St Giles Street

Lawnmarket

Parliament Square

◄ 6 James' Court
David Hume and James Boswell both lived here; Adam Smith and Dr. Johnson were visitors. The court, which has three entrances, was built between 1725 and 1727 by a wright, James Brownhill. The original, destroyed in 1857, was rebuilt.

▲ 7 Deacon Brodie's Tavern
This tavern was named after the infamous William Brodie, respectable citizen by day, burglar by night.

Across the street is Brodie's Close, named after William's father, a glass-grinder and burgess of the city. William lived there before his hanging in 1788

1 Parliament House and Statue of Charles II

This is the only surviving equestrian statue in Britain of this king. The building was completed in 1639 for the Scottish Parliament and used by it until the Union in 1707. It is now part of the Law Courts.

THE
ROYAL
MILE

High Street

▲ 3 The Heart of Midlothian (The Old Tolbooth)

The granite blocks embedded in the road mark the entrance to the old Tolbooth prison, demolished in 1817. The old custom of spitting on the heart survives today.

High Street

3

4

1

▲ 2 John Knox Statue
The religious reformer, whose zeal led to the establishment of the Protestant faith in Scotland, looks over the site of his grave in what was once St.. Giles' Churchyard.

▲ ▶ 4 St. Giles' Cathedral
Originally the city's only parish church, some parts date from 1100. It became a cathedral in 1633.

1 City Chambers
The City Chambers were built as the Royal Exchange with coffee houses, flats and a printing press between 1754 and 1757. The Town Council took it over in 1811.

2 Edwardian placard
One of a series of enamelled Edwardian advertisements from the front of the Waverley Cameron Pen Company Building in Blair Street, which can now be seen in The People's Story museum.

THE

ROYAL

MILE

High Street

3 Mercat Cross
The first cross, a focus for the market where royal proclamations were read, dates from 1365. The present one, paid for by Gladstone, used the shaft of a cross demolished in 1756.

5 Tron Kirk
Founded in 1637 by Charles I for those displaced when St. Giles became a cathedral, this church is named after a tron, or weighing machine, that stood on the site.

4 Parliament House
Built 1632-39, this was the seat of the Scottish Government until 1707, when the governments of Scotland and England became united. Since then it has been the seat of the Court of Session, the supreme court of Scotland.

THE

ROYAL

MILE

High Street

◀ **1 Museum of Childhood**
This sign gives a taste of the charms of a large and varied collection of historic dolls, games and hobbies inside.

▲ **2 Paisley Close**
These words, above the entrance to the close, were the cry of a boy trapped under rubble when tenements nearby collapsed in 1861

◀ **5 John Knox's House**
The house, possibly the oldest dwelling in the city, dates from 1490. It belonged to Mariota Arres and her husband James Mosman and their initials decorate the outside. Knox may have lived here from 1561 to 1572. It was bought by the Church of Scotland, became a museum in 1853 and was again restored in 1958.

◀ 3 Netherbow Port

The brass plate marks the position of the last Netherbow Port, one of six city gates, built in 1513 and demolished in 1764. The heads of criminals and preachers were displayed there.

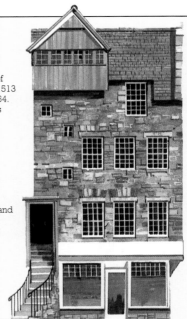

▶ 4 Moubray House

Built around 1462, this was a tavern in the eighteenth century, Daniel Defoe's office, and later Constable's bookshop. In 1890 the upper floors were a temperance hotel.

◀ 6 St Patrick's Church

Like many of the later public buildings of the Old Town, St Patrick's Church is tucked away in a close. Originally a Church of England chapel, it was consecrated as Episcopal Church, Cowgate in 1771; it changed its name to its present one in 1856, when it became a Roman Catholic church.

▲ 1 The Tolbooth

Built in 1591 as a council chamber, court house and jail, the tower of the Tolbooth is set with fearsome, but useless, gun ports. The clock was added in 1884.

THE ROYAL MILE

Canongate

◀ 3 Bakehouse Close

A property in the close was once owned by the Incorporation of Bakers of the Canongate. The archway was formed in 1570. Records from 1851 show that 230 people lived here.

▶ 4 Morocco's Land

This tenement is named after the stone, life-sized figure of a Moor, which was probably a late seventeenth-century merchant's sign, but the motto has long since been erased.

▶ **2 Huntly House**
Built as a row of sixteenth-century houses and remodelled by the Incorporation of Hammermen in 1647, Huntly House was rescued from ruin to form a museum in the 1930s.

Canongate

St John Street

1

5

2

3

▼ **5 Moray House**
The most opulent of the early town houses, built about 1625 by Mary, Dowager Countess of Home, Moray House is now a teachers' training college.

▲ **6 Chessel's Court**
Archibald Chessel, a wright, started building the Court in 1748 and Deacon Brodie was caught robbing here in 1788.

1 Canongate Church
This church was built in 1688 for those displaced when James VII and II converted the abbey at Holyrood for the use of the Knights of the Thistle.

THE
ROYAL
MILE

Abbey Strand

Canongate

Reids Court

Reids Close

3 White Horse Close
This close was used as the Royal Mews in the sixteenth century and in 1623 a merchant built an inn and coaching stables here, naming it after Queen Anne's white palfrey. Jacobite officers used the inn as headquarters in the 1745 rebellion. The close was restored in 1965.

2 Canongate Manse

Built in 1690 as a coaching inn, this building became a manse in 1789 and remained one until 1832. After having fallen into disrepair it was restored in 1958, and once again became the home of the minister of the Canongate Church.

▲ 4 Acheson House

Sir Archibald Acheson, one-time Secretary of State for Scotland under Charles I, built this house in 1633. It was restored in 1937.

◀ 5 Holyroodhouse Gates

Set at the entrance to the magnificent palace, the wrought-iron gates were part of the 1922 national memorial to King Edward VII.

At the foot of the Royal Mile stands one of the most imposing royal residences in the world. For over nine centuries Holyrood has been the scene of pomp and glory and of bloodshed and turbulence. It is still the official Scottish home of Britain's Royal Family.

The Palace of Holyroodhouse

The splendid royal palace that conceals a gruesome and grisly past

Glittering pageantry vies with a notorious murder and a splendid but grisly funeral in the crowded history of the Palace of Holyroodhouse, official Scottish residence of Britain's Royal Family. Down the centuries, the palace has seen dark events as well as grand designs, riot combined with revelry, fire and bloodshed along with the splendours of court life.

Bonnie Prince Charlie, Mary, Queen of Scots, Oliver Cromwell and the King he beheaded, Charles I—a note of grimness and tragedy runs through many of the names so inextricably linked with the fortunes of the Palace. It came into existence as a guest house associated with the medieval abbey which was founded in 1128 by King David I after a hunting accident that he barely survived. According to legend, the King was knocked from his horse and wounded in the thigh by a stag which then tried to finish him off. But a cross miraculously appeared between its antlers, the King clutched it, and the animal slunk away, suitably crushed. In thankfulness for his deliverance, David bequeathed the land to Augustinian canons then living in Edinburgh Castle and he ordered them to build the Abbey of Holyrood, known as the 'Church of the Holy Cross'.

The guest house for royal visitors was built to the west of the now-ruined abbey. Scottish kings lodged there in its earliest use as a royal residence, and James II was born, crowned, married and buried within its walls. In 1501 James IV decided to transform the guest house into a palace fit for a king and spent large sums on new buildings. An imposing four-storey corner tower was built with a gabled roof and balustrade—it is the northwest tower of the present building and still the most eye-catching feature. After James IV's death at the battle of Flodden Field, his son carried on the work of creating royal apartments and had reception rooms and bedchambers built above the ground floor vaults.

It was on the second floor that Mary, Queen of Scots had her rooms, and some of the original decoration survives in the painted ceilings and freize of her bedchamber. Mary, regarded by Catholics as the rightful Queen of England, was dining in her small supper room authoritative work 13.9 inches thick.

Right An aerial view of the Palace of Holyrood House, with the ruined abbey in the foreground. Originally built in the forests east of the town, the Palace was much more secluded than it is today. Salisbury Crags can be seen in the background.

in the west turret on March 9, 1566, along with guests who included her Italian secretary and hated favourite—David Rizzio. Protestant plotters accompanied by Mary's second husband, Henry, Lord Darnley, burst in over the Queen's protests and dragged Rizzio to an antechamber where they stabbed him to death. His body was left with over 50 dagger wounds. A brass tablet marks the spot.

The early Palace was only about 30 years old when, in 1544, an invading English army burned down most of it—and the adjoining abbey for good

measure—while laying waste to the countryside around Edinburgh. The great tower survived the flames, however, and after it had been repaired and extended the Palace buildings surrounded three courtyards occupying roughly the same site as the present ones. The palace stayed largely unchanged unto 1650, when an accidental fire reduced it to ruin except for the tower, whose massive walls saved it for the second time. Oliver Cromwell, who had quartered some of his troops there earlier that year while subduing the

rebellious Scots, ordered major rebuilding but in a style regarded as highly inferior to the original, and it stayed that way until the monarchy was restored with Charles II.

In 1661 Holyrood saw one of the most spectacular funerals in Edinburgh's history. The royalist Marquis of Montrose, who had been executed by Cromwell for high treason and had his limbs cut off for display around the country, was rehabilitated for a grand ceremony of farewell. One of his legs was brought from Aberdeen in an elaborate casket, his head from a spike in the capital, his other leg and his arms from Glasgow, Stirling and Perth, and the rest of his remains from the local gallows. After four months' lying in state in the chapel of Holyrood, the pieces of the Marquis were paraded through the crowded streets in a coffin carried by 14 earls and buried in the Kirk of St. Giles.

Although he never actually entered Holyrood, Charles II—the Merry Monarch—began building the existing Palace in 1671. It was a massive reconstruction which involved tearing down Cromwell's handiwork and erecting a new façade flanked at one end by the old tower put up by James

The Palace of Holyroodhouse

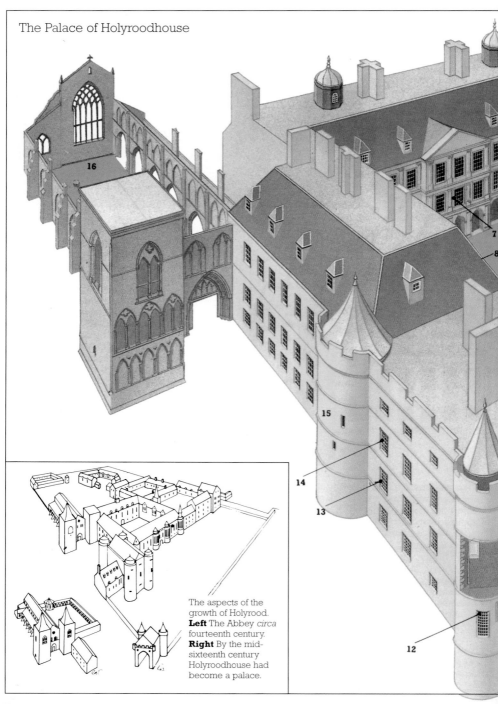

The aspects of the growth of Holyrood. **Left** The Abbey *circa* fourteenth century. **Right** By the mid-sixteenth century Holyroodhouse had become a palace.

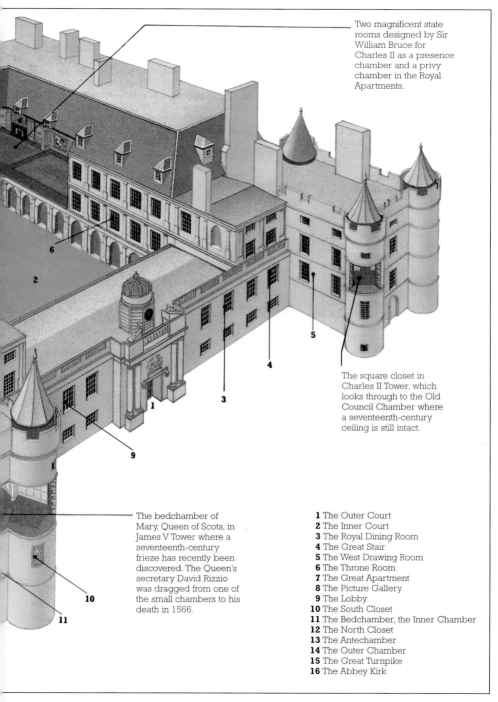

Two magnificent state rooms designed by Sir William Bruce for Charles II as a presence chamber and a privy chamber in the Royal Apartments.

The square closet in Charles II Tower, which looks through to the Old Council Chamber where a seventeenth-century ceiling is still intact.

The bedchamber of Mary, Queen of Scots, in James V Tower where a seventeenth-century frieze has recently been discovered. The Queen's secretary David Rizzio was dragged from one of the small chambers to his death in 1566.

1 The Outer Court
2 The Inner Court
3 The Royal Dining Room
4 The Great Stair
5 The West Drawing Room
6 The Throne Room
7 The Great Apartment
8 The Picture Gallery
9 The Lobby
10 The South Closet
11 The Bedchamber, the Inner Chamber
12 The North Closet
13 The Antechamber
14 The Outer Chamber
15 The Great Turnpike
16 The Abbey Kirk

IV more than 150 years earlier. The plans were drawn up by Sir William Bruce, a proven loyalist and fine architect, and the King's Master Mason, Robert Mylne, was called in to translate the design into stone. The total cost, sky-high for that time, was £57,000.

The Palace is built round an elegant, Italian-style courtyard quadrangle with an arcaded loggia and superimposed Doric, Ionic and Corinthian orders. On one projection there is a pediment bearing the Royal Arms, with its Scottish elements to the fore. The west front combines the medieval tower, which Charles II was anxious to retain, with the Renaissance classicism of the grass-covered courtyard. To achieve the effect he wanted, Bruce designed a matching tower on the southwest and linked the two with a screen dominated by a grand entrance of four Doric columns surmounted by the Royal Arms of Scotland. The motto 'In Defence' is emblazoned above the crest, while at its base are the Latin words *Nemo Me Impune Lacessit* (No one provokes me with impunity), motto of the Most Noble Order of the Thistle. The general style of Palace architecture is French, of the time of Louis XIV. The north side of the quadrangle contains the renowned Picture Gallery, with the State Apartments on the southern side.

Work on the new Palace was well under way by 1676 and three years later it was largely completed, with the truncated abbey becoming the Chapel Royal. The clock on the cupola over the gate bears the date 1680. A variety of non-Scots took part in the interior finishing.

Two Englishmen did the ornamental plasterwork, a Dutchman was responsible for the carving, and the decorative painting was by another Dutch-

Left This splendid fireplace of black veined marble is in the Morning Drawing Room. *Cupid and Psyche* are enclosed within the ornately carved wooden chimneypiece

Below The largest of the historical rooms, the Picture Gallery is still used for many state functions. Set into the panelling are the portraits of 111 Scottish monarchs.

man, Jacob de Wit.

De Wit's major legacy is to be found in the Picture Gallery—framed portraits of 111 Scottish kings and queens. A deed drawn up between Hugh Wallace, His Majesty's Cashkeeper, and de Wit 'binds and obleidges him to compleatly draw, finish and perfyte The Pictures of the Haill Kings who have Reigned over this Kingdome of Scotland... and to make them like unto the Originalls which are to be given to him'. De Wit set to with a will, but doubts have been cast on the accuracy of the likenesses he produced between 1684 and 1686 with the aid of old portraits supplied by the government. He was paid £120 a year for the work, which begins with King Fergus in the fourth century and ends with James VII—James II of England. A good deal of imagination seems to have gone into his masterpiece; more than 30 of de Wit's kings apparently never existed. Sir Walter Scott described the gallery as 'long, low and ill-proportioned, hung

Right The atmosphere of the seventeenth century is recaptured in Charles II's State Bedroom. The grand canopied bed dates from 1672.
Above The elaborate plasterwork on the ceiling is the work of Dunsterfield and Hulbert. It surrounds de Wit's *Apotheosis of Hercules.*

with pictures affirmed to be the portraits of kings who, if they ever flourished at all, lived several hundred years before the invention of painting in oil colours'. Undaunted, today's Royal Family holds state ceremonies in the gallery, which is the largest of the palace's 'historical apartments'. Representative peers of Scotland were elected in the gallery, which measures 150 feet (45 m)

long, 24 feet (7.2 m) wide and 20 feet (6 m) high. It was here that Bonnie Prince Charlie—otherwise Charles Edward, the Young Pretender—held sparkling levees during a stay in Edinburgh in 1745.

From the Picture Gallery, the State Apartments of the James IV Tower are entered through a chamber known as the Duchess of Hamilton's Drawing Room, which has ornamental ceilings and oval panels containing the cypher of Charles II. The Throne Room and drawing rooms all feature fine paintings, tapestries, furniture, panelling and ceilings. In the older part of the Palace are Lord Darnley's Rooms, consisting of an audience chamber, bedroom and dressing room with fireplaces of marble and Dutch tiles, portraits and ancient tapestry.

Queen Mary's corresponding apartments on the second floor are reached by a turnpike stair from Darnley's audience chamber. The public, by the way, has no access to a small private staircase by which the murderers of Rizzio entered the Queen's rooms on that fateful night in 1566. The supper room, where the attack on the Italian was mounted, is perhaps the most interesting of these apartments, at least for students of history. Coffered ceilings of oak are among the few fixed features left from Mary's time at Holyrood, but two panels embroidered in cross-stitch on linen canvas were genuinely

The richly carved ceiling of the Inner Chamber, or Queen's Bedroom, in James IV Tower is emblazoned with the initials of James V and his wife, Mary of Guise, mother of Mary, Queen of Scots. The panels were painted later, in the seventeenth century, and bear monarchs' emblems.

David Rizzio

Lord Darnley

Mary, Queen of Scots

The murder of Rizzio

Mary, Queen of Scots chose for her second husband in 1565 her cousin Henry Stuart, Lord Darnley. He was handsome and amusing and his claims to the English throne could bolster her own, but he was also violent, arrogant and had talents for making enemies, The royal pair soon quarrelled and when Mary was six months' pregnant with Darnley's child, he accused her of an affair with her Italian secretary. Jealous of the Queen's affection for the accomplished David Rizzio, Darnley found support for his hatred in those who thought the foreigner an undeserving, ambitious upstart. One cold night in March 1566 Darnley and his cohorts climbed the dark, hidden steps to Mary's chambers and dragged the screaming Rizzio from the Queen's supper table. In the corridor outside they stabbed him again and again. Rizzio died at Mary's feet with more than 50 wounds in his body. Darnley's dagger stood deep in his heart, left there for all to see by Darnley's accomplice, Lord Ruthven. Mary was distraught at the Italian's death but suspected that Darnley had wanted her dead too. He was killed by his enemies in an explosion at Kirk o'Field in 1567.

worked by the Queen during her imprisonment in England, where she was eventually put to death at the order of Elizabeth 1. Her work is signed with her monogram, MR.

The outer room, known as Queen Mary's Audience Chamber, 24 feet (72 m) long and 22 feet (66 m) wide, has a splendid display of heraldic symbols representing the arms of James V, King of Scots; his Queen, Mary of Guise; Mary, Queen of Scots; her first husband, the Dauphin of France; and his father, King Henry II of France. At the east end there is an oratory, and part of the freize which adorned the walls in Mary's time has been uncovered. Other panels contain the crowned initials of James V and his Queen. The initials recur in the inner chamber, called Queen Mary's Bedroom, which has panelled compartments with the emblems of Scottish sovereigns in the ceiling. The walls are hung with tapestry. More tapestry, much decayed, hangs in a small dressing room

The House of Stuart

Elizabeth Mure m(1) ROBERT II, King of Scots m(2) Euphemia of Ross
of Rowallan   d 1390

John Earl of Carrick (ROBERT III King of Scots)

Walter

Robert Earl of Fife (later Duke of Albany and Governor of Scotland)
— Murdoch Duke of Albany

Alexander

David Earl of Strathearn
— Euphemia m Sir Patrick Graham
— Malise Graham Earl of Strathearn

Walter Earl of Atholl
— James Master of Atholl   Alan
— Robert Master of Atholl

David Duke of Rothesay

JAMES I m(1) Joan Beaufort m(2) Sir James Stewart
King of Scots d 1437   The Black Knight of Lorne

JAMES II m Marie of Gueldres King of Scots d 1460   daughters

John Earl of Atholl

James Earl of Buchan

Andrew Bishop of Moray

JAMES III King of Scots d 1488 m Margaret of Denmark
— JAMES IV King of Scots d 1513 m Margaret Tudor m(2) Archibald Douglas 6th Earl of Angus

Alexander Duke of Albany
— John Duke of Albany (Regent) osp

John Earl of Mar osp

Mary m(1) Thomas Boyd, Earl of Arran osp m(2) James, 1st Lord Hamilton
— Elizabeth m Matthew Stewart 2nd Earl of Lennox
— John Stewart 3rd Earl of Lennox

James Hamilton 1st Earl of Arran
— James Hamilton 2nd Earl of Arran & Duke of Châtelherault (Regent)
— James Hamilton 3rd Earl of Arran d 1609

JAMES V m(1) Madeleine King of Scots of France d 1542 osp m(2) Marie de Guise

Lady Margaret m Matthew Stuart ★ Douglas 4th Earl of Lennox (Regent)

John Stuart 5th Lord d'Aubigny
— Esme Stuart 6th Lord d'Aubigny & 1st Duke of Lennox d 1583

MARY, Queen of Scots m Henry Stuart Lord Darnley ex 1587

HOUSE OF STUART

JAMES m Anne of Denmark
VI of Scotland and I of England d 1625

★ This Earl of Lennox took French nationality in 1537. From him derives the French spelling of the surname 'Stuart'

Henry Prince of Wales osp 1612

Elizabeth d 1662 m Frederick V Elector Palatine
— Sophia d 1714 m Ernest of Hanover

HOUSE OF HANOVER

CHARLES II d 1685 m Catherine of Braganza (no legitimate issue)

Mary m William of Orange
— WILLIAM III m MARY II d 1702 osp d 1694

CHARLES I m Henrietta Maria ex 1649

JAMES VII of Scotland m(1) Anne Hyde m(2) Mary of Modena and II of England d 1701

ANNE d 1714 (no surviving issue)

JAMES VIII and III m Maria Clementina d 1766 Sobieska
— CHARLES EDWARD ('Charles III') d 1788 m Louise of Stolberg (no legitimate issue)
— HENRY BENEDICT Cardinal Duke of York ('Henry IX') osp 1807

osp = died without children

which adjoins the bedroom and occupies the eastern turret of the tower. Tapestries in the State Apartments came from the looms of Flanders, Brussels and Paris in the sixteenth and seventeenth centuries, but much of the furniture dates from a later period.

Sir William Bruce's scheme for the State Apartments involved more rooms than Charles II finally decided to have. Bruce wanted to keep to the tradition of a separate suite of rooms and private stairs for the King and Queen. In each suite there was to be a guard hall, a 'presence chamber', a bedroom, dressing room and closets, planned so as to bring the bedrooms near to each other. But the King chose the eastern section for his apartments because he wanted to look out towards a garden he had made on the site of the demolished abbey's cloister. Except for her bedroom, the Queen's rooms were constructed in the southern range of the Palace. Charles also ruled out having the private chapel on the ground floor of the tower, insisting that the chapel should be at the eastern end of the long gallery where private family prayers could be said near his presence chamber.

With the building near completion, work was held up by political uncertainties and a lack of funds. The south and west quarters of the Palace were left unfinished, and a good deal of the oak panelling and plasterwork to be seen now is modern. But it fits in well with the original work—sympathetic treatment which has been credited to the Royal Family's interest since the Palace became their home in Scotland's capital.

A sun dial made in 1633 by a royal master mason graces the garden to the northwest of the James IV Tower. It has carvings of various royal heraldic badges and the crowned initials of Charles 1. The fountain in the palace forecourt was put up by Queen Victoria, and a small building called Queen Mary's Bath House stands in a corner of the one-time garden. She was reputed to have bathed there in wine.

During Bonnie Prince Charlie's stay in 1745, the Palace became the focus of a glittering court life, most notably the grand levee he staged in the long gallery. But then Holyroodhouse fell into disuse as a regular royal residence. The Duke of Cumberland lived there for a short time in 1746 after a punitive campaign in Scotland, but 50 years then went by before royalty came back in the person of a refugee from the French Revolution, Count d'Artois. He lived there for four years and later returned as the exiled King Charles X, staying for three more years. James Boswell, the author and traveller, described Holyrood as 'a virtuous place where no monarch dwells'. The tide turned in 1822, however, when George IV—the first Hanoverian king to set foot on Scottish soil—held a levee in the Palace but failed to take up residence because he found it uninhabitable. Queen Victoria and Prince Albert stayed in the royal apartments in 1850 and enjoyed their visit so much that they made a habit of resting at Holyroodhouse on their travels to and from Balmoral Castle.

Repair works prevented King Edward VII and Queen Alexandra from moving into the Palace in 1903, a year after their coronation, but they delighted Edinburgh society by holding a levee there. Holyroodhouse came more frequently into royal use with the accession of King George V and Queen Mary, who paid seven state visits between 1911 and 1934. Much redecoration and renovation were authorized by the royal couple, who had several

The sumptuous bedchamber of Mary, Queen of Scots was linked to Lord Darnley's below by a private staircase in James IV Tower. The Queen's room has since been changed and the bed moved to the King's Suite in the newer part of Holyrood Palace commissioned by Charles II.

Mary worked two of these panels when she was in the custody of George Talbot, 6th Earl of Shrewsbury. The cat and mouse expressed her own situation. Bess of Hardwick, George's wife, embroidered the third.

uncompleted state rooms panelled in oak to harmonize with the original designs. The kitchens were entirely remodelled and Queen Mary personally directed the refurnishing of many rooms. More lavish and colourful ceremonial revived under King George VI and Queen Elizabeth, the present Queen Mother. They took up residence and held a whole series of state functions in the Palace shortly after their coronation in 1937. Their many further visits have been emulated by the present Queen and Prince Philip, Duke of Edinburgh, since she succeeded to the throne.

Since 1929, the palace has had the official designation of the Palace of Holyroodhouse, a title first used centuries ago. Since its triumphant return to royal favour, the days seem long past when Robert Louis Stevenson wrote in 1896: 'The Palace of Holyrood has been left aside in the growth of Edinburgh and stands grey and silent in a workmen's quarter between breweries and gas works.'

However, all that now remains of the glory of the medieval 'fair Abbey of Holyrood' is reflected in its ruined nave. Only a section of the north wall and the roofless nave are from the original twelfth-century chapel. The magnificent window of the east wall dates back to the seventeenth century, when the abbey was partially restored for the coronation of Charles I. The abbey's story is one of destruction and

violence. The transepts and choir were brought down by church order in 1569 and the vaulted ceiling of the nave collapsed during a storm in 1768, felling the main arcading on the north side. The western front is generally in the English style, with intrusions of later Gothic. Gravestones pave the floor of the nave, and among the tombs is that of Sir James Douglas, who killed the Earl of Arran in 1596 and was himself stabbed to death by Arran's nephew in the High Street of Edinburgh 12 years later.

Rioters played their part in the abbey's long descent to ruin. The trouble erupted after James II fled from his throne and William and Mary arrived from Holland in the 'bloodless revolution' of 1688. Supporters of the Dutch Orangeman overwhelmed a company of musketeers defending the Palace and rampaged through the royal apartments, tearing out all the furniture and ornaments of the private chapel. Then, in a passion to purge the abbey of Roman Catholic ornaments, they burst into the kirk and smashed it up. The lids of lead coffins in the royal burial vault were stolen for their high market value, and the bones of kings and princes were said to have been left exposed for many years. The mob built a huge fire in the outer court, burning books, images and every last symbol of Catholicism—or so they thought. In fact, the altar vessels were saved and are now held by the Scottish hierarchy of the

Catholic Church. The royal vault was restored by Queen Victoria in 1898. Occupying the east end of the south aisle, it contains the remains of such Kings of Scots as David II, James II, James V and of Lord Darnley, consort of Mary, Queen of Scots.

For almost four centuries the abbey was a haven for debtors —not only paupers but professional men like doctors and lawyers who had fallen on hard times. Even the exiled King Charles X of France stayed there at one time. Debtors began seeking refuge in the abbey in the 1530s, and a small township grew up nearby with shops, taverns and markets. Inhabitants were under strict rules: they had to secure a place to sleep and report to the man in charge, the bailie, within 24 hours of arriving, but after that they were safe from the law.

The leave was allowed between midnight on Saturday and midnight on Sunday, and one debt-ridden minister used to walk 20 miles to preach in his parish and then trudge back again within the time limit. The last debtor recorded as having entered the abbey for sanctuary was an Edinburgh solicitor in 1880.

When it was founded in 1128, the abbey was in fact part of a sanctuary stretching from the base of the present-day Royal Mile to Duddingston Loch and covering what is now known as Holyrood Park. Today, despite its ravages, it remains an oasis of peace and serenity not far from the bustle of the city.

The Old Town

The tumult of ages has bequeathed old Edinburgh a brooding appeal

Winding alleys, dark lanes and thoroughfares steeped in history make up the Old Town of Edinburgh. It stretches from the Castle to the Palace of Holyroodhouse down the Royal Mile, main street of the medieval burgh. Built on a ridge ending with the towering Castle Rock, where Picts first founded a settlement in prehistoric times, it has captured the imagination of travellers through centuries of high drama. The antiquity and charm of this area have never been overshadowed by the New Town, the spacious and graceful city extension conceived in 1752. The main reason has to be a brooding appeal which stems from its history of violent death, of folly and betrayal, of noble patriotism and religious dedication.

Some of its history can be seen underground. Mary King's Close had shops, houses and taverns but was abandoned in the mid-seventeenth century after a plague epidemic. It is now part of the foundations of the City Chambers and guided tours are given (by advance appointment only). You can also take 'Auld Reekie's Underground City Tour', leaving daily from the Tron Church, which includes 'a pagan temple' and 'the haunted vault'. You have been warned!

Perhaps most evocative of the good—or bad—old days are the Grassmarket and the Cowgate, lying south of the Castle and the High Street. Cowgate, an extension of

Holyrood Road leading from the Palace, was originally a country lane along which cattle were driven to pasture. This narrow and somewhat sombre road has known its ups and downs in the life of the Old Town. In the fifteenth century it began to be a fashionable suburb with lavish mansions and private wells to provide acceptable drinking water for the gentry. Cowgate was described by the writer Alexander Alesse in the early sixteenth century as the place 'where the nobility and chief citizens dwell and the greatest in the land have their palaces, where nothing is cheap or mean but all things are magnificent'.

Some of the rich residents apparently disliked the road's somewhat earthy name, and the street degenerated over the years to the point where traveller Alexander Smith wrote in 1865: 'The inhabitants are morally and geographically the lower orders. They keep to their own quarters and seldom come up to the light of day. Many an Edinburgh man has never set his foot in the street. The condition of the inhabitants is as little known to respectable Edinburgh as are the habits of moles, earthworms and the mining population.' At the eastern entrance to the Cowgate stands the Magdalen Chapel, which was erected about the middle of the sixteenth century and contains what are regarded as the best examples of rare pre-Reformation stained-glass windows in Scotland. The

chapel now serves as the headquarters of the Scottish Reformation Society and can be viewed by the public.

Farther to the east stands St. Cecilia's Hall, which has a world-famous collection of over 30 keyboard instruments including harpsichords, clavichords, fortepianos, spinets, virginals and chamber organs.

On the south side once stood the Blackfriars Monastery, a Dominican friary founded as far back as 1230.

Cowgate then passes under an arch of South Bridge and into a valley between the Sheriff Court House on the south and the National Library of Scotland to the north. The library, opened by Queen Elizabeth II in 1956, contains more than three million books and manuscripts, the largest and most valuable collection of its kind in Scotland.

Take note of Guthrie Street, on the south side. Sir Walter Scott was born there in 1771, in a house long demolished and now marked by a stone tablet. After passing under George IV Bridge, Cowgate opens into the Grassmarket, a stately 230-yard (210 m) long rectangle standing in splendour under the lofty heights of the Castle. The tree-lined Grassmarket is a pleasant place now, but it has to be set against a bloody back-cloth of murder and execution. At the east end, a small enclosed garden marks the place where the public gallows stood until 1784, when a halt was ordered to executions in the Grassmarket.

'Common criminals' died in their hundreds on this spot, along with high-born leaders and rebel Covenanters—of whom at least 100 were hanged between the years 1661 and 1688. The site of the gallows is marked by a St. Andrew's Cross, in rose-coloured cobblestones, which bears the inscription: 'For the Protestant faith on this spot many Martyrs and Covenanters died.' The particular irony of the inscription is that, in the complex religious divisions of that era, it was other Protestants who ordered the executions. When one Covenanter stood on the gallows and refused to recant his faith in the face of death, the Duke of Rothes is said to have remarked: 'Then let him glorify God in the Grassmarket.'

The Grassmarket's most notorious inhabitants were infamous murderers. In Tanner's Close, long vanished, William Burke and William Hare carried out their trade of supplying corpses to surgeons for medical research. They lured paupers and prostitutes to their lodging house and strangled them. Hare finally turned against his companion in crime and got away with murder, but Burke was hanged in the Lawnmarket on 28th January 1829. The judge who sentenced him said in court: 'I trust that if it is ever customary to preserve skeletons, yours will be preserved in order that posterity may keep in remembrance your atrocious crimes.' The judge's remark was heeded, and Burke's body was delivered to the Department of Anatomy at Edinburgh University, where many of his victims had ended up. His skeleton may be seen at the Medical School today (by advance appointment only).

Murders, riots and executions apart, the Grassmarket had an important trading role in the life of the Old Town. In 1477 King James III granted a charter

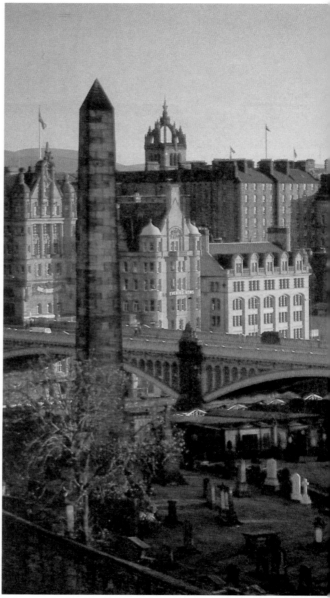

Spires emerge from the Old Town, viewed from above Calton churchyard.

for a weekly market which was held regularly until 1911, when it was removed to Saughton in the west of the city. Circuses, cockfighting and other so-called entertainments were once a feature of the bustling market-place nestled into a hollow at the base of Castle Rock. A plaque commemorating the 500th anniversary of the charter was unveiled in the west end of the

Grassmarket in 1977.

What a marvellous place the old marketplace must have been. Printers, tanners, brewers, tobacconists, corn merchants and 'such trades as prepare cat gut from the intestines of animals' all lived, worked and sold their goods there. On Fridays, the main market day, the area was so crowded that travel was almost impossible between the Grassmarket and the Cowgate. And yet this is still the largest open space in the Old Town. From the West Bow, so named because it was within arrow shot of the Castle, it extends just over 230 yards (210 m) to King's Stables Road.

In the heart of the Old Town you find tall, crammed buildings, dating from the fifteenth to the seventeenth century and almost Dutch in appearance. But only the occasional summer fair brings back the atmosphere of the ancient market. Perhaps the best example of the Grassmarket's age and architecture can be seen half way down the north side, before you reach Castle Wynd. A stairway entrance, only three feet (0.9 m) across, carries the inscription: 'Blessed by God for all his giftis.' Fascinating little shops abound here, and just up from the Grassmarket in West Bow and Victoria Street. Some offer cookery books, some offer clothes, new or second-hand. Others have coffee or cheese (Victoria Street is the best-smelling street in Edinburgh). One old-established shop sells every variety of brush you could ever want.

In a passage at the southwest corner of the Grassmarket is a section of the Flodden Wall, which was painstakingly built around Edinburgh after the Scots suffered a dreadful defeat by the English at the battle of Flodden Field in 1513. Some authorities say that the legendary caution of Edinburgh folk is exemplified by the fact the wall took the best part of 50 years to build. Nevertheless, it defined the limits of the burgh for 250 years; it now serves as the western boundary of the grounds of George Heriot's School, founded and endowed in 1628 by the goldsmith to King James VI.

There is another special sight to see on the north side of

the Grassmarket. It is the White Hart Inn, an early eighteenth-century hostelry which has beautiful wallhead gables to the front and two semi-octagonal stair towers at the rear. Among noted guests at the inn were the poets Robert Burns and William Wordsworth.

Before leaving the Grassmarket, do have a look at what is now the Apex Hotel, erected in 1968 to be part of Heriot-Watt University, on the site of the old Corn Exchange.

At its southeast corner the Grassmarket joins ancient Candlemaker Row and the southern part of the Old Town; it connects with the fragment of West Bow which now runs into Victoria Street. West Bow formerly led to the heights but was remodelled in the nineteenth century to join the George IV Bridge.

At the upper end of Victoria Street stand the India Buildings, erected in 1867 and now a Registrar's Office.

Candlemaker Row was named in recognition of one of Edinburgh's great crafts, which flourished from 1488 until gas lighting emerged early in the nineteenth century. The hall of the ancient Corporation of Candlemakers can be found at the head of the row. It was built in 1722 and restored in 1929. At the road junction in front of the hall is a memorial to 'Greyfriars Bobby', the Skye terrier who kept a 14-year vigil at the grave of his master in the adjoining churchyard. The main entrance of the churchyard, once the garden of a Franciscan monastery, can be reached through a lane at the top of Candlemaker Row.

More than any other place of worship in Edinburgh, Greyfriars Kirk reflects the turbulent history of the Church of Scotland from the Reformation in 1559 to the establishment of the Protestant faith in 1689. Its history is particularly closely

The old craft of candlemaking revived with a modern touch.

associated with the Covenanters. The church was opened in 1620—the first built in Scotland since the Reformation. It owned two 'repentance stools' on which worshippers with a record of unseemly behaviour were forced to sit during services. One of these stools has survived and is now to be seen at the National Museum of Antiquities in Queen Street. During the 1650s, when Oliver Cromwell's troops occupied Edinburgh, Greyfriars was used as a barracks. The congregation was unceremoniously kicked out. The church suffered badly at the hands of the soldiers, and a collection for repairs was taken at all the places of worship in Edinburgh when Greyfriars was handed back to the congregation in 1653. The church suffered yet again in 1718, when gunpowder stored in the tower by the city fathers exploded. The event was recorded by the Court Clerk in this way: 'On Wednesday the 7th of May instant 1718, about a quarter of an hour before Two of the Clock in the morning, the Grayfriar Church Steiple was blown up, which Surprized and allaramed the whole City, more particularly the Grayfrier Congregation. By which the Grayfrier Church sustained so great

damage as it was rendered unfit for the Congregation to assemble therein for publick worship . . .' After fresh repairs the kirk was reduced in sizeand a new church was built as an extension in 1721, with a dividing wall. It also suffered serious damage in a fire in 1845. Eventually the entire church was restored, the dividing wall was removed in 1938, and now the united congregations worship in the Kirk of the Greyfriars.

Today the church is architecturally quite unremarkable, a somewhat featureless oblong with an interior in a simple Gothic style. Its unbroken nave extends for 150 feet (45 m). But it stands in an historic enclosure —the churchyard occupying a spectacular site between the George IV Bridge and the Grassmarket. Its fame is chiefly associated with the signing of the National Covenant in 1638. Here, on February 28, in what is now the churchyard, the entire congregation gathered with Edinburgh's noblemen and merchants to put their names to the Covenant, which pledged all its signatories to fight anyone trying to establish the 'papist' religion in this country.

In effect, it professed loyalty to King Charles I but warned him not to interfere in the affairs of the Scottish Kirk. The Covenant, which also called for a free Scottish Parliament, was said to have been signed on a tombstone in the churchyard—sometimes in blood. Copies were later signed in churches all over Scotland.

On the side of the churchyard backing onto Candlemaker Row is the Martyrs, Monument, erected in 1688 to the memory of Covenanters who had been executed in Edinburgh more than 20 years earlier. Its inscription reads, in part: 'Here lies interred the dust of those who stood gainst perjury, resisting unto blood, adhering to the Covenants and laws . . .

Public executions were witnessed from these windows on the north side of the Grassmarket.

Their lives were sacrificed unto the lust of prelatists and abjur'd.'

The majority of the martyrs were buried in the churchyard, ironically not far from the tomb of the man who ordered their torture and execution. He was Sir George Mackenzie, a Lord Advocate—or royal prosecutor —who came to be known as 'Bluidy Mackenzie'.

In the southwest corner of the churchyard is the Covenanters' Prison. Some 1200 Covenanters, captured at the battle of Bothwell Bridge, were imprisoned for five months here—under open skies and through the grim Edinburgh winter of 1679.

Rigorously guarded, the inmates were allowed a daily ration of one 'penny loaf', but in many ways they were better off than their leaders—who were condemned to enslavement in the American plantations.

Round the churchyard walls are a range of stately monuments and ornate tombstones commemorating famous

citizens of old Edinburgh. Here are the last resting places of William Adam, the classical architect; Joseph Black, renowned physicist and chemist; George Buchanan, tutor to Mary, Queen of Scots; John and George Watson, who founded the hospitals (i.e.,charity schools) that bear their names; Gaelic poet Duncan Ban McIntyre; James Craig, architect of the New Town; and Dr Thomas McCrie, church historian and biographer of John Knox. But it must be said that most visitors head straight for the grave of Greyfriars Bobby, the faithful terrier. The spot is marked by a headstone provided by the 'American Lovers of Bobby'.

To the south, on the western side of the rural-sounding Middle Meadow Walk, stands one of Britain's leading hospitals, the Royal Infirmary. It started in a humble way in 1729 as a 'hospital for the destitute sick', with only six beds. The site is marked by a plaque at the top of Infirmary Street. A second royal infirmary was completed in 1748, starting with about 70

beds but growing as funds increased. Between 1762 and 1765, according to medical records, 15,600 patients were admitted, of which about 75 percent were discharged as cured. The records show that about 750 patients died under treatment, and quite a few 'left of their own accord'. The foundation stone of the present building was laid in 1870 by the Prince of Wales, later Edward VII, and the new hospital was opened nine years afterwards. There was a major extension in 1939, when the Royal Simpson Maternity Pavilion was opened. Nowadays the Royal Infirmary is one of the most important centres in the country for training doctors. The Infirmary, however, is scheduled to move to Little France, on the outskirts of Edinburgh, around 2002.

There is quite an inspiring story about the building of the first infirmary. Its true creator was George Drummond, who was elected six times as Lord Provost (Mayor) of Edinburgh and is regarded as the father of the city. Drummond struck a chord among the residents when he appealed for funds to meet this crying need in eighteenth-century Edinburgh. Money poured in from firms as well as individuals, from church-door collections and social groups who had the name of 'dancing assemblies'. Well-off citizens provided cash in response to Drummond's appeal. Landowners and quarrymasters gave stone, slates and timber. Farmers supplied carts for carrying materials to the site. Some English companies gave glass for the windows— and many Edinburgh workmen toiled there without wages for one day a month. The sacrifices were made out of a genuine desire for progress and one wonders whether such dedication could emerge today in a different but no less traumatic climate.

The New Town

The prime mover for the New Town, its inspiration and drive, was the city's Lord Provost, George Drummond.

Drummond, who had the idea from one mooted at the time of Charles II a century earlier, started planning the extension to the city when he was first elected Lord Provost in 1725. In his biography the Reverend Thomas Somerville quotes a fascinating conversation he had with Drummond:

'I happened one day . . . to be standing at a window (in the Old Town) looking out to the opposite side of the North Loch, then called Barefoot's Parks, in which there was not a single house to be seen. "Look at these fields", says Provost Drummond. "You Mr. Somerville are a young man and may probably live, though I will not, to see all these fields covered with houses, forming a splendid and magnificent city. To the accomplishment of this nothing more is necessary than draining the North Loch and providing a proper access from the Old Town. I have never lost sight of this object since the year 1725 when I was first elected Provost".'

But it was not until 1752 that his 'Proposals' were published and 14 years later a competition for the final plans opened. It was won by an unknown 23-year-old architect, James Craig, son

Detail of a Charlotte Square window (**above**) and the Moray Estate (**left**).

of an Edinburgh merchant. Only six had entered the contest and the prize was the freedom of the city and a gold medal. For James Craig there was also overnight fame.

The cause of all the planning was the great increase in population (the Scots economy was improving) to about 50,000 who were crammed within the ancient city walls on an area of 138 acres (55.2 ha). Conditions were gruesome, disease rife and crime high. It was clear something had to be done.

Drummond, six times Lord Provost between 1725 and 1764, was met by plenty of traditionalist opposition to his visionary ideas but he was shrewd enough to push them through in well-spaced stages.

First came the publication of the 'Proposals' in 1752, setting out the intention to build on the green fields overlooking the city to the north. Then in 1765 a contract was awarded for the building of North Bridge to take a new road across the valley of Nor' Loch to the port of Leith and at the same time give access to the New Town land (much of which had been bought already by speculating city officials).

A year later, the year of Drummond's death, the competition was announced and in 1767, only two weeks after Parliament in Westminster had passed the Act to extend the city limits, Craig's win was announced.

The first stage

Craig's plan was classic and grand, with its grid-iron pattern of squares, gardens and parallel streets. But it was simple, too, and without any detailed drawings for the rows of houses that were to come. That was left to other architects.

The street names were an integral part of the design and symbolized the parliamentary union between England and

Above Craig's triumphant design in the 1776 competition for a New Town plan. **Left** The 23-year-old winner at work. **Far right** The architect Robert Adam in profile. **Below** One of the finest examples of his genius, Register House, designed in 1772. **Right** Interior of Register House.

Scotland, glorifying George III and the House of Hanover. George Street, the main axis, linked two magnificent squares that were to be St. George's and St. Andrew's, the patron saints of England and Scotland, but Queen Charlotte thought differently and the former was soon renamed after her.

The outer streets were Princes and Queen Streets and were crossed by Frederick (George's son), Hanover and Castle Streets. The ones in between, where the trades and craftsmen were to thrive, were Thistle and Rose Streets, named after the national emblems of Scotland and England.

There was, though, a reluctance on the part of the townspeople to build in the New Town area and the city's council soon came to the conclusion that incentives would have to be offered.

Mr. John Young, who built his house at Thistle Court, off St. Andrew Square, was awarded £20 for being the first to make his home in the New Town. The silk merchant John Neale was exempted from city rates when he built the first house in Princes Street in 1769.

In 1777 advertisements invited plans 'by which buildings might be erected in the most regular, handsome and commodious manner'. Plain-fronted tenements, double flats and houses began to spring up but there was no uniformity of style and by 1782 the city decided to impose a few rules. Every house on the main streets, for example, was to be three-storeyed with a sunk basement and a frontage of not more than 48 feet (14.4 m). Failure to comply meant a £30 fine and immediate removal. But the more elaborate houses were designed by the notable architects of the day and the New Town became the fashionable place to live.

By now Robert Adam had

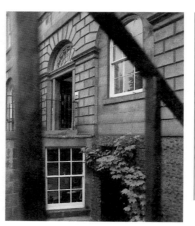

Above Charlotte Square in detail from the air; and the original elevation plan drawn by Robert Adam for the north and south sides (only the north was built). **From the left:** The view of West Register House from the square, the square's surroundings; intricate old street lamps; and an elegant dooway.

made his reputation as a stylish young architect in England and had made some very influential friends. But he returned to his native Scotland (which he had left calling it 'a narrow place') for the chance to design great public buildings.

Register House, where the historic and administrative records of state are kept, was started in 1774 from designs of Robert's and his brothers James and John. Robert did not actually move to Edinburgh but, as the building progressed, John kept an eye on it and Robert visited. It took more than 12 years to build and cost the government £31,000 but it is still one of the most remarkable architectural features of the city with its huge dome and splendid frontage. The former home of Sir Laurence Dundas flanks the east side of St. Andrew Square. This square is one of the richest in the world due to the number of banks and insurance headquarters there. In the centre is a statue of Henry Dundas, 1st Viscount Melville, a powerful Scottish figure in the 1780s.

At the other end of George Street, balancing St. Andrew Square, is Charlotte Square, the most spectacular and beautiful of Adam's achievements. It was designed by Robert Adam who had been commissioned by the town council in 1791 to produce a unified scheme of frontages for the houses in the square – something quite new to a city where only a similarity in style had been attempted.

Robert died the following year and a letter written by his brother James afterwards asks for payment on account of a promise to Robert of 200 guineas for the elevations for Charlotte Square. But, accounting difficulties aside, the building went ahead and the rectangular square, with streets entering at each corner, one side of elegant frontages mirroring its opposite side and

The beauty of the Royal Bank of Scotland, formerly Sir Laurence Dundas's home, designed by Sir William Chambers in 1772. The star shapes cut in the ceiling allow light in. Light, this time at night, illuminates the Assembly Rooms (**right**).

the gardens in the middle, is a major achievement in European civic architecture.

Princes Street, once regarded as the most beautiful street in Europe, grew up rather haphazardly, starting at the beginning of the building of the New Town and not ending until 1805. It has a glorious open view on the south side across the gardens to the Castle. But this now much-admired view was once under threat. Town officials, greedy for the profits

of development, discussed a plan to enclose the south side of the street and, after a running battle, the gardens' owners were smart enough to take out a 99-year lease on the land in 1771, which prevented any building at all.

During the building of Princes Street's north side the excavated earth from it, and other streets, was used to fill in the already drained Nor' Loch to make private gardens for the residents. These were jealously

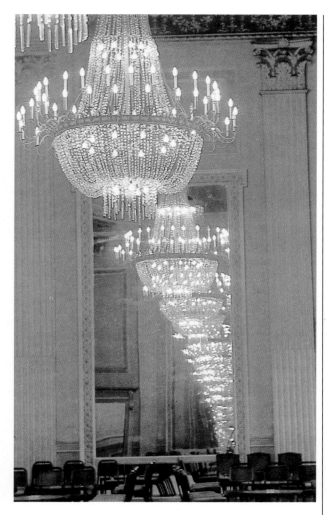

lost his fortune after a divorce and a disastrous second marriage.

It was Miss Burns' custom to take an evening walk along Princes Street where she attracted much attention. But it was her behaviour at her home that caused enormous trouble – particularly to a Lord Swinton whose back windows overlooked hers. The matter ended in court where Bailie – later Lord Provost – Creech heard the case and expelled her from the city on pain of six months in a House of Correction, 'drumming' through the streets and further expulsion. But she appealed to higher courts and won the right to stay.

Baile Creech's dislike of the 20-year-old beauty was well known and the matter prompted comment from many. Even Robert Burns has his say on the lady:

> Cease, ye prudes, your envious railing:
> Lovely Burns has charms – confess:
> True it is she had one failing:
> Had a woman ever less!

The second stage

By the close of the eighteenth century the New Town had become the fashionable place to live and in the 1820s the Governors of Heriot's Hospital, who owned the land immediately to the north, embarked upon a speculative extension to the New Town. This second stage was largely residential and has remained so. The scale therefore is more homely and the downhill sloping site gave magnificent views across the Forth to Fife. The whole development was largely under the control of Robert Reid, the Master of the King's Works in Scotland, and William Sibbald, Superintendant of Works in the City, and thus has more architectural unity than the first stage.

guarded from the public – possibly because it was the owners who had to pay for planting and laying them out.

The garden owners were issued with keys, for £1 each, to get into the gardens but it was not long before a Rose Street locksmith was producing replicas and a builder of houses in Castle Terrace gave his buyers keys which just happened to fit the garden gates!

The Mound, which divides the gardens, was begun by a Lawnmarket clothier, George Boyd, in 1781, as a shortcut for his New Town customers. His mud brig was officially sanctioned by the Town Council and more than two million cartloads of soil from the foundation of New Town houses were dumped there in his time.

Rose Street was also the centre of a scandal which shocked the local residents. In about 1789 a young lady called Miss Burns moved to the street from Durham where her father had

It too is based on a grid system. The outward-looking Heriot and Fettes Rows flank Northumberland, Cumberland and Great King Streets, which lead onto the massive open spaces of Drummond Place and Royal Circus.

Royal Circus was the work of William Playfair, possibly the most prolific and influential of Edinburgh's architects. He was born in London in 1789, the son of a Scots architect, and when his father died in 1793, William was sent to Edinburgh to his uncle John, professor of mathematics and, later, of natural philosophy, at the city's prestigious university.

William first gained attention when he won a competition for a design which would complete the university, largely planned by Robert Adam. He went on to do a massive amount of work until his death in 1857. Donaldson's Hospital was his largest work but the others were scarcely inconsiderable: the National Gallery, the Calton Hill scheme (the National Monument and New Observatory) the Royal Institution (now the Royal Scottish Academy), the Royal College of Surgeons. The list is almost endless–even the Princes Street railway line was his design.

This phase, too, met with great opposition. Robert Chambers, writing his *Walks in Edinburgh* in 1825, says the building of Heriot Row was thought by many to be a mad speculation. And an English traveller, Sir John Carr, said the fine view from Queen Street was beginning 'to be interrupted by the recent elevation of new streets and particularly by the houses on a piece of ground called Heriot's Row.'

The lesser streets run parallel to the main ones, and Northumberland and Cumberland Streets, which have marvellous Georgian features, have been extensively restored.

Another, Jamaica Street, was inferior and deteriorated so badly that it was eventually demolished. But it did have one claim to posterity. For a time, the young Thomas Carlyle tried to find the tranquillity he needed for his writing in a top flat there but his window overlooked Royal Circus and he wrote, in 1821, that 50 masons were 'chipping away'. He moved to more peaceful rural surroundings in Spey Street on the road to Leith.

The East End and Calton Hill
The area that earned Edinburgh the title of 'Athens of the North' is Calton Hill. There is an odd array of buildings and monuments, begun in 1776 and finished in 1830.

The Old Observatory came first, designed by Craig and made to look, it is said on the suggestion of Robert Adam, like a fortress. It is his only surviving building in the city and is basically a tower with Gothic windows. He planned it in 1776 but it was not completed until much later – in 1792.

Nearby is the New Observatory, Roman Doric and in the shape of a cross, begun in 1818 and designed by William Playfair. There is also a monument in Grecian Doric form to his uncle, John Playfair, who was also president of the Astronomical Institution.

William Playfair was also responsible for the monument to Dugald Stewart, another Grecian-style construction like a small circular temple. Stewart succeeded Adam Ferguson as professor of moral philosophy at the university in 1785. Both his memorial and that to Burns on the lower slope of the hill near Regent Road, designed by Thomas Hamilton (1830), were copied from the monument of Lysicrates in Athens.

Above them rises the column of Nelson's Monument, a rather Gothic design by Robert Burn

The glories of Calton Hill. **Far left**: The neo-classical memorial to the philosopher Dugald Stewart by William Playfair (1822). **Near left** Nelson's Monument (1807) by Robert Burn. **Below** The ribs of the intended National Monument, started in 1822 and never completed because of lack of funds.

The steady expansion of the New Town over the years is marked by distinctly separate stages of development.

The First New Town

The Second New Town

Moray Estate

Stockbridge and the Dean Valley

The West End

The East End and Calton Hill

Further Extensions

and supposed to represent an upturned telescope. On top of the 106-foot (31.8m) tower is a time ball which drops daily at 1.00 pm, at the same time the Castle cannon is fired.

But the National Monument which stands on the summit is the one that grabs the eye. Funds with which to complete it were not forthcoming and it stands now not as a memorial to the Scottish soldiers and sailors who died in the Napoleonic Wars as was intended but to the hasty enthusiasm of those who conceived it.

It was supposed to be an exact copy of the Parthenon to be used as a grand memorial church with catacombs beneath, a sort of 'Scottish Valhalla'. C. R. Cockerell designed it originally but Playfair was ultimately responsible.

In 1822, when part of the money had been collected, the foundation stone was laid with great ceremony but only the base and 12 columns were built —at the cost of £1000 each. Ever since, the structure has been called all sorts of names: Scotland's Pride and Poverty, Edinburgh's Disgrace and Edinburgh's Folly.

Waterloo Place, which leads from Princes Street to the hill, was conceived to give access to the new prison on the south slope. In 1815, the year of Wellington's victory, Robert Stevenson started work on the street. Old houses had to be cleared, a gorge crossed and tons of rock removed from the hill. Now all that is left of the jail is the little 'fortress' of the governor's residence and the underworks that support St. Andrew's House.

Further east is the old Royal High School. The school was founded in 1128 and originally supervised by the abbots of Holyrood. But by the early nineteenth century, when a new building was considered,

it was the responsibility of the city fathers. The site at Calton Hill was chosen in 1825 after much discussion. Thomas Hamilton, a former pupil, was asked to plan it and he kept the cost down to £24,000. Building was completed in 1829 and it is generally regarded as one of the best of the city's neo-classical edifices.

The New Town to the east was mooted as far back as 1811 on ground belonging largely to Heriot's and Trinity Hospitals, and Mr. Allan of Hillside. Once again Playfair took over a project, this time from his master William Stark, who had stressed the importance of trees and landscape in his discussions. Stark died in 1818 and the following year Playfair completed his design. It is very spacious and Royal Terrace, on the north side of the hill, is the grandest part of the triangle. It is the longest continuous frontage in the city—very nearly a quarter of a mile—and was built between 1821 and 1860.

Regent Terrace, which looks south over the Old Town, is an impressive continuous block which climbs to make a grand sweep around the end of the hill. It is decorated with a wrought-iron balcony which runs the whole length.

In between, the triangular garden was designed for the proprietors' use with the idea that it would be more attractive than the scheme at the West End.

The West End

The story of this area, bordered by Queensferry Road and Haymarket Terrace, Belford Road and Atholl Crescent, is spread over many years. James Gillespie Graham produced a master plan in 1813 but progress was confused by the feudal rights of landowners and an enormous number of architects. Building in the area went on until 1907.

Robert Brown designed most of the area from Melville Street to Coates Crescent for the Walker family in 1813. In the middle of the street, where it is crossed by Walker Street, is Melville Crescent, laid out by John Lessels in 1855 with a grandiose statue of the 2nd Viscount Melville in the centre.

At one end of the street is St. Mary's Episcopal Cathedral, designed by Sir George Gilbert Scott in 1879, a solid soaring edifice to Victoriana. It is the largest ecclesiastical building erected in Scotland since the Reformation.

The Misses Walker of Easter Coates were largely responsible for the creation of the massive cathedral. They left their grand old manor house—and the fortune they made by letting off the bulk of their estate during the latter stages of the building of the New Town—to the Church. The result was the cathedral with its two western towers, finished in 1917, named Barbara and Mary after them.

Atholl Crescent, by Thomas Bonnar (1824), was the home of William Gladstone's father, Sir John, who lived at Number 11. Across the road, in Coates Crescent, an earlier block by Robert Brown built between 1813 and 1823, is the W. E. Gladstone Memorial, moved there from its original site in St. Andrew Square in 1955. Atholl Crescent is interrupted by Canning House, the last of the office towers to be built in Edinburgh's centre before they were banned in 1974.

The two crescents lead into Shandwick Place where Sir Walter Scott lived for two years at Number 6. He left when he gave up his post as clerk of session in 1830.

Scott was instrumental in helping his literary neighbour, in Manor Place, Mrs. Grant of Laggan, acquire a pension of £100 a year from George IV.

The lady, who wrote *Letters from the Mountains,* held many parties for celebrities of her time and the profits from her writing, together with bequests from deceased friends and the pension paid through the Civil Establishment of Scotland, made her later years comfortable. She died in Manor Place in 1838 at the age of 84.

Manor Place leads into Rothesay Place, built by John Watherston between 1876 and 1907. There were strange disturbances reported by one owner who had brought home a piece of wood from a friend's cottage in the north of Scotland. Drawers opened and closed of their own accord, teapots fell off the table, and a pervading smell of tobacco lingered. It was all blamed on a sailor called Merry Jack Tar who was supposed to be haunting the flat above the old Theatre Royal.

In the theatre itself ghosts apparently re-enacted plays on stage after the manager and his family had retired to their upstairs flat. This story, also linked with Tar, was mentioned in a pamphlet marking the closure of the theatre in 1859.

The Moray Estate

In 1822, the same year work began on Royal Circus, Lord Moray advertised his estate for a development. It had been bought 40 years before by the previous Earl of Moray to use as the family's suburban home. It was an odd-shaped piece of land, north of Charlotte Square, bounded by the deep gorge of the Water of Leith on its further side.

The Earl, in the conditions he set for the sale of his grounds, had determined to make the new area of the highest quality. He had, in the architect's words, done 'everything in his power, consistent with his own interest, to render the plan ornamental to the City and convenient for the inhabitants'. He had ensured, equally, that none of the

expense of streets, sewers, boundary walls or pleasure gardens would fall on him but, proportionately, would be the purchasers' responsibility.

The plans for the new estate were drawn by James Gillespie Graham. For a fee of five guineas he supplied drawings of each house front, including full-size details, which would grace the newest part of the New Town. He even designed the railings which had to be of a standard pattern—a distinctive double rail with wreaths in between—for the price.

Gillespie Graham shied away from the grid-iron pattern of Craig and created instead the majestic curves of Randolph Crescent, Ainslie Place and the many-sided Moray Place, connected with short avenues to the streets of Craig, Reid and Sibbald.

All the building that was going on was quite a surprise to many of the townspeople. An anonymous diarist wrote, in March 1823, that the sale of the Earl's grounds 'which commenced last year, is likely to lead to the formation of a third grand division of our new town. The addition of from 700 to 800 new dwelling-houses in Edinburgh every year for some years past, one would think, must through time over-stock the market and lower the rents, but this state of matters has not yet taken place.'

In October he was still astonished at the progress: 'The most remarkable increase as to buildings of expensive architecture are those on Lord Moray's ground. . . . Now a great part of three or four sides of the Octagon are visible.' Moray Place, the grandest of circuses, is,' in fact, 12-sided. Only two sides can be seen at a time and each has a tuscan portico, alternatively plain and pedimented. Lord Moray took one of the houses, Number 28, for his own home.

Most of the house-plots had been sold by 1827 although a few plots on the south side of Great Stuart Street and Ainslie Place remained undeveloped until the middle of the century.

On the steep, wooded slope that led from the houses to the Water of Leith, the land was planted with shrubs and pathways were made. It became known as Lord Moray's pleasure-ground. It, too, was paid for by the householders who enjoyed it and who contributed to its upkeep. Their successors still use the gardens for a stroll along the cliff whose retaining walls are now ivy-decked.

Stockbridge and the Dean Valley

Across the Water of Leith, beyond the city boundary, there was building too. The villages that had existed for centuries were swallowed up by new streets but they were not digested and still remain—black, old and incongruous in the middle of the grey eighteenth and nineteenth century serenity.

The earliest development of these outlying villages began in 1813 when the portrait painter Sir Henry Raeburn began to sell house-building plots in the street that he had given to his wife Ann, and named after her. It is rather grand in the middle but the houses at the two ends of the street have a doll's-house charm with long front gardens, a rare thing in Georgian streets. Tradition maintains that Raeburn designed it himself but it may have been the work of the architect James Milne.

In nearby Henderson Row on July 1, 1823, the foundation stone of the new Edinburgh Academy was laid despite the opposition of the Town Council. The Council maintained that distinctions of wealth would be introduced if there were a rival to the high school where children from all walks of life had studied together. But Sir Walter Scott was behind the new school, together with other powerful voices like the judge, Henry, Lord Cockburn. Both men joined the first board of 16 directors, whose chairman was Robert Dundas of Arniston.

The Council were furious but could do nothing. There was a rumour, though, that the Council deliberately chose the site for William Playfair's massive St. Stephen's Church to block the view of the new academy which could be seen from the whole length of Howe Street.

Where Henderson Row meets Hamilton Place is the district of Silvermills. In 1607 quantities of silver were found at Linlithgow, 15 miles away from the city, and ore was refined on the banks of the Water of Leith. Traces of the mills, bought by James IV with the mines, remain on both sides of West Silvermills Lane.

In 1824 the Lord Provost Learmonth proposed a new bridge to his newly acquired estate of Dean, north of the river near the west end of town. He had ideas of development too and employed Thomas Telford to build Dean Bridge, begun in 1829, which was one of the highest of its era. But a recession had set in and it was another 20 or 30 years before the streets like Oxford and Eton Terraces were built—in Victorian style.

The old village of Dean, west of the bridge, has partly survived almost hidden in the gorge of the Water. It was, in the sixteenth and seventeenth centuries, a very busy milling centre where there were 11 mills and many 'baxters' (bakers) of Edinburgh.

City Life

The most extraordinary thing about all the energetic, speculative building and investment that went on in the whole of the New Town was that the common people were starving.

At the turn of the nineteenth century the city streets were infested with beggars, there was widespread unemployment and famine—and ugly violence followed.

War with France and poor harvests made food scarce and dear. The 'meal mobs'—famished townspeople—attacked shops to provide grain for their malnourished families. In 1800 Parliament was forced to allow the town's authorities to raise £10,000 to give food to the impoverished but it wasn't enough and further riots, in the Grassmarket and Cowgate, followed. Permanent soup kitchens and cash handouts had to be made for those in need.

In 1811 Hogmanay was, in the words of diarist W. M. Gilbert, 'disgraced by a series of riots, outrages and robberies'. Two people died in the riot and a reward of 100 guineas was offered for the arrest of the murderers. Three youths, all under 18, were hanged.

There was also the problem of professional beggars; those who refused to work in a House of Industry (the work house) were sent to Bridewell Prison and the special society formed to deal with beggars heard 622 cases in its first year of operation, The Committee for the Relief of Workmen out of Employment helped a few with work on the roads project, costing £10,000 at Calton, and on the Union Canal to Glasgow.

Properly trained police were brought in to replace the much-criticised town guard and they were certainly well occupied by those, not finding work, who fought and looted in the streets.

Despite the problems of the city, the poverty and lack of public funds, the New Town grew to be acclaimed as a huge architectural and town planning success, much admired throughout the Europe of the era and still renowned today.

Unusual in the New Town is the rural feeling that has been captured in the pleasant development of Ann Street. The artist Sir Henry Raeburn, whose wife was called Ann, started laying out the land in 1813 with unusually long gardens in front of the rather formal Georgian houses.

The Georgian House

An English tradition brought style and quality to Edinburgh living

Towards the end of the eighteenth century the building of the Edinburgh New Town with its terraces of spacious Georgian residences permitted a style and quality of living previously unthought of in Scotland. The new residents of this extension to the city were consciously Anglophile in their admiration of all things English and wished to reproduce the high standard of living they glimpsed on their very occasional visits to London. Some of the grandest of their private dwellings stood on Charlotte Square at the west end of James Craig's New Town plan.

The north side of this square was designed by Robert Adam and its building begun before his death in 1792. It is a masterpiece in the Georgian neo-classical style. Under the influence of ancient Roman architecture Adam created an impressive 'palace' façade to dominate the handsome square. Heavily rusticated at the base and decorated with a variety of light ornament on the upper levels, this symmetrical façade embraces separate houses, all of which underwent drastic interior alteration during the Victorian period. Now, one of them—No. 7—has been completely restored to the style of the late eighteenth century.

Its owners and keepers, the National Trust for Scotland, went to enormous lengths to guarantee the authenticity of the restoration. Appropriate furniture and fittings were acquired from all over the country; suitable paintings either given or borrowed; layers of paint removed from walls and woodwork in an attempt to discover the original colour scheme; floor-boards dry-scrubbed in the original style; and eighteenth-century pattern fabrics specially woven for curtains and coverings. The result for the visitor is a genuine experience of the lifestyle of such a house around 1800.

In every room there is a fascinating array of artefacts. The dining room, its table prepared for dinner with Wedgwood dinner service and Sheffield plate; the adjoining bedchamber (reconstructed here, as it would have been in the late eighteenth century, on the ground floor) with its wonderful four-poster bed dominating the room; and, perhaps most magnificent, the formally arranged drawing room stretching the entire width of the house. Do not miss the kitchen in the basement, and try to imagine a small army of servants needed to run such a grand, sophisticated house.

Another feature makes a visit to No. 7 Charlotte Square an extraordinary pleasure. This is the absence of ropes cordoning off the valuable 'exhibits'. You can stroll freely around the house. Touching the furniture is, of course, forbidden but the lack of obvious restrictions makes for a more relaxed atmosphere.

Right The contents of the dining room date mainly from the last quarter of the eighteenth century. Note especially the harlequin set of chairs.
Left This Wedgwood dinner service was made around 1830.

Above No kitchen was complete without a mortar and pestle. This large specimen is made from marble.
Right The kitchen was painted blue as it was believed that this colour contained something to ward off flies.

Viewpoints

Enjoying Scotland's capital city from the summits of seven hills

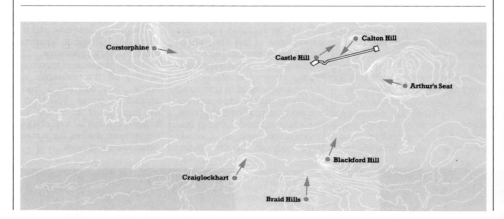

Corstorphine • →   Calton Hill •

Castle Hill   • Arthur's Seat

Blackford Hill •

Craiglockhart •

Braid Hills •

Calton Hill

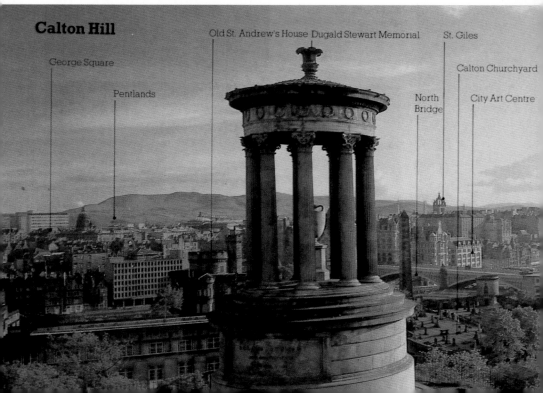

George Square   Old St. Andrew's House   Dugald Stewart Memorial   St. Giles

Pentlands   North Bridge   Calton Churchyard

City Art Centre

Edinburgh was described by her native son Robert Louis Stevenson as a 'precipitous city'. Like Rome, she is built upon seven hills, though perhaps without the craggy magnificence of her southern counterpart. Nevertheless, Edinburgh's 'mountains' do provide an amazingly variegated panorama of street and building, close and park.

The hills are all named:

Blackford	539ft (164m)
Braid	675ft (206m)
Castle	435ft (133m)
West Craiglockhart	575ft (175m)
Arthur's Seat	823ft (251m)
Calton	328ft (100m)
Corstorphine	531ft (162m)

The highest is Arthur's Seat, named in the fifteenth century with the revival of interest in the Arthurian romances. An extinct volcano of red igneous rock, Arthur's Seat offers panoramic views over the city to the Pentland Hills and the Firth of Forth.

Calton Hill, as Stevenson noted, is the best place from which to view both the Castle and Arthur's Seat. The views along Princes Street and of the Old Town are truly magnificent. It slopes rather abruptly on the northwestern ridge.

Blackford Hill was described by Scott as the spot where Marmion stood gazing with rapt wonder and delight on the scene below. Overlooking the gentle southern suburbs of the city, it is located in a park with a pond and assorted birdlife. It is also the home of the Royal Observatory.

Craiglockhart Hill, of hard basalt, overlooks the southwestern part of the city. The village of Swanston is still much as it was when Stevenson described it.

Braid Hill gives fine views of Ben Lomond to the northwest and the slopes of the Pentlands to the south.

Corstorphine Hill offers a wide panorama of the city. The Clermiston Tower was built to celebrate the centenary of the birth of Sir Walter Scott (1771). The crest of the hill figures in Stevenson's *Kidnapped* and is the site of the Edinburgh Zoo.

Castle Hill is perhaps the most commanding spot in Edinburgh. Since it was the starting point for the city, almost the whole of both the Old and New Towns are visible, and the parapets make for an infinite variety of viewpoints.

For the energetic, fit and trim, the hills can be mounted over the course of a couple of days. Transport is easily arranged by bus, foot or car.

Outlook Tower
Bank of Scotland
Edinburgh Castle
Balmoral Hotel
Scott Monument
Greenside Village
Caledonian Hotel
St. Mary's Cathedral
Register House
West Register House
King James Hotel

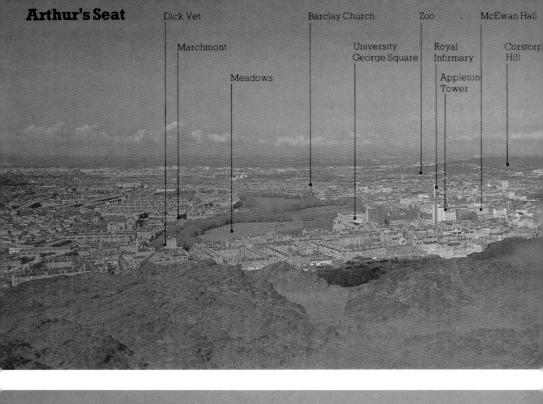

Arthur's Seat

Dick Vet

Marchmont

Meadows

Barclay Church

University, George Square

Zoo

Royal Infirmary

Appleton Tower

McEwan Hall

Corstor[Hill]

Blackford Hill

Granton

West Register House

St. Gile[s]

[C]astley Ainslie Hospital

Edinburgh Castle

Royal Infirmary

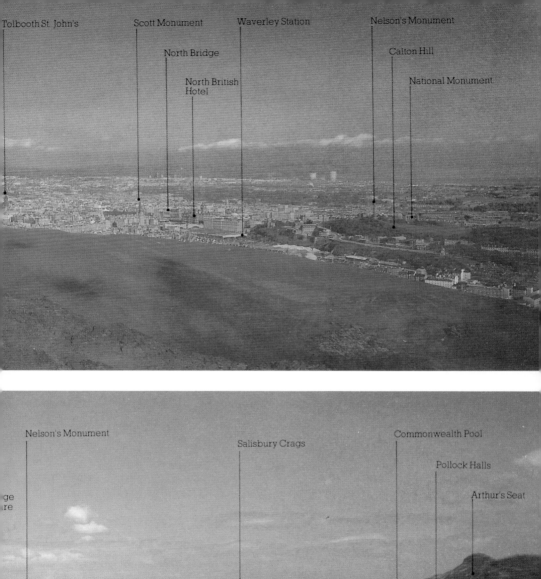

Tolbooth St. John's   Scott Monument   Waverley Station   Nelson's Monument

North Bridge   Calton Hill

North British Hotel   National Monument

Nelson's Monument   Salisbury Crags   Commonwealth Pool

ge re   Pollock Halls

Arthur's Seat

Braid Hills

Forth Bridges

Corstorphine Hill

Granton

Wester Craiglockhart

Fife

Firth of Forth

Donaldson's School

St. Mary's Cathedral

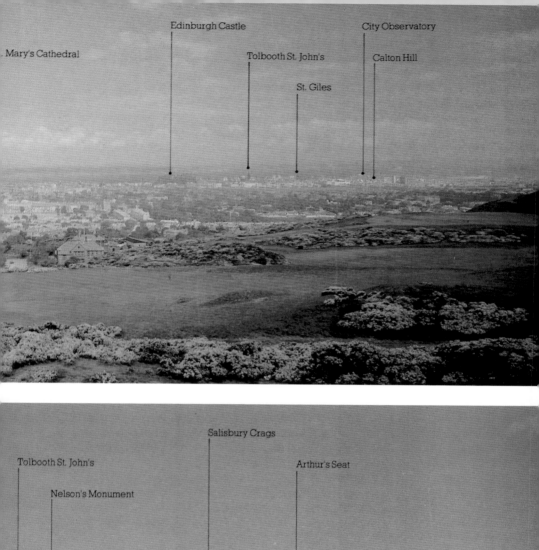

Mary's Cathedral

Edinburgh Castle

Tolbooth St. John's

St. Giles

City Observatory

Calton Hill

Tolbooth St. John's

Nelson's Monument

Salisbury Crags

Arthur's Seat

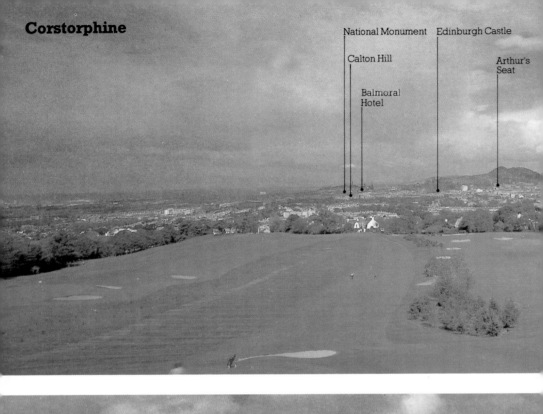

Corstorphine

National Monument

Calton Hill

Edinburgh Castle

Balmoral
Hotel

Arthur's
Seat

Castle Hill

Dundas
Monument

St. Andrew's House

Scott Monume

Princes Street

Princes St
Gardens

National
Gallery

Royal
Scottish
Academy

Calt
Hill

National Monument

Nelson's Monument

Waverley Station

Royal High School

North Bridge

The Mound

Bank of Scotland

Assembly Hall

Ramsay Lodge

St. Giles

Section of Castle

Tolboot St. John's

Villages of Edinburgh

The other Edinburgh: a patchwork of rural life, history and tradition

To most visitors, historic Edinburgh consists of the Castle and Holyrood Palace with the Royal Mile in between and the New Town to the north. Such a view does no justice to the other sections and deceives the people who hold it.

In the first half of the eighteenth century, there were as many as 46 villages spread out over the area which Edinburgh now covers. Although over the next two centuries, the boundaries gradually melted away, there are still many semi-rural communities with independent histories and traditions in existence today. Dean Village, with its riverside tranquillity, is very much a country town, while the coastline villages have a completely different character, and could be miles away. It is this blending patchwork of communities which has to be understood for Edinburgh to be fully appreciated. And without the villages Edinburgh would lack much of her charm.

Dean Village

The romantic informality of Dean Village contrasts vividly with the classic regular style of its neighbour, the New Town. Set in a valley with steep wooded slopes on either side, the distinctive red pantiled roofs of the village buildings may be seen clearly from many vantage points around it. The apparent uniformity of the bright rooftops is deceptive however and a closer inspection reveals an eclectic architectural approach to building with varied wall finishes and a diversity of period, style and condition. This is not surprising. It is natural that a village which has existed for 800 years or so has some changes.

Accessibility to the Water of Leith resulted in a mining community being established here as far back as the twelfth century and, for a long time, the city and the Incorporation of Baxters (Baker's Union) operated 11 watermills and two granaries in the area. Numerous relics of those times remain today.

Bell's Brae House, originally built as an inn in 1640, was the Baxters' meeting place and in the northeastern wall is the bakers' stone with symbolic wheat sheaves, the ripening sun and bakers' shovels.

At the bottom of Bell's Brae stands the Baxters' Tollbooth, built in the same century and the official headquarters and granary of the incorporation. It is typical of Scottish domestic architecture of the time, with stair towers and cut-away corners over the window lintels and on a wall adjoining Dean Bridge parapet is a stone with the inscription: 'Blessed be God for all his gifts'. This came from Lindsay's Mill of which only three grindstones remain on its site by the riverside path formerly called Miller's Row. Jericho Mill, almost completely destroyed by a fire in 1956, has been restored as offices.

Before the building of Telford's Dean Bridge in 1832, the village was also important as a crossing point, for Bell's Brae was the main road out to Queensferry and the north. In 1751, the road was turnpiked with a toll bar at the top of the hill and some distance down it were the stables and coach houses. Both have now been restored as offices.

Many other buildings, including some houses in Dean Path and a seventeenth-century building near Dean Bridge, have also been sympathetically modernized. Others have gone completely but have been replaced by suitable worthwhile structures. Well Court, a great square of red stone buildings, designed by Sydney Mitchell in 1884, was built on the site of some old cottages to provide community housing in a highly experimental way. Dean House has also gone. In its place stands the cemetery, where Lord Cockburn and other great personalities rest.

Baxter's mills of yesteryear in Dean Village by the Water of Leith

Corstorphine

Despite rapid expansion in the twentieth century, bringing modern office blocks, shops and houses in its wake, the spirit of old Corstorphine lingers on. Situated on the southwest side of the city, Corstorphine today is clearly a residential area, surrounded and interspersed by parks and wide open spaces. But it has, like other villages, a main street and several historic features of interest.

For centuries farming was the mainstay of the local economy—mostly wheat and potatoes in the eighteenth century, then market gardening some time later. Owing to the presence of a spring of 'weak sulphurous water' reputed to have medicinal properties until it became polluted as a result of reclamation of the loch which once existed here, Corstorphine also had its day as a fashionable spa with its round of balls and concerts for the wealthy families of Edinburgh.

In 1910, an important craft industry was set up by the son of William Morris, making 'dovecot tapestries'. In 1946, it became the Edinburgh Tapestry Company and still continues in business today.

Of Corstorphine Castle, once lived in by Adam Forrester to whom the estate belonged, little remains, except a few relics found by local houseowners through the years, and an ancient stone dovecot, circular in shape, which still has some 1060 nests to provide 'fresh food for the laird' and 'fertilizer for his crops' had he been there.

Not far away and probably part of an avenue of trees once leading to the castle is an old sycamore tree, 55 feet (16.7 m) high and 12½ feet (3.8 m) girth, always veiled with beautiful foliage in summer. Legend has it that the ghost of Christian Nimmo, who stabbed her lover, James Lord Forrester, by the tree in 1679, still haunts it.

Dover House in St. Margaret's Park was built in the mid-seventeenth century and displays characteristically Scottish crow-stepped gables. The ornamental gate pillars at the east High Street entrance to the park were probably once the entrance to the castle.

Corstorphine Kirk, another relic of the Forrester reign, contains some interesting early tombs of the family, with carved stone effigies and heraldic panels. A lamp, high on the building, placed there to guide travellers coming along the marsh or along the loch late at night in days of yore, has now been replaced by a symbolic electric light. In 1905, the church was successfully modernized to harmonize with some of the earlier structures and now, considered to be the 'Corstorphine Heirloom', is a source of pride to the community-conscious inhabitants.

Morningside

Traditionally a salubrious part of Edinburgh (the accent is said to have derived from Irish elocutionist, Thomas Sheridan, father of the famous playwright), Morningside actually had its origins in agriculture and it was only the advent of the railways at the end of the nineteenth century that brought about its considerable change in status.

Many years ago, the village was centred on the small area now occupied by the Public Library and the Merlin pub. The Old Tollhouse was built on the lawn surrounding Braid Church on Morningside Road and has now been rebuilt as a gatehouse at the entrance to the Hermitage of Braid Drive. Number 259, its original number, can be seen on a lintel at the rear of the building.

Later, the nineteenth century influx of wealthy people brought with it a great growth in the building of beautiful villas in the district of Cluny, Hermitage and Braid. Each villa had resident servants, usually spinster ladies, and at that time the population ratio of Morningside was two females to one male.

Of these buildings not many remain, although Number 6 Morningside Place, home of the Misses Balfour, aunts of Robert Louis Stevenson, still stands complete with the author's initials which he himself carved on a cupboard door. Of the humbler and older residences, a group of old stone cottages in Springvalley Terrace remain, as do some cottages at 160 Morningside Road, one of which has an outside stone staircase. Two large square stones with holes to support gibbets in Braid Road were the scene of public executions.

Monumental stones in the churchyard

This old dovecot houses 1060 nests

The residents also knew how to enjoy themselves, however, and Carter's Parade, on the first Friday in April, was the excuse for great festivity, usually ending up in the Volunteer's Rest (now Volunteer's Arms or the Canny Man). This pub, standing at the corner of Canaan and Morningside Lanes, has a complete range of copper whisky blending jugs and measures as well as an accounts book (dated 1892-93) in which regular customers were each allocated a page and there are such entries as 'George the joiner—glass of whisky—4d'. One of the customers, the painter Sam Bough, presented the inn with a two-sided oil painting for use as a sign board, today displayed in-

Morningside serenity

side the pub. Perhaps he did not want to see his name entered in the book. Today, Morningside is a spacious suburb which in many ways still retains the well-to-do air of the turn-of-the-century. The wide streets and well-preserved buildings reflect the comfortable standing of the residents. Trees and wide open spaces, many of them hospital and school grounds, break up the unfolding vista.

Not only does Morningside preserve this atmosphere, people also still demonstrate many of the characteristics that have made their village celebrated. The Morningside accent, for instance, with its 'refained' vowels, is still a city landmark.

Colinton

Today, the affluent 'village' of Colinton, with its beautiful villas surrounded on all sides by the serenity of the unspoilt countryside, makes it hard to believe that at the turn of the nineteenth century it seemed to be in decline. Although agriculture was the main source of employment, many people depended on the distillery, skinnery and water mills powered by the Water of Leith as a means of livelihood. The former two died a natural death, while the latter was no competition for the steam-operated machines now being used elsewhere.

The coming of the railways in 1875 turned the course of events. Now that Colinton was within commuting distance of the city centre, wealthy people started building villas here. This was not surprising. The rural beauty of the area still survives today. The Pentland Hills, the starting point of the Water of Leith, and Colinton and Craiglockhart Dells, with ivy-entwined sycamore trees, wild hyacinths and pink hedgerows

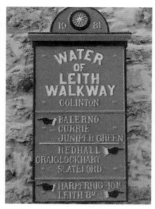

Walking by the waters

of dog rose, have always been outstandingly beautiful.

Despite its expansion, many relics of Colinton's past remain, emphasizing the village spirit of the area. Colinton Brig, the main road into the village, retains much of its character, and the ruins of Colinton Castle may still be seen in Merchiston Castle School. The Parish Church, first erected in 1771 on the site of an earlier building and mod-

ernized in 1968, has many features of historic interest. An old mort safe, to prevent bodies from being dug up for medical research in bygone days, still stands to the left of the entrance gates, while ancient tomb-stones in the churchyard provide material for perusal. James Gillespie, mill-owner and public benefactor, lies buried here, as does Reverend Dr. Lewis Balfour—maternal grandfather of Robert Louis Stevenson and once minister of the church. Indeed, the novelist spent much time in Colinton and his grandfather's manse and old yew tree (seen from Dell Road, over the wall and across the graveyard) are mentioned in *Kidnapped*.

Many other buildings of note are to be found throughout the village, some of them designed by Sir Robert Lorimer. Glenlyon and Almora in Pentland Avenue, distinguishable by their semi-circular towers, are two such examples. Across the road, built in 1898 but Scottish seventeenth century in style are the 'Sir William Fraser

Swanston

Separated from the rest of Edinburgh by half a mile of farmland, Swanston, nestling on the lower slopes of the Pentlands, with fields or golf courses on all sides, is in truly splendid rural isolation.

This unspoilt hamlet remains much the same as when Robert Louis Stevenson and later Edwin Muir knew it. The T-shaped wood behind Swanston, planted by a Trotter as a memorial to a descendant of the house who fell in battle, is still

green and lush. The village centre with its old-world charm has also not altered much in the last century or so.

A group of seventeenth-century white-washed cottages, with blue paintwork, black chimney pots and thatched roofs have been sympathetically restored and modernized. The old farmhouse, the heart of the village, now being used as a bothy, and the White House, the old school, are still there.

A later addition was some

stone cottages with slated roofs around a square. Some distance away is Swanston Cottage, described as a 'rambling infinitesimal cathedral' by Stevenson in *St. Ives*. It was used as a summer cottage by the Stevenson family from 1867 to 1880 and the house on the left of the drive leading to the cottage belonged to Alison Cunningham, known as 'Cummy' to the novelist, his 'first wife and second mother'. John Todd, a Swanston shepherd provided

The parish church dating back to 1771

Rural glades surround the village

Homes', originally founded by a wealthy merchant for the rent-free use of retired ladies.

Of the humbler abodes, several small cottages are still in evidence. Those at the foot of the long steps near the church have unusual porches, rough-finished façades and moss-covered pantiles. Others of a similar ilk are on Spylaw Bank Road which also has the old station master's cottage connected by wooden steps (Jacob's Ladder) to the platform of a former station. Redhall Mill is still in use today and the Old Boag's Mill which produced bank notes in 1735, later turning to the grinding of oatmeal and barley, also still stands.

Seventeenth-century cottages in Swanston

the writer with many anecdotes of his working life and some of these stories are also depicted in the author's book, *St. Ives.*

Apart from Swanston Golf Club and the new Swanston Farm, there is little else of the village. It truly earns its reputation of being tiny and unspoilt and, now classified as a Conservation Area, it will probably remain so. Within the village, the small white houses stand out against the lush green background, while from the outside, screened on all sides by high trees, it is an oasis of quiet retreat and a delightful contrast to the vital beat of the city centre.

Duddingston

*L*ocated between Duddingston Loch and Arthur's Seat, with Holyrood Park to the west, is the village where a sense of enclosure prevails. The high walls, tall trees and remains of the old stone boundary all contribute to the intimacy of the old village centre.

At the beginning of the eighteenth century, the cottage weaving industry was the main

Duddingston Loch and the village

Portobello

*I*t was a battle in Panama's Puerto Bello in 1739 which gave rise to the name and possibly the development of this village. A returning sailor built a house called Porto Bello in a spot where the Baptist Church in High Street now stands. He or his successor in the house dabbled in saddlery and coach repairing and the last pottery works, in Bridge Street, was moved to Crieff in 1972.

In order to attract more custom in 1753, he advertised that a horse race would be run 'at Porto Bello, in the midst of the Freegate Whins'. Thus began the growth of a community.

By the end of the eighteenth century, the village was developing in two ways. William Jameson 'Father of Portobello' started an important pottery industry using the extensive beds of clay lying on its beaches. The site soon became a service station for itinerants.

The bracing air and miles of golden sands had the potential of attracting another market which John Cairns was quick to spot. He acted promptly and, in 1795, advertised 'bathing machines on the sands'. These proved most popular and brought about the spread of the many simple Georgian houses,

Greenside

*B*ecause of its minuscule size, it is hard to believe that Greenside was ever a village, much less such an interesting one. Lying below Calton Hill's western slope and Leith Walk, and including today's Blenheim Place and Greenside Row, it was given to the sporting fraternity by James II to practise the art of mimic warfare. Thus it became a Tilting Ground and, later, in the nineteenth century was the place for holding open-air plays and revels. Until 1769, it was also a popular site for the burning and hanging of criminals and witches. Indeed, there are records showing that in 1717, a certain Robert Irvine had both hands cut off *before* he was executed here. His body was then flung unceremoniously into a quarry hole at the east end of Royal Terrace.

In the mid-sixteenth century a Carmelite monastery is said to have existed here and still to this day an official in the Convent of the Carmelites in Rome bears the inimitable title 'Il Padre Priore di Greenside'.

A hospital for lepers was established in the building left unoccupied by the nuns.

Greenside has changed much since those days and even since the 1960s a lot has means of support for most people living in the area, when the manufacture of a flaxen cloth—Duddingston Hardings—was at its peak. By 1845, severe competition had brought this to a halt and gradually the old weavers' cottages on the Causeway (the main road) were also demolished. Later the pits, breweries and the mills provided jobs for the men, and where Duddingston Road crosses Braid Burn, some of the mills may still be seen, although only brewing still thrives.

The Sheep's Heid Inn, said to be the oldest licensed premises in Scotland, is in the Causeway. It is said that James VI frequented the inn and in 1580 presented the landlord with an embellished ram's head. By the inn is an old skittle alley and the Sheep Heid Trotters founded in 1882 meet here.

Duddingston Kirk, built in Norman style, is the oldest building in the village. A watch tower, to guard against body snatchers, stands in the churchyard, and at the gate are some old jougs—iron collar and chain, to punish evil-doers—and a loupin-on-stone—to help old or obese horsemen to mount.

There is a seventeenth-century building where Bonnie Prince Charlie is said to have slept before the Battle of Prestonpans. Duddingston House, designed in the eighteenth century by Sir William Chambers is surrounded by a 200-acre (81 ha) park and golfers make use of the grounds while famous Duddingston Loch is now a bird sanctuary.

usually used as summer homes for visitors. Between the High Street and the sea and especially at the east end of Bath Street, many, of these may still be seen.

The Victorians also found Portobello a relief and they too built villas—this time large baroque ones—and also established parks and bandstands and erected a wide promenade along the sea front to 'take the airs'. Later, numerous 'amusements' were added to the existing features and so Portobello became known as the 'fun place' of Edinburgh.

Personalities of note visited or lived here too: Sir Walter Scott came to stay with friends in what is now known as Bellfield Street and it was in Portobello that he completed the first canto of *The Lay of the Last Minstrel*. The Scots comedian, Harry Lauder, lived at 3 Bridge Street for a time and the King's Road was named after George IV when he rode down the street to review his troops.

Despite its past glory, by 1967, it was evident that much had to be done to aid Portobello's deteriorating condition. The Victorian mansions had deteriorated, as had the miles of golden sand, such an attraction in former days.

By the beginning of the 1970s, the Beach Nourishment Scheme had taken effect and tons of sand from a nearby beach were poured onto Portobello's shores. This not only improved the appearance of the beach but also protected the promenade wall and sea front. Many buildings such as the George Cinema were listed for preservation, while others were at least refurbished.

been demolished. On the site of the Tabernacle, a baptist church of some repute, stands the Playhouse, first built in 1929 for use as a cinema and now a popular theatre.

Of other places and events only historic and literary records remain to fill in gaps from the past. James Nasmyth, inventor of the steam hammer, as a small boy often accompanied the servants to the bleaching green on Calton Hill and in his writings he mentions the 'blacksmiths, coppersmiths and brassfounders busy in the

'Church on the Hill'

Greenside workshops'.

Robert Louis Stevenson was also a frequent visitor. His paternal grandfather, an elder at Greenside Parish Church, the 'Church on the Hill' still standing today, once occupied the house at Number 1 Baxter's Place—of which the novelist writes in picturesque terms of its 'great size, infinity of cellars, garrets and apple lofts'. On the death of the grandfather, Robert Stevenson, his three sons bequeathed a section of their garden to the church, on which was later built a chapel, now demolished.

Queensferry

Situated at the narrowest point of the Forth, nine miles (14.4 km) west of the city centre, Queensferry (often erroneously known as South Queensferry) still has the feel of a Scottish east coast town with a small, tightly-knit community.

The name has ancient associations with Queen Margaret, for it was just west of the town at Brinks Rock that she disembarked in 1067 as the bride of King Malcolm. Legend has it that her footprint may still be seen on the rock on which she landed. The scene has been commemorated in the Burgh Arms.

Queensferry has been an important crossing point for many years. To the north of the Church of St. Mary of Mount Carmel, built over 500 years ago and one of the oldest Carmelite Houses in Great Britain still used for Christian worship, there is a line of rocks stretching to the Firth, showing traces of cutting to form landing stages for the ferry boats. The first ferry service was not officially opened until the time of King David I in 1129, however, and Queen Elizabeth II and Prince Phillip were the last to use it in 1964, just prior to the opening of the New Forth Bridge. The Ferry Fair, which is still held in the second week in August, features the Burry Man, who is completely covered in burs from the burdock plant and visits householders for donations.

A feature of Queensferry has always been its terraces and it is in East Terrace that the oldest house in the town, the Black Castle, built in 1626, still stands. Typically Scottish in character, it has crow-stepped gables and ornamental dormer windows and the narrow staircase in the east gable is reputed to be a smugglers' stair. Next door is the Forth Bridge Hotel, also dating from the seventeenth century, which was much modernized after a fire in 1910.

The Burgh Chambers, which was once a hotel, is now the Burgh Museum.

The Tollbooth, with its pointed steeple and outside staircase was originally a prison. The four-faced clock was added to commemorate Queen Victoria's jubilee.

The other main church in Queensferry, the Kirk, completed in 1635 but renovated in the

Cramond

Cramond's view of the River Almond

Nestled around the estuary of the River Almond 4½ miles (7.2 km) northeast of the city centre and backed by an attractive rural hinterland, Cramond is one of the prettiest villages lying along Edinburgh's 9 miles (14.4 km) of coastline.

Conclusions drawn from archaeological digs in the area point to beginnings as far back as AD 142 when Antoninus Pius established a fort here. A plan of the fort can be found next to the Kirk, itself partially constructed from Roman stones, while various Roman artefacts are at the Huntly House Museum in the city centre. A chance discovery in 1976 on the site of a proposed car park brought to light an exceptionally well-preserved Roman bath-house. One of the most important Roman finds in Britain took place in 1996 when a 5 feet (1.5m) long sandstone sculpture of a lioness eating a man was found in the River Almond by the ferry steps. It dates from the 2nd or early 3rd century AD and is thought to be from the tomb of an important Roman official.

Despite these relics of a Roman heritage and even the ghost of a Roman centurion which supposedly roams the bottom of the village steps frightening local dogs, the village is predominantly eighteenth century in character. The Industrial Revolution did not pass it by. Water-driven iron mills were put in harness for the production nineteenth century, also still stands today. It had great influence within the community and parishoners were actually fined for being absent from worship or for taking a boat across the ferry on the Sabbath.

Despite the strict religious background, a distillery flourished here at the beginning of the nineteenth century. It was situated near the pier, between the present Stag Head Hotel and the Queensferry Arms Hotel, and parts of the original building still remain.

Dominating the skyline of Queensferry are the two bridges: the Forth Railway Bridge and the Forth Road Bridge. The Railway Bridge was opened in 1980 and at the time was the biggest bridge in the world. The opening of the Road Bridge in 1964 brought to an end a ferry service which had existed for almost 800 years.

The old buildings of East Terrace

Newly restored house

of iron implements such as nails and shovels, to be gradually replaced by paper and furniture some years later in the mid-nineteenth century. Some of these original mills still stand, as do many of the workers' white-washed cottages which, although much modernized, still retain their old-world charms.

Other buildings date from earlier times. Cramond Kirk and Cramond Tower are both medieval in origin, the latter having once been the property of the Bishops of Dunkeld when it was used as the basic part of the earliest house.

Cramond Inn is a popular watering hole reputed to have connections with Stevenson's *St. Ives*, while Cramond House is said to have provided the setting for his *House of Shaws*.

The bridge crossing the River Almond carried traffic between Edinburgh and nearby Queensferry and one of the old tollhouses still stands today. Legend has it that King James V was once being attacked by gypsies on the bridge when a local miller, Jock Howieson, came to his aid. Howieson's reward was the land of Braehead, on condition that his descendants would wash the hands and feet of all new sovereigns on their first visit to Scotland. In 1952 Elizabeth II was the last recipient of this quaint gesture.

Interesting though the history is, it is the scenery which first catches the eye and there is a wide variety of walks in the area made all the more enjoyable by the bracing sea air. Northwards towards Hound's Point (so called because of the dog which supposedly haunts it) and Queensferry, a walk passes several interesting features en route, one of which is the first Gothic Revival building in Scotland – Dalmeny House. At low tide one can walk to Cramond Island, inhabited only by birds and mammals. A wide, open promenade leads to Granton and Silverknowes, while a delightful route through leafy glades along the river goes to Barnton.

Newhaven

To many people Newhaven still conjures up images of traditional fish-wives clad in colourful costumes, their cry of 'Caller Ou' resounding through the streets. Unfortunately, these ladies, immortalized in Sir Walter Scott's *The Antiquary*, are no longer there, the last one having retired in 1977 at the sprightly age of 89. The village, which has undergone extensive re-development, survives, however, and much has been preserved for the appreciation and enjoyment of many generations to come.

Newhaven was originally established at the beginning of the sixteenth century when James IV, at war with England, decided to build a Scottish navy of his own. Its flagship, to be called the *Great Michael*, could not be constructed in Leith owing to insufficient depth of water and so new dockyards were laid out at 'Novus Portus de Leith' (Newhaven) and

Vessels in harbour

Flemish, Dutch and French workers brought in to build the ship. The death of James at the Battle of Flodden brought an end to the ship-building industry which had started to flourish here but soon afterwards the Society of Free Fishermen was founded, adding further to Newhaven's increasingly significant

standing as a fishing village.

As an offshoot of this industry, a reputation for the preparation of seafood was established in the eighteenth century and in 1767, a wine merchant, Thomas Peacock, petitioned Edinburgh for a few of the links and cottages where the food was prepared. The Peacock Hotel, named after him, still stands.

For a short time in the late 1700s, Newhaven also became the most important ferry and packing station in Scotland, although competition from nearby Granton, established in 1835, soon put this to an end.

Fishing again came to the rescue, this time in the unlikely form of oysters. A bowl of them cost 6d—2½p—and that included the bowl. Newhaven Fish Market came into being in 1896 and the stalwart Newhaven Fisherwomen's Choir was established during the First World War.

Today, the tramlines and old

Leith

Despite its proximity to the city centre, Leith has always been entirely distinct from it and some animosity has prevailed between the two. Today, many locals bemoan the changes which have taken place here, but its vital—if chequered—history more than compensates for the steps it has taken under the name of progress.

In the fourteenth century Logan of Restalrig was allowed to establish the little village of Leith as a burgh of the barony, with fewer privileges than a royal burgh, but holding the right to have incorporations (trade guilds).

Even then, trade rivalry between Leith and the city existed and was not improved when, desperate for money, the laird finally sold the superiority of the shore and harbour to Edinburgh. The powerful Leith incorporations were not recognized by the city and friction prevailed until 1833 when Leith gained its independence only to lose it again just after World War I.

Because of its standing as a port and nearness to the city centre, Leith was often the first glimpse of Scotland many royal visitors ever had. It was here that George IV landed with such pomp and ceremony. Mary of

Gueldres, Queen Madeleine, Mary of Guise and of course Mary Queen of Scots also arrived on its shores and it was in Lamb's House (now used as a centre by the Edinburgh and Leith Old People's Welfare Council) that the latter rested.

The royal procession would go through Kirkgate, the main street, passing the Church of St. Mary (today, South Leith Church in the churchyard of which are recorded the names of Leith's merchant princes and mariners in the great days of sail). Some stayed for a time and Charles I played golf on what is now

Fisherfolk's cottages in the old port

towering lamp-posts which were still in the Main Street in 1948 are no longer there, and most of the buildings have either been restored or completely demolished and new ones put in their place. This on the whole has been done with taste and the cottages on the north side of the Main Street have been restored to retain many of their original Flemish features, with red pantiled roofs and external staircases. Other restored areas include Lamb's Court, Fishmarket Square, Peacock Court and the fishermens' burial ground.

Newhaven was declared a conservation area in 1978.

The Newhaven Heritage Museum opened in 1994. It tells the story of Newhaven and its people through reconstructed sets of fishwives and fishermen, displays of objects and photographs and first-hand written and spoken accounts of people's lives. Although it is no longer a fishing village Newhaven is still a distinct community.

---

known as Leith Links.

Leith was once a popular bathing resort with a bathing machine on the sands as early as 1750. Shipbuilding was also important and *Sirius*, the first British steamship to cross the Atlantic, was built here in 1837.

Trinity House, belonging to the guild of the sea-faring community, still stands today. Part of it is a Maritime Museum and a Raeburn portrait of a famous Leith admiral hangs on one of its walls. The original Custom House in Commercial Street is also still there as is the Boundary Bar, half-way up Leith Walk, complete with brass plate marking the boundary between Leith and Edinburgh, before 1920.

Much has also disappeared.

The Auld Gaiety, a music hall, is no longer there and neither are the fiddlers, organ-grinders and beggars, including Commodore O'Brien who sat daily on the east side of Leith Walk, in a little masted boat given him by order of George IV.

There has recently been a revival of interest in preserving what remains of historic Leith while at the same time providing the facilities for a surge of commercial activity.

Many old buildings have been restored, including the Old Leith Bank at the corner of Bernard Street and Constitution Street, and King's Wark, an early eighteenth-century building nearby. Old warehouses and cooperages have been converted into expensive flats. Advertising agencies, public relations firms and artists of various kinds are finding Leith a congenial place in which to work. In 1995 the Scottish Office moved into impressive new premises on Victoria Quay, relocating staff from three buildings in other parts of the city.

Landscaping and tree-planting have made a difference to the open spaces. Leith is now well known for its restaurants (including a floating restaurant) and upmarket wine bars and pubs.

Whether all Leithers are in favour of this transformation is perhaps another matter, but there is no doubt that Leith is popular with visitors from near and far.

The Scottish Office, Victoria Quay, opened in 1995

Plan of Leith. 1883 **Opposite** The Shore, Leith

The National Gallery of Scotland

Scotland's premier collection of Old Masters and indigenous artists

In contrast to immense galleries like the Louvre in Paris and the National Gallery in London, with their labyrinth of rooms and endless corridors, the National Gallery of Scotland, designed by W.H. Playfair, is entirely accessible and human in scale.

The collection of paintings is not enormous, although it contains the most important group of Old Masters in Great Britain outside London and is studded with rarities and masterpieces from almost every major period in Western art. The collection was begun in the 1830s by the old Royal Institution and given its international significance in 1946 by the loan of the Duke of Sutherland's collection—one of the finest collections in Great Britain—containing major works by Raphael, Titian and Rembrandt. In 1995 the National Gallery and the Victoria and Albert Museum in London saved a major work of art from going abroad by jointly purchasing *The Three Graces*. This marble statue by Antonio Canova depicts Aglaia, Euphrosyne and Thalia from Greek mythology who embody qualities of beauty, gracefulness and youth.

A wing on the lower level houses a Scottish collection which may well surprise the visitor. It has its fair share of curiosities but also includes the work of Scottish painters of international repute: Ramsay, Raeburn and Wilkie.

The most recent change to the Gallery has been the internal decoration. The octagonal ground floor rooms now have claret-painted walls and a green carpet. This decorative scheme is a copy of the original design by Playfair and his collaborator D.R. Hay in 1859.

The following selective tour through the gallery traces the major European artistic movements illuminated by some of the most important and interesting pictures in the gallery.

This page *The Three Graces*, by Canova, owned jointly by the National Gallery of Scotland and the V & A in London who will share its display on an equal basis.
Opposite The *Bridgewater Madonna* by Raphael, part of the collection on loan to the Gallery from the Duke of Sutherland.

Early Italian and Early Northern Art to c.1530

This includes some of the earliest paintings in the gallery. If they all look very different from one another it is because they were painted during the Renaissance, one of the most revolutionary periods in the history of art.

The Renaissance was a dramatic cultural upheaval—literally a rebirth of learning—and affected every sphere of Europe's creative life. In the great city-states of Italy—Florence, Rome, Siena—scholars rediscovered the literature of ancient Greece and Rome. The Christian ethos of the medieval world was gradually replaced by a new confidence in man's ability to organize his own cosmos. The repercussions on painting were enormous. The flat, decorative late medieval style was abandoned as artists struggled to represent mankind in a believable, naturalistic way. To this end they studied anatomy and practised drawing from life. By 1500 an artist's ability was judged by his skill in painting the figure. A new discovery, scientific perspective, was used to create the illusion of three-dimensional settings.

The medieval tradition of artist as craftsman is exemplified by the thirteenth-century *Tuscan Triptych*. Painting was only one of the artist's skills. His aim was to create a valuable and awe-inspiring object of worship. In this case a large amount of goldleaf has been employed; the small figure scenes stand outlike jewels against the rich background. An altarpiece like this was meant to be closely observed—the scenes of Christ's Passion on the side-panels, for example, are clear and very detailed.

The small late fifteenth-century panel fragment depict-

Verrocchio's *Madonna and Child*

ing the *Death of St. Ephraim* attributed to Giuliano Amedei presents an interesting stylistic contrast with the much earlier triptych. By the time this small panel was painted, artists were studying their environment far more closely. The painter of the triptych made no attempt to place his small figure groups in naturalistic settings, but here the artist has surrounded his group of mourners with a believable, if stylized, landscape. The figures interact one with another; one can almost hear the murmur of conversation. Unlike the consistently stylized drapery in the triptych, their robes fall into natural folds.

The stylistic contradictions of Lorenzo Monaco's *Madonna and Child* are the result of an incomplete assimilation of Renaissance ideas. The Madonna herself is of an older tradition —rather like a Byzantine icon —but the child is much more believable. The artist attempts to model the faces and hands but he treats the Madonna's robe in the stylized medieval way. Incidentally, the strange colouring of the Madonna's face was not intentional. Centuries of kissing by the devout has worn away the surface to reveal the green underpaint.

There is no painting here by the greatest Renaissance genius, Leonardo da Vinci. However, a *Madonna and Child* by his teacher, Andrea del Verrochio, is a particularly tender treatment of this subject. The Madonna gazes down at a very life-like baby fidgeting and sucking his finger. Behind her, Verrochio displays his knowledge of the new perspective in his depiction of an ornate Roman ruin. The drawing of the Madonna's hands, for which Verrochio was particularly noted, is beautiful. This kind of sweet Italian painting was especially appreciated in Victorian England and this example was owned by John Ruskin.

The background of Raphael's *Bridgewater Madonna* has been overpainted at some time, but the figures show why Raphael was considered one of the greatest Renaissance painters. Not only are they beautifully drawn but they are juxtaposed in perfectly harmonious balance.

Scotland lost nearly all of its religious art during the Reformation and the *Trinity Altarpiece* is almost unique in its survival. Nobody is sure of the original function of the two remaining panels though they were once thought to be organ shutters. More likely, they are the flanking wings of a triptych, the central section of which was destroyed. We do know that they were specifically painted for the Collegiate Church of the Holy Trinity, which stood, until the railway came, on the present site of Waverley Station. We also know that they were not painted by a Scottish artist but by the fifteenth-century Netherlandish painter Hugo van der Goes. He was greatly esteemed for his draughtsmanship and fluid use of oil paint, a technique which had recently been refined in Flanders. The commissioning of such a work by a major artist says a great deal about the cosmopolitanism of fifteenth-century Scotland.

The panels are painted on both sides and mounted on a mechanism which turns them at 30-minute intervals. In their closed position, Sir Edward Bonkil, first provost of the Collegiate Church, is depicted kneeling in front of the patron saint of music, St. Cecilia, conventionally portrayed at the organ. The Bonkil portrait is astonishingly realistic and full of character, and was probably painted from life when he travelled to Ghent to arrange the commission.

The panels open to reveal King James III of Scotland and his wife Margaret of Denmark kneeling in front of their country's respective patron saints —St. Andrew and St. Canute. The fine painting of fabrics and the rich opulence of the backgrounds are typical of Flemish painting though the execution of the royal portrait heads suggests that they were inserted by a local artist after the paintings were shipped to Scotland. It was undoubtedly because of the royal portraits that the panels survived the Reformation. The subject of the missing centrepiece remains a mystery and one can only guess at its splendour.

16th Century Venetian
The main centres of the Rennaissance in Italy were Florence, Rome and Venice. Michaelangelo, Leonardo and Raphael worked mostly in Florence and Rome where accurate observation and fine drawing were valued above all else. However, in Venice there was a greater emphasis on colour and the free handling of paint. Absorbing the achievements of Florence and Rome, the Venetians used them to create a far more sensuous style of painting and the great master of the sixteenth century was Titian. He dominated the scene for most of the century and no major painter could escape his influence. The five Titians which hang here are on loan from the Duke of Sutherland and span the artist's long career.

The Three Ages of Man was painted when Titian was in his early twenties. It is typically

Diana and Actaeon by Titian

Venetian in concept—a poetic work in which landscape is combined with figure painting. A master of the nude, he painted the male figure with an absolute sureness of touch. Titian also invented a new type of female nude exemplified by the *Venus Anadyomene*. Voluptuous and potentially erotic, she recurs in the work of every painter to specialize in the nude from Rubens to Renoir.

In the 1570s Philip II of Spain commissioned Titian to paint a series of mythological subjects. Well aware of his patron's erotic tastes, Titian took the opportunity to show off his mastery of the female nude. The two pictures from that series which hang here represent scenes from the legend of Diana the huntress. In *Diana and Actaeon* the youthful Actaeon accidentally interrupts the godess while she is bathing at a fountain in a forest glade. It is an essentially voyeuristic scene. The intruder strides in from the left plunging Diana's naked attendants into disarray while the goddess herself raises a cloth in a gesture indicating anger rather than modesty. Through the arch on the distant horizon a little hunting scene foreshadows Actaeon's fate—Diana turned him into a stag and his own dogs tore him to pieces.

Vengeance is once more the theme in *Diana and Calisto* where the goddess chastises her pregnant handmaiden for her carnality. Here Titian has evolved in style from the smooth finish of *The Three Ages of Man* towards a much more impressionistic and free approach. Paint is applied unevenly over the picture—in some places it is just skimmed over the canvas while in others it is applied densely. The movement and drama are underlined by the immediacy of the technique.

The recent cleaning of Jacopo Bassano's *Adoration of the Kings* has revealed its brilliance—real Venetian colour. Its exuberance is also typical of Venice—the nativity is just an excuse for a full-scale costume pageant. Everything—colours, patterns, texture—conspires to produce a gorgeous spectacle, but don't be too dazzled. The young Bassano also excelled in portraiture and there are a number of fine portrait heads set into the tumult of robes and accessories. Bassano's attempt at an architectural setting is little more than a caprice.

Tintoretto is most famous for his large-scale mural decorations in which he attempted to combine the drawing of Michaelangelo with the colour of Titian. His *Deposition of Christ* really belongs in the dark of a chapel in the Venetian church of St. Francesco della Vigna. There the candlelight in which the scene takes place would have appeared even more eerie. Tintoretto has managed to give Christ's limp body a real feeling of weight and one can sense the struggle involved in manoeuvering it down from the Cross. The two crouching figures in the foreground are derived from Michaelangelo's sybils from the ceiling in the Sistine Chapel.

Sixteenth and Seventeenth Century European Art

Spanish art is poorly represented in the gallery, though there are two paintings by El Greco, one of the first and most distinctive of the great Spanish masters. *The Saviour of the World* truly shows his visionary power. But even this has a certain sweetness which detracts from the potency of the image. Christ has the hieratic appearance of the icons from El Greco's native Crete, combined with the elongated

and mannered drawing style of Tintoretto whose work influenced the young Greek when he was studying in Venice. *Fabula (The Fable)*, a work of haunting beauty c.1580, represents a rare departure by El Greco from religious subject matter. A figure blows on a burning ember whilst a man and a monkey (traditionally a symbol of evil) watch. This painting is the latest and most brilliant of three versions of the subject by El Greco.

Valazquez painted *An Old Woman Cooking Eggs* when he was only 19 years old. He was to become one of the greatest portrait painters of all time and, although this picture

El Greco's *The Saviour of the World* painted in the 1590s

is a genre piece, the realism of the head painting is quite remarkable. Spanish tradition was essentially realist and Spanish painters excelled at the depiction of surface textures. The still-life in the foreground rivals the best Dutch still-lifes.

Some of the paintings in these rooms are by seventeenth century artists working in Rome. *Landscape with Apollo and the Muses* is the largest landscape ever painted by the French-born artist Claude Lorraine. Claude worshipped classical Rome

Bassano's *The Adoration of the Kings*

and at an early age decided to spend his life among her ruins. His pictures are not depictions of actual places but idyllic dreams of perfect landscapes peopled by mythological figures.

Two of the smallest and rarest pictures in the gallery are the work of a German expatriate living in Rome, Adam Elsheimer. Elsheimer worked in oil paint on a copper surface—a technique which gives his colours a striking luminosity. In *The Stoning of St. Stephen* the shiny metal underneath makes the bloody gash on the martyr's forehead horribly vivid. *Il Contento* is his masterpiece. An agitated crowd is trying to prevent Zeus abducting the goddess of happiness, unaware that he has replaced her with the goddess of discontent. The picture is

filled with movement and dramatic contrast. In spite of the miniature scale of his work and his early death at the age of 32, the vitality and atmosphere of Elsheimer's style inspired a host of younger painters from Rubens to Rembrandt.

Poussin's Seven Sacraments

A Frenchman, Nicholas Poussin spent his working life in Rome where he was influenced by antique friezes and the figure style of Raphael. He dedicated his life to developing a detached, unemotional style through which he could express his deep religious and philosophical convictions.

The Seven Sacraments is a second version of this unusual subject. By freezing all action and subduing the colour, he aimed to induce a quiet,

contemplative response. The meaning of each of the sacraments is emphasized by the symmetrical composition which focuses attention on the central action—in the Baptism for example, the pouring of the water onto Christ's head.

Massys' *Portrait of a Notary*

17th Century Dutch Art

Seventeenth-century Holland was a thriving trading nation and the art of the period reflects Dutch bourgeois preoccupation with everday life.

Dutch landscapists were the first artists to paint naturalistic landscapes. Avercamp's atmospheric *Winter Landscape* is thronged not with classical figures, but with ice skaters. There are no antique ruins in *The Banks of a River* by Jacob van Ruisdal, only a real Dutch town in the distance.

Peter de Hoogh shared Vermeer's interest in the depiction of ordinary rooms and objects. His simple picture of a *Courtyard with an Arbour* would have been unthinkable to the Italians.

Frans Hals of Haarlem was almost exclusively a portrait painter. The pair of *Portraits of a Gentleman and His Wife* are extremely fine examples of his mature work, the figures clearly proclaiming in confident poses their wealth and security.

Hals' deftness of touch was second only to Rembrandt's. Rembrandt's earlier portraits are very tightly painted—*Portrait of a Young Woman with Flowers in Her Hair*, wearing a minutely detailed lace collar, shows how precise he could be. However, he was not satisfied only to represent the surface appearance of things and his later work—particularly his self-portraits—shows his obsession with inner character at the expense of expected standards of finish. The *Self-Portrait* is alive with his brush-work.

But Rembrandt was also much moved by biblical stories and often used them as subjects for his paintings. The sentiment of *Hannah and Samuel* is touching because of the tender relationship between

Rubens' *Feast of Herod*

the old woman and the boy—the more convincing because the model was probably the painter's own son. The picture on the easel, *Woman in Bed*, was probably meant as part of a larger biblical composition. The model is thought to be Geertje Dircx, who lived with the artist.

At the height of his fame Rembrandt had many pupils, not all of whom were to develop the same free technique as their master. Gerrit Dou was intrigued by light and reflections and painted exquisitely detailed little pictures

The Lomellini Family by van Dyck

such as *Interior with a Young Violinist*. Very different from Rembrandt's later work, this is obviously a young man's painting, carefully detailing the

usual paraphernalia associated with students. Books are strewn around and there is an up-turned beer tankard lying on the floor—things haven't changed much in 350 years!

J.M.W. Turner

Every January the famous Vaughan Bequest of watercolours by J.M.W. Turner is on view in Room VIII. Regularly changing exhibitions, sometimes selected from the permanent collection, are held in this room at other times of the year.

17th Century Flemish and Dutch Art

Painting north of the Alps was always quite distinct from Italy. Painters in Germany and the Low Counties were more pragmatic and their figures are individual, not generalized, types. They were less inclined to experiment than the Italians and medieval traditions per-sisted longer. But by the beginning of the fifteenth century, Renaissance ideas began filtering through.

Bernard van Orley was a Brussels painter who did his

Il Contento by Elsheimer

best to imitate the new southern style. He may have visited Italy and certainly saw Raphael's tapestry cartoons which came to Brussels to be woven. His work may not look much like Raphael to today's viewer, but in his day he was known as 'The Raphael of the Netherlands'. The bulky figure of Christ in *Before the Crucifixion* is similar.

Quentin Massays, a leading Antwerp portrait painter, obviously knew about Leonardo's accomplishments. *Portrait of a Man* has an intimate, naturalistic air to it. The notary (if that is what he is, for nobody has explained his halo) sits in front of an arcaded window behind which recedes a beautiful rocky landscape similar to Leonardo's in *The Mona Lisa*.

Here are works by the two greatest Flemish painters of the seventeenth century, master and pupil—Sir Peter Paul Rubens and Sir Anthony van Dyck. Both worked in

Elsheimer's *The Stoning of St. Stephen*

England for the ill-fated Charles I and were knighted for their services.

Rubens was a multi-talented genius: diplomat, courtier and linguist, he is one of the most attractive personalities in art history. As a young man he travelled throughout Europe and he thoroughly absorbed the grand Venetian decorative manner, imbuing it with his own passionate temperament. The result was a colourful, ebullient style—full of energy and movement. Rubens satisfied the demand for his work by organizing his workshop on factory lines. Though he was responsible for the overall design of the pictures much of the work was carried out by assistants.

The *Reconciliation of Jacob and Esau* is the sort of small oil sketch Rubens always made for a larger painting. The colour and brushwork is fresh and spontaneous and his composition is full of exotic detail—note the camels in the top right-hand corner.

The full-size *Feast of Herod* is a hugely enjoyable banquetting scene. Rubens has converted one of the most horrific of biblical tales into a brilliant costume piece. Salome sweeps across the picture carrying the head of John the Baptist. After his assistants had completed their tasks it is likely that Rubens himself worked over his canvas, for the bravura brushwork bears his unmistakable stamp.

Van Dyck's *St. Sebastian Bound for Martyrdom* is an early work painted in the exuberant baroque manner of his master. However his reputation was made in England as a portrait painter to Charles I and his court. The painting of the Genoese Lomellini family was done in Italy before he settled in England. He was never averse to flattering his subjects and they look down on us with amused disdain.

If you are acquainted with the work of the Dutch painter Vermeer, *Christ in the House of Martha and Mary* may come as a surprise. It is the earliest of his known works and its biblical theme and large scale make it quite unlike the tranquil domestic interiors for which he is so famous. The existence of one religious picture caused art historians to presume that Vermeer had done others which have since been lost. This prompted the famous Dutch forger van Mee-

gren to produce a number of fake Vermeers in the style of the Edinburgh picture. The

Detail of Poussin's *Baptism*

Detail of Poussin's *Mystic Marriage of St. Catherine*

sombre tonality of the picture is characteristic of a group of Dutch painters who imitated the dramatic contrasts of light and shade of the Italian painter Caravaggio. A more typical example of his school's work is Hendrik Terbrugghen's *Beheading of John the Baptist*—possibly the most depressing picture in the gallery.

18th Century British, Italian and French Art

During the eighteenth century the English aristocracy developed a passion for portraiture, and many gifted painters specialized in giving the public what it wanted. Perhaps the greatest was Thomas Gainsborough, who gave his clients good value for money.

The Honourable Mrs. Graham was only 18 when she sat for Gainsborough, so we can be sure that her youthful bloom had nothing to do with flattery. But young faces present even the finest painter

with a difficult problem—they can so easily appear bland and characterless. Gainsborough has coped by making a great play of the costume—a dazzling piece of work. *Mrs Graham* was shown at the Academy in 1777 and we can be sure that she outshone her rivals.

Gainsborough's chief rival was Sir Joshua Reynolds, first president of the Royal Academy and one of the most respected figures in English art.

In matters of theory Reynolds was the most erudite man in the country, but when it came to painting portraits he lacked Gainsborough's vitality, though his pictures of women and children have an attractive sweetness. *The Ladies Waldegrave*—three fashionable sisters —are portrayed with an appropriately flattering eye.

In France, J.B.S. Chardin is distinguished from his contemporaries by his unaffected and direct approach to subject matter as can be seen in his *Still Life: The Kitchen Table*. Nor could anything be simpler than *Vase of Flowers*, his only surviving flowerpiece. It is a minor masterpiece.

In contrast fellow Frenchman Antoine Watteau has painted supremely artificial works. His imaginary scenes of costumed ladies and gentlemen cavorting in prettified pastoral settings are really *bon-bons*. This is not to belittle his talent, for Watteau was a fine draughtsman and kept albums of his beautiful drawings from which he selected the figures for his compositions. *Fêtes Venitiennes* is not only one of his finest pictures, it is also one of the best preserved.

The Italian-based painters of this era are well represented in

Self-Portrait from 1657, one of several painted by Rembrandt

the gallery. At that time no gentleman's education was considered complete unless he went on the 'Grand Tour' and visited the artistic centres of Europe. Rome was the high-light of the trip and the painters resident there profited from the lucrative tourist trade. It was the height of fashion to have one's portrait painted in Rome— often with a typical Roman back-ground such as the Colosseum. Pompeo Batoni's portrait of *Princess Benedetto Guishani* lacks the fashionable landscape backdrop, but in the strong characterization and delicacy of handling you can see why he was the most popular portrait painter in the city.

The Scots painter Gavin Hamilton worked on a grandiose scale and one cannot imagine even the most enthusiastic tourist carrying home his *Achilles Lamenting the Death of Patroclus*. Hamilton was a dealer in antiquities who spent most of his life digging up Rome. His unparalleled knowledge of ancient art was the main influence on his painting, though his figure style owes a great deal to Poussin.

In complete contrast to the academicism of Hamilton is *The Finding of Moses* by the Venetian painter Giovanni Battista Tiepolo. There is nothing pedantic about this bravura romp by one of the greatest decorators of the eighteenth century. Tiepolo makes absolutely no attempt at historical accuracy. Although this scene is supposed to have taken place in ancient Egypt, he has dressed Pharaoh's daughter in sixteenth-century finery and her attendants—especially the dwarf—are straight out of a Renaissance court.

The style of the Spanish painter Francisco de Goya

Achilles Lamenting the Death of Patroclus by Hamilton, 1763

El Medico (The Doctor) by Goya

also owes someting to Tiepolo although he lacks the Italian's frivolity. Indeed his later work was exceedingly dark and pessimistic. *El Medico* is an unusually light-hearted picture of a doctor on his rounds warming himself over a brazier and is a tapestry design meant for a decorative scheme in one of the Spanish royal palaces.

Nineteenth Century British and American Art

The emphasis is mainly on early nineteenth-century English painting, so Frederick Edwin Church's *Niagara Falls from the American Side* is decidedly out of place. Church was one of the leading lights of the

emergent nineteenth-century American landscape school which sought to celebrate the natural wonders of the New World. He could hardly have found a more awe-inspiring subject than Niagara and represents the full force of its torrents on a suitably enormous canvas.

John Constable's *Vale of Dedham* is positively serene by comparison. It is based on a classical composition by Claude Lorraine though it does contain precise features of Constable's local landscape such as the tower of Dedham Church and the meandering River Stour. This is a highly finished exhibition picture worked on at length in the studio and quite different from the loosely treated little

Detail of Gainsborough's
The Hon. Mrs. Graham

Chardin's *Still Life*

Constable's *The Vale of Dedham*

sketch *On the Stour* which was probably executed in a few minutes direct from nature.

However, the most magnetic picture here, far out-shining Church's bombastic Niagara, is J.M.W. Turner's *Dream of Italy*, the paint surface of which seems almost dissolved in light. Unlike Constable who adored the English landscape, Turner was besotted by Italy. His pair of Roman views, *Modern Rome* and *Rome from the Aventine*, are full of topographical details such as the Colosseum, yet they remain poetic evocations of a golden Mediterranean world.

In the early nineteenth century pure landscape was considered a minor art and Turner was obliged to include mythological or historical figures to make his pictures acceptable to the Royal Academy. Constable refused to compromise his authentic view of rural England and, unlike the successful Turner, he gained little official recognition. Despite these differences, in Turner's and Constable's freedom of handling and preoccupation with light effects they can be seen as precursors of the Impressionists.

Eugene Delacroix, the greatest romantic painter of nineteenth-century France, admired both Constable and Turner although he was preoccupied with monumental figure composition rather than pure landscape. Like all romantics, he was intrigued by exotic Eastern subject matter and *The Chess-players* gives us a hint of the opulence of his colour and technique.

Raeburn and West

A great eighteenth-century Scottish portraitist, Sir Henry Raeburn made his reputation entirely in Scotland, immortalizing the leading lights of the eighteenth century cultural revival. Had he shown more in London, perhaps his inter-national reputation might now stand higher, for at his best he has the freshness and fluidity of Goya.

The Edinburgh-born artist painted most of the notable Scotsmen and Scotswomen of the day. The portraits of Sir Walter Scott, Sir John Sinclair and Niel Gow may be noted.

A portrait like *Sir Patrick Inglis* shows Raeburn at his most natural. Executed quickly and simply in broad brush-strokes of fresh colour without fussing over unnecessary detail, in it he has captured the whole character of his sitter.

In contrast his magnificent portrait of *Colonel Alastair McDonnel of Glengarry* in full highland dress seems rather over-worked. But it is a costume piece and must have looked very dramatic high on the wall of some dark baronial hall.

On a less serious note, who can fail to be charmed by Raeburn's portrait of *The Rev. Robert Walker Skating on Duddingston Loch*? The incongruous sight of this dour minister skating is one of the most memorable images in the gallery.

Benjamin West, an Anglo-American eighteenth century painter, is a near contemporary of the more famous Raeburn. West practised portrait painting in America, and after three years in Italy, settled in England in 1763. His painting *Alexander III Rescued from a Stag* is a large canvas illustrating the legend of Colin Fitzgerald, an Irish refugee saving the life of Alexander III, King of Scotland, from an enraged stag. There is no real basis historically for the story, but it is symptomatic of a real interest in Scots history. West's Roman training shows in this picture with its combination of medieval myth and a classical historical piece.

Eighteenth and Nineteenth Century European Art including French Impressionists

All these paintings are the work of artists who, in one way or another, rejected the authority of the French Salon. Their experiments and investigations were to transform people's ideas about painting and sow the seeds of an aesthetic revolution they could have scarcely foreseen.

Gustave Courbet's small canvases, *View of Ornans with Church Tower*, *River in Mountain Gorge* and *The Wave* may look harmless enough—even conventional—to modern eyes. But in the 1850s their painter represented all that was revolutionary in French art. Courbet waged war against the Academy and all it stood for. When his works were accepted for exhibition in the annual Salon, they incurred bitter criticism on account of what was seen as their vulgarity. If his work failed to be accepted he characteristically set up an alternative show—erecting a tent and charging admission! Courbet offended against official taste both in his choice of subjects and the way in which he painted them. He chose 'down to earth' things—a local burial or men breaking stones for example. Not for him historical or mythological subjects, false sentimentality or overt moralizing. Something of this direct approach can be seen in these three small pictures; especially in the simplicity of his sea composition with its broad use of palette-knife. The unprettified, sober townscape is a view of Ornans—the artist's hometown. Courbet's attitude to his art was influenced in no small way by his political idealism. A convinced socialist, perhaps the most bizarre episode of his extrovert career occurred in 1871 when he was held responsible for the destruction of the Vendôme Column during the Paris Commune of that year. His last years were spent in exile in Switzerland.

The other small landscapes hanging here alongside the work of Courbet represent another—less violent—anti-Academic trend in mid-nineteenth-century painting. *Soleil Couchant* and *Cottages at Barbizon: Evening* by Charles Daubigny and *Pool in the Forest* by Narcisse Diaz are both typical, in their freshness and intimacy, of the pictures produced by a group of landscapists working in the Fontainbleau woods south of Paris. Centred on the village of Barbizon, they have become known as the Barbizon School and anticipate the Impressionists in their dedication to working directly from nature out of doors.

They admired Dutch seventeenth-century landscape painting and the work of John Constable, and the spontaneity of many of their small pictures recalls that of the English artist. The charming picture *Entrance to a Wood* was painted by the group's chief mentor, Camille Corot, and is a fine example of the subtle, poetic type of landscape which made him the most popular and influential landscape painter of his generation. Building up a picture with small areas of soft tone, Corot produced a very indistinct romantic effect, paying scant attention to precise line-drawing and concentrating on the atmosphere of a subject. This aspect of his work not only endeared him to the Impressionists but also made him a favourite with generations of forgers who made sure that 'Corots' continued to come onto the market long after his death in 1875.

Pictures by the Impressionists are so often reproduced that the shocking effect they must have had on the public in the 1870s can easily be forgotten. But, even here, where they rub shoulders with the pictures of the Barbizon school, their brightness—the high pitch of their colours—produces a shattering contrast.

The spirit of the group is epitomized by Auguste Renoir's *La Promenade*. Such a delightfully casual subject would have been unthinkable earlier in the century. The naturalism of the picture is a result of Renoir's acute observation of the effect of light filtering through the trees and dappling the strolling couple. And it was light and the difficult technical problem of rendering its transitory effects that obsessed the Impressionists. Claude Monet spent his whole life grappling with the problem. In the 1890s he painted entire series of works—almost scientific studies—of the same subject seen at different times of day and in different weather conditions. *Poplars on the Epte* and *Haystacks: Snow Effect* are from two such series. The picture of haystacks is a very good example of the Impressionist belief that the shadows of objects are tinged by the object's complementary colour.

In the painting of poplar trees the form of the trees is broken up by the shimmering light rendered with small agitated brushstrokes. These small dabbed brushstrokes became a hallmark of Impressionist pictures. Alfred Sisley produced some of the prettiest of them. *Mosley Weir: Hampton Court* was painted when, along with several other of the Impressionists, he fled to England during the 1870s in order to escape the political turmoil of France.

Together with Monet, Camille Pissarro was to become one of the most dedicated and consistent practitioners of Impressionism, but his large *River*

The Wave by Courbet

Haystacks by Monet

Landscape hanging here was executed before he had fully developed his ideas. *The Kitchen Garden at the Hermitage, Pontoise* is a more typical work.

Edgar Degas' *Portrait of Diego Martelli* displays all the characteristics which set him

Degas' *Diego Martelli*

apart from other Impressionists. The picture's greatest strength is the superb drawing of Diego Martelli (note the delineation of the crumpled trousers). Degas was a magnificent draughtsman, traditionally trained, and this love of drawing always tended to make him antipathetic towards the Impressionists' overwhelming preoccupation with light. For Degas light was a dramatic tool with which to compose arresting pictures in the quiet of his studio and not something to be slavishly copied out of doors. But in spite of his more conventional attitude towards picture-making, he was in many respects an innovator. One of the first painters to use the camera extensively in his work, he became fascinated by the unusual appearances of things seen from unexpected angles. Extending the Impressionist range of modern subjects, he painted the races, women in hat shops, laundresses. The ballet, in particular, gave him endless scope to compose interesting groups of contorted figures and the artificial theatre lights

prompted him to explore exciting, unnatural combinations of colours. Note how deftly Degas is able to contrive a composition like *Group of Dancers* from a severely limited palette of greens and oranges. While some of the Impressionists

Gauguin's *The Vision of the Sermon (Jacob Wrestling with the Angel)*

escaped to England to avoid the deprivations of Paris under seige by the Prussians in 1870-1871, Degas stayed on, enduring dreadful hardships. As a result he soon began to lose his sight. *Nude Study for 14 Year Old Dancer, Dressed* is a bronze taken from one of the sensitive wax models he made when his almost total blindness prevented him from painting.

A comparison between Paul Gauguin's *Vision of the Sermon: Jacob and the Angel* and the previously discussed Impressionist pictures will give some idea of the extreme reaction against Impressionist naturalism which occurred in the 1880s. Before he found his very personal voice Gauguin worked in an Impressionist style, exhibiting with the group in their later exhibitions. *The Vision* is his first overwhelming anti-naturalistic picture—an imaginary subject painted in flat brilliant colours.

The convoluted shapes of the Breton women's headdresses are silhouetted against a field of strident vermillion. The diagonal thrust of the tree across the picture plane is inspired by similar compositions found in the Japanese prints popular in France at this time. The overall effect of Gauguin's picture is closer to that of medieval stained glass than the work of the Impressionists and it was, indeed, the emotional impact found in medieval work which Gauguin wanted to emulate in his picture. Gauguin continued his visionary painting in the South Seas. The serene mood of a picture like *Three Tahitians* gives no indication of the inconveniences and hardships he suffered there.

Gauguin eventually abandoned the small brushstrokes of the Impressionists to paint in flat areas of vivid colour but Van Gogh chose to develop them into a violent personalized calligraphy. *Olive Trees* vibrates with the artist's disturbed personality. The brushstrokes of colour writhe over the surface of the canvas. What might have been a rather charming scene in the hands of one of the Impressionists has become an emotional expression of the artist's state of mind. Like Gauguin, who fled from the bourgeois life of a stockbroker to dedicate himself to art, Van Gogh came to painting late in life. For a very short period in 1888 the two painters even tried

Apart from the similar way of applying paint, Seurat's art is in almost every other respect alien to that of the Impressionists. Unlike them he had no interest in capturing the fleeting moment but wanted to compose harmonious classical pic

lem of describing the simple underlying forms of nature—the solidity of an apple or a mountain. In his later years he lived a hermit's life near Aix-en-Provence, constantly analysing a very narrow range of subjects. The underlying structure and

Van Gogh's *Olive Trees*

living together but this experiment was not a success.

The Impressionist method of building up an image with small strokes of paint of precisely the right tone and colour had always been a more or less instinctive process. George Seurat investigated the actual scientific basis for the theories vaguely espoused by Monet and the other Impressionists. Under the influence of various optical theories current in the 1880s, he developed a way of placing small dashes of pure colour alongside one another, intending them to fuse into correct areas of tone to the eye.

tures. The small study hanging here is a free sketch for the monumental depiction of a contemporary bathing scene (now in the National Gallery, London).

Whatever the virtues of Impressionist painting, it could never really defend itself against the criticism that it was lacking in form. Impressionist pictures were painted quickly in an effort to capture a particular moment—the transitory effects of light on things. The structure of things was more or less irrelevant. Paul Cezanne began by painting in a more formless manner than any of the Impressionists but gradually became obsessed by the prob-

shape of *Mont St. Victoire* was a source of constant fascination for him. Using natural brushstrokes and a limited palette, he repeatedly tried to find some equation for its form on canvas. Many of these attempts are unfinished, like the example here, almost as if the task was too daunting to be successfully accomplished. Cezanne's single-minded dedication to solving this problem influenced a generation of artists. The first great movement of the twentieth century, Cubism, developed as a result of his research and he is now generally regarded as one of the most influential artists of the last 100 years.

The Scottish Collection

The downstairs extension houses the gallery's Scottish collection. These few rooms offer a quick survey of eighteenth- and nineteenth-century Scottish painting which should not be missed. It is an uneven group of paintings but the best pictures certainly rank alongside many of the masterpieces of European painting upstairs.

Keeping company amidst a number of undistinguished early portraits we meet with the haunting eyes of the French philosopher *Jean-Jacques Rousseau*. The painting is by Rousseau's friend Allan Ramsay who exemplifies the sophisticated, cosmopolitan, eighteenth-century Scot. Ramsay made a considerable reputation in London, eventually becoming court painter to George III. This was an appointment much resented by Reynolds whom contemporary critics considered superior in male portraiture. Reynolds never produced anything quite so perceptive as this characterization of the quicksilver Rousseau. Rousseau was upset that Ramsay had made him look too 'shifty'. Reynolds' admirers, however, conceded that Ramsay was without equal in the portrayal of female beauty.

Sir David Wilkie's reputation was made in London where he became a member of the Royal Academy. The honest realism of his early work comes straight from Dutch art. The narrative and attention to detail in such story pictures as *The Letter of Introduction* and *Distraining for Rent* made him enormously popular in his own day. However, in later life after suffering a breakdown of health he visited Spain where he came under the influence of Spanish painting. These last pictures are the antithesis of all his early work—large in scale and loosely painted. Unfortunately, he mixed bitumen with his paint to make his dark colours richer and this has caused these pictures to crack dreadfully.

The remaining rooms are fitted with a plethora of lochs, beasties and elders of the Church. Enjoy wandering through for they are great fun, if not exactly high art. Marvel at Noel Paton's enamelled fairy paintings crammed with hundreds of tiny female nudes —in reality, Victorian soft pornography. Thrill to the drama of James Drummond's costume pieces, starring the ill-fated Mary, Queen of Scots. Do not miss the tiny tempera panels of William Dyce whose exact technique and sincere approach to religious subject matter influenced the English Pre-Raphaelites.

Sir William McTaggart, Scotland's greatest landscape painter, was one of the same generation as the French Impressionists. He understood the Impressionists' theories before any other British painter, and his brushstrokes and fresh colour point the direction of modern Scottish painting.

His early work was influenced by the brilliant colour

and detail of the Pre-Raphaelites, but from the 1870s his painting bore a steadily decreasing resemblance to anything produced in Britain at the time.

McTaggart painted with feeling and imagination scenes of Scottish country life, sea pieces and portraits. *The Storm* is a large Impressionistic picture of the west coast of Scotland. Many of his later works were of the endlessly repeated advance and fall of the Atlantic breakers on the west coast beaches. In these, colour and brushwork combine to create a powerful conception of rhythmic movement in space.

An early Glasgow School painter, Sir James Guthrie produced work which, like McTaggart, is cosmopolitan in style. The square brushstrokes style of the Glasgow School is evident in his painting *A Hind's Daughter*, a delightful picture of a young girl in a bed of blue-green Brussels sprouts.

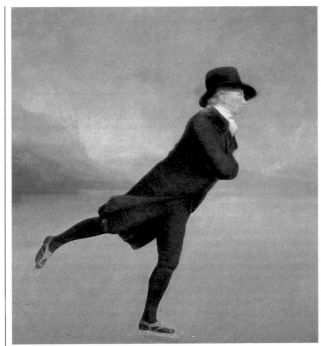

Far left *The Quarrel of Oberon and Titania* by Paton, 1849.
Above *Rev. Robert Walker Skating* by Raeburn.
Below *The Storm* by McTaggart, dated 1890.

Scottish National Gallery of Modern Art

Masterpieces of twentieth-century painting, sculpture and graphic art

In the Summer of 1984 the Gallery moved to premises in Belford Road. It is now housed in the former John Watsons School, a neoclassical building designed by William Burn in the 1820s. The tury, the earliest prints belonging to Max Klinger's portfolio 'On the Finding of a Glove', first published in 1881, while the earliest painting is an oil of c. 1892—Edouard Vuillard's 'La Causette'.

I. There are pictures from the various phases of the career of Pablo Picasso, probably the most universally acclaimed artist in history; a tiny canvas 'Mother and Child' from his famous 'Blue Period', a cubist

A general view of the Scottish National Gallery of Modern Art.

spacious grounds show off the Gallery's sculpture collection.

In spite of the inflated price of modern art, the Scottish National Gallery of Modern Art has succeeded in building up a very respectable collection since its founding in 1959. The collection spans about a cen-

The core of the collection is a small group of works by the pioneer artists of the twentieth century. 'Candlestick' by George Braque is a very good example of the work of the cubist movement he developed along with Picasso in the years leading up to World War

still-life of 1912/13 called 'Guitar, Bottle and Gas Jet' and two still-lifes, 'La Table de Musicien' and 'The Soles', both painted in later, contrasting styles. Do not miss 'La Leçon de Peinture' by Henry Matisse. It is an uncharacteristically sombre picture by an artist famed for his bright colours, a picture composed of simplified decorative shapes. There are a number of fascinating surrealist works: pictures by Rene Magritte, Picabia, Joan Miró, Max Ernst, Duchamp and Giacometti. The works of German and Russian artists are displayed alongside the French work. Note the chilling nude by Otto Dix.

The gallery is also famous for its comprehensive selection of British twentieth century painting. All major figures are represented from Matthew Smith, with his very personal interpretation of French Fauvism, to David Hockney, one of the most popular artists in Britain today.

A unique feature of the Scottish National Gallery of Modern Art collection is its group of works by Scottish painters. Relatively unknown in the rest of Britain, painters in Scotland at the beginning of this century were often closer to continental developments than their counterparts in England. They form a specifically Scottish school known as the Colourists. Look our for paintings by Peploe, Cadell, Hunter and Fergusson. Recent acquisitions include the first oil painting by Lucian Freud, more than 250 drawings by Joan Eardley, and a watercolour and a piece of furniture by Charles Rennie Mackintosh.

Reclining Figure 1951, in bronze, is one of two by Henry Moore in the grounds.

Hanson's *Tourists* are very popular with visitors.

Cadell's *Lady in Black*.

Scottish National Portrait Gallery

The Scottish National Portrait Gallery, in Queen Street, opened its doors to the public in the summer of 1889. It was almost entirely the result of the munificence of John Ritchie Findlay, proprietor of the *Scotsman* newspaper. It was an extraordinary act of private patronage that has never been equalled in Scotland in the sphere of museums and galleries, involving the expenditure of some £70,000 on the elaborate red sandstone, neo-Gothic building designed by Sir Robert Rowand Anderson.

The many ideas which, since the eighteenth century, were to lead to a new manifestation of national identity came to fruition late in 1882 when the Board of Manufactures undertook responsibility for the foundation of a gallery devoted to national portraiture. The collection began to grow quite quickly and by 1885 some 156 portraits were on show in a temporary building on part of the site where the Portrait Gallery was being erected.

The first catalogue of the collection appeared in the same year, the work of the Gallery's first Curator, John Miller Gray, a former banker and dedicated antiquarian and art critic. His reputation as one of Scotland's finest art historians rests principally on his unsurpassed book on the portrait medallionists, James and William Tassie.

The collection now amounts to some 2,800 items. In addition, there are 340 long-term registered loans. The Gallery's collecting policy has evolved to include, as well as the basic collection of portraits of historically important Scots, topographical paintings (like the view of Falkland Palace painted by Alexander Keirincx about 1635) and depictions of great historical events (such as Tilleman's view of the Battle of Glenshiel in 1719). A radical departure from previous policy has been, since 1983, the acquisition of portraits of distinguished contemporaries, many of them commissioned by the Gallery. Temporary or touring photographic exhibitions are also held, such as a collection of photographs by Annie Liebowitz and the John Kobal Photographic Portrait Award. There is a programme of lunchtime lectures.

As you go in make sure that you look up at the wonderful processional frieze in the central hall.

Among many others there are portraits of Robert Burns, Flora Macdonald, Prince Charles Edward Stewart at age 12 and in old age, David Hume the philosopher, James Watt

Perhaps best known for his role as James Bond, actor Sean Connery can now be seen in the Scottish Portrait Gallery, painted by John Bellamy.

the engineer, Sir Walter Scott, Lord Byron, Thomas Carlyle and Robert Louis Stevenson.

Although famous Scottish artists such as Allan Ramsay, Sir Henry Raeburn and David Allan are represented, many of the portraits were painted outside Scotland by artists including Luttichuys from Holland, American John Singleton Copley, and Gainsborough, Romney and Reynolds from England.

The gallery of twentieth century portraits includes Sir Winston Churchill, Ramsay MacDonald, Sir Compton Mackenzie, Sir Alex Douglas-Home, poets Hugh MacDiarmid and Norman MacCaig, film director Bill Forsyth, writer Muriel Spark, British Caledonia founder Sir Adam Thomson, footballer Danny McGrain, fashion designer Jean Muir (a ceramic sculpture of her head), conductor Sir Alexander Gibson by John Houston and writer Molly Hunter by Elizabeth Blackadder.

From the world of entertainment—but perhaps the first time they have appeared together—there are portraits of Fife musician Jimmy Shand and Edinburgh-born actor Sean Connery.

Artistic Tradition in Scotland

The long traditions of Scottish art are linked with those of Europe in certain respects, but, in others, they are unique. The national tradition of painting really begins with the Renaissance—or, rather, the lack of it, for the Renaissance spirit of artistic independence totally failed to spread to Scotland at the time. Unlike England, where itinerant Continental painters such as Holbein and Van Dyck took the place of the monkish artists expelled by the Reformation, Scotland had little such input. The chief reason for this was the sheer distance from the centres of European art, though the climate and the dour Scottish character may have had something to do with it as well.

Thrown back on their own resources, the Scots developed their own native art style. Mostly, Scottish painters worked in portrait—a tradition that was to expand and flower until it reached its peak in the work of the eighteenth-century artists Allan Ramsay and Henry Raeburn. These were the painters of the first great Celtic revival, even though Ramsay made his reputation in London and eventually became Court Painter to George III.

As this tradition reached its peak with Raeburn, another tradition was being founded with the work of the young David Wilkie. His development marks the beginning of a new movement in art which was not just of Scottish, but also of European, importance. Wilkie's adoration of the Dutch and Flemish schools led him to adopt the genre style in his painting. This, sometimes in a slightly debased form, became a cult in Victorian times. Wilkie was described by Millais as the greatest Scottish painter; he became so fashionable that when his painting showing the return of the veterans from Waterloo was exhibited at the Royal Academy, London, barriers had to be erected to keep back the crowds.

The style became part of the Scottish Academy tradition, together with good portraiture, following Raeburn's example. By the mid-nineteenth century the former was becoming steadily more romantic—subjects included scenes from Scott's novels, border ballads and the like—and centred on landscape.

It was at this time that yet another tradition started, which has deeply influenced Scottish art down to the present day. This was a painterly version of the Auld Alliance, demonstrating the continuing Scottish love of things French and of French culture in particular.

In reaction to the conservatism of the Scottish Academy, a group of young painters started looking to France and, in particular, to the work of the Impressionists. Gradually, the link grew. Sir William McTaggart, for instance, was the first notable painter in Britain to work in the Impressionist style.

McTaggart was joined by a group known as the Colourists. This group was Glasgow- and Edinburgh-based (the first Academy rebels had been from Glasgow). Scotland's painters still show their influence; it is notable, for instance, in the work of Joan Eardley, one of Scotland's most important twentieth-century painters.

The story of Scottish art is made up of many strands and themes. Some Scottish artists took the prosperous road south; others, like Raeburn, have been neglected in Britain, though acclaimed on the Continent and in the USA. One factor remains constant—the fact that individuality has been preserved in Scottish art. Its great flowering was almost as much a reaction to external circumstances as the result of the gifts of the painters themselves. The guiding light, in art as in much else since the Union of Parliaments, has been the determination to make painting an integral part of an independent national heritage. In pictorial form, this shows itself in the free handling of paint; in attitude, it shows itself in a spirit of fierce independence which has persisted to the present day.

National Museums of Scotland

Royal Museum of Scotland

Travel the world and go back in time under one roof

As might be expected of the capital of a proud and ancient nation, Edinburgh's museums are treasure-houses of national, as well as local, importance.

The Royal Museum of Scotland was founded in 1854. Since 1865, when the first part of the building in Edinburgh's Chambers Street opened, there have been several name changes. In 1985 it became the Royal Museum of Scotland.

The Museum of Scotland is scheduled to open in November 1998. Visitors can

approach it through the Royal Museum of Scotland but it will also have its own entrance on Chambers Street. It will be the first museum to tell the story of Scotland and its people, from its geological beginnings to the present day. The Museum of Scotland will house about 14,000 objects, some of which

have never been on display before due to lack of space. There will be fossils and other natural history exhibits and large working machinery from the last century. There will be works of art, archaeological pieces and interactive computers to help interpret the displays. From roof-top terraces there will be magnificent views of Edinburgh Castle and the city skyline. While the Royal Museum has an international collection of objects from around the world the new Museum will house the Scottish

The huge natural history section displays elephants, the skeleton of a blue whale (**left**) and the dodo of the Indian Ocean (**above**). The attractive iron galleries of the Main Hall are shown on the opposite page.

collections and present them in a purpose-built setting.

When visiting the Royal Museum of Scotland visitors are advised to pick up a 'What's On'. As well as the permanent exhibitions and collections there is a vigorous programme of temporary exhibitions. The Museum Guides

provide a programme of tours, gallery talks and study sessions to further the appreciation and enjoyment of the collections. Small visitors can borrow steps to stand on so that they don't miss anything of interest in the cases; it is worth checking during holiday times for special children's events.

'Art and Industry since 1850', a permanent gallery on the ground floor, opened in 1996. Visitors are challenged to re-examine some familiar, and not so familiar, objects and question how the item was made, how it functions and why it was styled in a particular fashion. A grand piano painted by the artist Phoebe Anna Traquair, a modern oil-can transformed into a light, a Mies Van der Rohe chair, and a selection of footwear from the past 100 years are just some examples. And with nostalgia back in fashion there is much here which will be familiar—a 1970s Afghan coat, toys, kitchen utensils, bicycles and cars. The nostalgia theme is further emphasised with a series of multi-media programmes which illustrate the music, fashions and pastimes of the 1950s, 60s, 70s and 80s.

The gallery shows the work of artists, engineers, craftspeople and scientists over the last 150 years. All the exhibits were subject to the process of design which was intended to make them look better, perform better or sell better. 'Art and Industry' invites the public to question what constitutes successful design. It wants them to be aware of the significant changes that have occurred since 1850 and to appreciate the complex interplay between art and industry.

The 'World in our Hands' exhibition uses a multi-media approach to: explain how plants and animals keep the planet working; show how people are threatening these processes; suggest what we can do to prevent further environmental damage. The Biodome has a film introducing 'World in our Hands' and explains why planet Earth is special. In the 'Planet Earth in Peril' section interactive devices are used to deal with such problematical questions as global warming and ocean pollution. The exhibition shows a range of extinct and endangered animals and plants from all over the world. See the Quagga and the 4m tall Great Moa—both now extinct —the Museum's reconstruction of the long-dead Dodo and the endangered Giant Pandas in their forest home. The part people have played in the downfall of those species is explained. Habitat loss is also looked at. Whereas occasional extinctions are not a threat to Earth's life-support systems, the loss of habitats such as coral reefs, oceans and tropical rain forests is far more serious. The good news is that there is much that individuals can do to help the environment, from recycling materials to joining environmental organisations.

On the second floor you can experience the fascinating cultures of China, Japan and Korea in the Ivy Wu Gallery. This unique collection of East Asian treasures, many on display for the first time, illustrates the international importance of these ancient and influential civilisations.

From China there are sumptuous costumes and textiles, laquer thrones, richly decorated screens, jade and ivory. Visitors will realise the richness and diversity of this vast country, which at one time led the world with its techniques in printing, design and decoration.

In the Japan section, western images of Japan, 17th century Japanese views of Europeans, the Scottish connection, Japanese art and the armour of the Samurai are among the key themes. The museum has an extensive collection of art in miniature (sword furniture, netsuke and lacquer inro), ceramics, costumes, textiles and musical instruments.

Korea has a rich tradition of pottery making and beautiful lacquer and woodwork. This

Skeleton of boa constrictor

Some of the fascinating encounters that await the visitor to the Royal Museum of Scotland are pictured here. They are representatives from the four main departments of the museum—art and archaeology, geology, natural history and technology.

The departments generally are not restricted to one area but have exhibits on several floors.

Scottish silver box 1736

Fish fossils, 350 million years old

Relief of Pharaoh Akhenaten 1365-1348 BC

Locomotive *Wylam Dilly* 1813

Model of Bell Rock lighthouse 1833

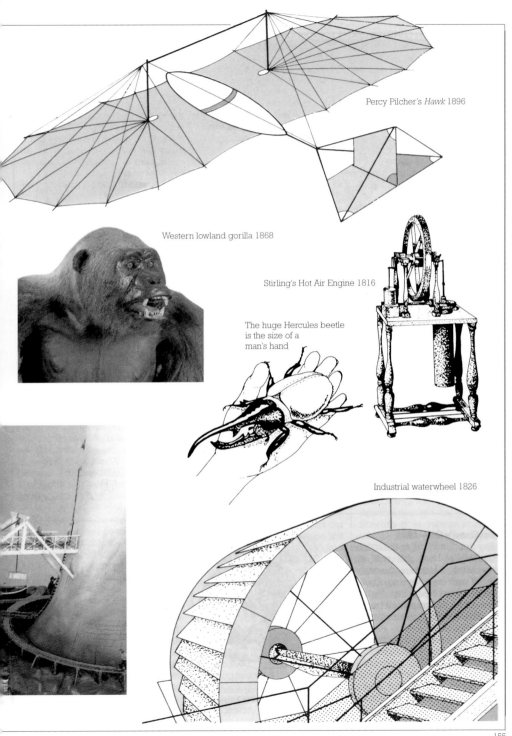

Percy Pilcher's *Hawk* 1896

Western lowland gorilla 1868

Stirling's Hot Air Engine 1816

The huge Hercules beetle
is the size of a
man's hand

Industrial waterwheel 1826

part of the Gallery provides a window on the history and art of Korea, in particular the importance of celadons or green glazed stonewares, the role of men and women in a Confucian society and the use of decorated chests for storage.

In the Tribal Art Gallery look for the helmet mask from New Ireland, which is 600 kilometres (400 miles) east of New Guinea. Although many New Ireland traditions no longer survive, the important funeral ceremonies held every four or five years, known as Malagan, still persist in certain villages. The spirits of the dead, thought to remain among the living, are celebrated or appeased. The mask, which is made of wood and painted in traditional colours, was prob-ably worn during the Tananua, a sacred dance which is part of Malagan.

An 11th century astrolabe from Moorish Spain can be seen in the Instruments of Science Gallery. This is a complex scientific instrument which played a vital role in the leading medieval science, astronomy. Its primary use was in undertaking calculations but it was also used to cast horoscopes. This example is particularly rare and precious, the oldest known signed and dated astrolabe made in Europe and a symbol of the revival of science in the West.

Among the many fascinating displays in the Skeleton Gallery perhaps there is none more so than the boa constrictor. The fossil record shows that snakes were the most recent of the reptilian groups to evolve. It is generally believed that the long limbless body was for burrowing but it also suits other activities such as travelling above the ground, climbing and swimming.

Other galleries include: Minerals and Gems, Geology, Rocks and Minerals, Within the Middle East, Arms and Armour, Ceramics, Glass, Fish, Insects and Molluscs, Ancient Egypt, Modern Jewellery and Costumes.

Allow yourself plenty of time for your museum visit because there is so much to enjoy. There is a tea-room at the back of the building and a cafe on the ground floor when you need a refreshment stop—or you can sit by the fountains in the foyer and watch the world go by.

An artist's impression of the new Museum of Scotland.

1

2

3

Some of the treasures
which will be on show in
the new Museum of
Scotland.

1 Two beakers
2000-1600 AD
2 Two silver-gilt chapes,
part of the St. Ninian's
treasure
3 The Hunterstone Brooch
circa AD 700
4 Roman iron helmet mask
with traces of silver plating,
late 1st century AD
5 Pictish symbol stone
7th-8th century AD
6 Three carved stone
balls and a macehead
circa 2000 BC
7 Gold collar and earring
circa 2000-1700 BC

4

4

6

7

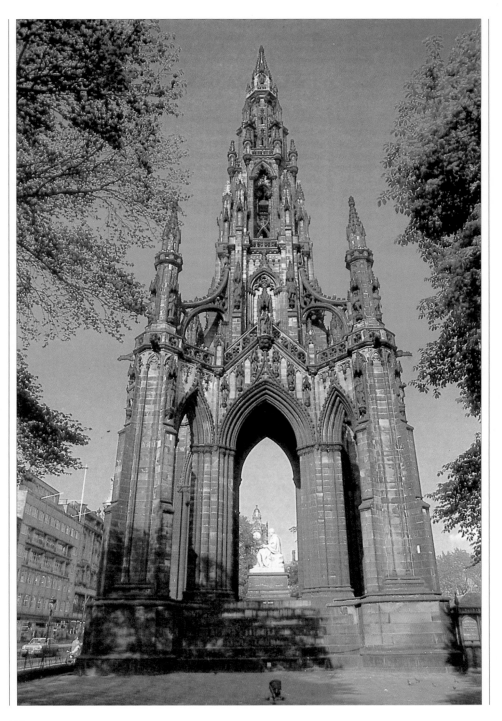

Statues and Monuments

A miscellany of the many memorials Edinburgh has raised to heroes

The Gothic fantasy of Sir Walter Scott's monument dominates east Princes Street, towering over the gardens at the foot of St. David's Street.

Designed by George Meikle Kemp, a joiner and draftsman, and with a twice-life-sized statue of the seated Sir Walter by the sculptor Sir John Steell, it is a legacy of the romantic Gothic Revival popularised by Scott.

The competition for the design of the monument, announced in 1836, caused enormous controversy over the design and the winner: Kemp was accused of plagiarism—and he was an unknown from the lower classes. But his monument was inaugurated after interminable squabbles and delays on August 15, 1846, and immediately became one of the major attractions of the city.

Kemp designed the monument, inspired by Melrose Abbey and Gothic memorial crosses, in only five days and it was chosen by the Memorial Committee despite designs submitted by illustrious architects like William Playfair.

The monument is 200½ feet (601.5m) high, and the 55-square-feet (5m2) base rests on a foundation of solid rock 52 feet (15.6m) below street level.

Above the foundations, rising seven steps on each side, is a quadrangular platform where the statue of Scott and his dog, Maida, rests. It is carved from a solid block of Carrara marble that originally weighed 30 tons and was, in fact, the first marble statue in Scotland.

At each corner of the platform, four massive piers of clustered shafts are joined by pointed arches and the space

above is vaulted over with ribbed arches. The vaults are supported by four external buttresses, rising 90 feet (27m). A gallery surmounts the four principal arches and contains a central room, the Museum Room, completed in the 1870s.

Above the gallery the main tower rises steeply and contains a further three galleries with connecting stairs. The uppermost gallery is a climb of 287 steps but the view from the top is spectacular.

The exterior is highly decorated with 64 characters from Scott's novels and a further 16 statuettes are of Scottish poets.

The monument is made of sandstone from the Binny Quarry and it was decided to re-open the Quarry in 1997 for stone to use in restoration work.

David Livingstone

At the Waverley Bridge entrance to East Princes Street Gardens stands this statue to David Livingstone, the nineteenth-century explorer and missionary. After discovering the Zambezi River and Victoria Falls, he was awarded the Gold Medal by the Royal Geographical Society, shortly after which he was made an honorary burgess of Edinburgh. Livingstone died in 1873 while searching for the source of the Nile, and his body was returned to Britain to be buried in Westminster Abbey. Three years later this bronze statue was erected. It is the only statue in the gardens sculpted by a woman, Amelia Robertson Hill. Although it was said to be an 'admirable likeness', many present at its inauguration thought this statue to be too small for the open air and more suitable for the interior of a building.

Allan Ramsay

The marble statue showing this eighteenth-century wigmaker turned poet wearing a silk nightcap was sculpted by Sir John Steell, who carved it from a solid block that weighed 18 tons. Ramsay, who moved to Edinburgh from his native Lanarkshire, became a great success in the capital through his writing and bookshop and

was among the pioneers of lending libraries, opening one in the High Street in 1725. This, and his involvement with the theatre which he fought to have legalized in Scotland, made him very unpopular with the Presbyterian Church.

The statue, erected in Princes Street Gardens West in 1865, was commissioned by one of his descendants, Lord Murray, who appears on one of four medallions on the plinth. General Ramsay, the poet's grandson, the poet's wife and two great-granddaughters are depicted on the others.

Charles II

In Parliament Square the Merry Monarch, Charles II, prances near the grave of the Gloomy Reformer, John Knox, whose remains were buried here when it was St. Giles graveyard. Charles's statue is the oldest in Edinburgh and the oldest equestrian statue, dated 1685, in Britain. It is thought to be of Dutch origin but the sculptor is unknown. No one knows quite how much it weighs but when it was built no supporting struts were inserted. As a result the horse is buckling at the knees and has to be repaired frequently: a long-term reinforcement programme is planned.

The statue was removed during the nineteenth-century renovations to St. Giles and was put back again in 1835 when Robert Mylne, the King's Master Mason in Scotland, added the plinth.

John Knox

An ironic memorial to the reformer of the Scottish church, John Knox, stands against the wall of St. Giles in Parliament Square. 'He sleeps', wrote Robert Louis Stevenson, 'within the call of the church that so often echoed to his preaching.' The bronze statue of Knox, who campaigned tumultuously against 'graven images' in churches, was designed by Pittendrigh MacGillivray in 1902 and cast in 1906. The statue marks the approximate site of the dour man's grave (this area used to be St. Giles graveyard) and seems to look accusingly at the nearby statue of the Merry Monarch, the libertine King Charles II.

George IV

Designed by Chantrey in 1831 to commemorate the King's famous visit in 1822, this statue stands in Hanover Street. George's visit was very popular and he was rapturously welcomed, even though he wore pink silk tights under his kilt. The royal tour, the first since the Scottish defeat at Culloden, was seen as a recognition of Scottish participation in the union as a partner rather than a vanquished nation.

Melville Monument

This 150-feet-high (45.7m) stone column, topped with a statue of Henry Dundas, 1st Viscount Melville, has a rather turbulent history. Building began on the column, a copy of Trajan's Column in Rome, in 1821. The money, £3,500, was raised by officers, petty officers, seamen and marines who served Melville during his time as First Lord of the Admiralty, but it ran out before completion, and the city was forced to help out financially. However, it is still not certain that building debts have been cleared.

There was also a squabble over the siting—first it was to be at Calton Hill, then its present site in St. Andrew Square was chosen; followed in 1823 by hot debate whether or not it should be completed at all. Others suggested it should be rededicated to William Pitt. Finally, in 1837 after 14 years of argument, Melville, so powerful in his day that he was nicknamed King Harry the Ninth, triumphed and a statue was designed by Sir Francis Chantrey and carved by Robert Forrest.

Dundas, a man of indefatigable industry, was Solicitor General for Scotland at the age of 24, Lord Advocate between 1775 and 1783, Treasurer to the Navy under William Pitt from 1784-1800 and then First Lord of the Admiralty.

Scottish American War Memorial

The Scottish American War Memorial Committee dedicated this statue to 'the Scottish effort in the Great War' in 1927. The bronze cast had taken the designer, Professor R. Tait Mackenzie of Philadelphia three years to complete and it is entitled 'The Call'. It shows a kilted soldier on a plinth looking at a frieze where volunteers from all walks of life are represented. Above the frieze are two intertwined wreaths, one with a shield of the Stars and Stripes and the other with the shield of St. Andrew's Cross.

At the Beginning of World War II the statue, in Princes Street Gardens West, was covered in sandbags to preserve it. The bags were ceremoniously removed during a memorial service on May 30, 1942.

Alexander and Bucephalus

Sir John Steell first modelled this huge statue 50 years before it was finally cast in bronze—in 1883, the cost paid for by subscribers. It shows the Macedonian king Alexander taming his warhorse Bucephalus as a representation of 'mind over brute force' and was unveiled in 1884 on the west side of St. Andrew Square. In 1916 it was moved to its present position outside the City Chambers in the High Street because it was a traffic hazard. The Gladstone Memorial Committee paid the cost of the move as they replaced it with a statue of Gladstone but this, too, had to be moved in time.

Earl Haig Memorial

A Bombay parsee, Sir Dhumjibhoy Bomanzi, commissioned this bronze statue of Earl Haig and his horse 'in admiration of the services rendered to the British Empire by the Field Marshal'. Haig was Commander in Chief of the British Army in World War I. The statue was designed by George Wade and unveiled in 1923 on the northern edge of the Castle Esplanade, alongside a parade of memorials to Scottish soldiers and regiments.

Adam Black

The politician and publisher was Lord Provost of Edinburgh from 1843 to 1848 and is depicted by John Hutchison, the sculptor, in his robes of office. Black, who also represented the city as a Liberal Member of Parliament, refused the knighthood normally offered to retiring Lord Provosts, with the words, 'I have no need of a title for my wife to be called "my lady" (she was already a Lady) and I have enough heirs to do without airs and graces.' He was one of the city's most prominent publishers, founder of A & C Black, and had acquired the copyright for some ot the early editions of the *Encyclopaedia Britannica* and Scott's Waverley Novels. The statue, cast in bronze, was erected in Princes Street Gardens East in 1877.

Duke of Wellington

This statue, outside Register House in Princes Street, so pleased the Duke of Wellington that he wanted a copy for his London home. But as the complete equestrian sculpture weighed 12 tons, he had only the bust cast.

Known as the 'Iron Duke in bronze by Steell', it was among the first successful models of a

prancing horse, cleverly using the tail as means of support. The Duke's war horse, Copenhagen, was unavailable as a model for the sculptor, Sir John Steell, so he borrowed a horse of a similar breed from the Duke of Buccleuch's stables at Dalkeith Palace, to which he again resorted for models for the Albert Statue in Charlotte Square.

Sir William Chambers

When the Town Council commissioned a statue of their former Lord Provost William Chambers there was heated argument about the suitability of the design—a recumbent figure that was to have lain in St. Giles Kirk. But the Kirk authorities objected and the council were forced to find an alternative site. A competition for a new design was launched and the sculptor John Rhind won with his model of Chambers, brother of the publisher, standing in his Provost's robes. The bronze statue was erected by the Town Council in 1891 and unveiled by the then Lord Provost John Boyd in Chambers Street.

The Royal Botanic Garden

The largest section of the Royal Botanic Garden is the Arboretum, where visitors can wander or rest in the shade of trees and shrubs from all over the world. Some of the most brilliant flowering is in the nearby Rhododendron Walk.

$\mathcal{F}$ew cities in the world can boast a park or garden of over 70 acres (28 ha) only a 10-minute bus ride from the centre. As you pass through the East Gate, Inverleith Row, you can see what makes Edinburgh's Royal Botanic Garden different; the emphasis on woodland and wild areas contrasts completely with the formality of mansion gardens.

The Garden contains a remarkable collection of more than 34,000 living plants. Work at the Garden focuses not only on flowering plants and conifers but also on ferns, mosses, fungi, lichen and algae. The botanists and horticulturalists are engaged in a race against time to determine what still exists and how best to conserve plants on which we depend for our survival. This involvement spans the globe—from the jungles of Malaysia to the mountains and valleys of the Himalayas, and from the deserts of Arabia to the uplands of Scotland.

The Royal Botanic Garden is primarily a scientific research institution—a place of learning. The plant collection is complemented by three further vital resources. Housed in the complex of the Science buildings are: the Herbarium—a reference collection of over two million preserved plant specimens; the Library containing nearly 100,000 books and periodicals; and the Laboratories with their state-of-the-art facilities for microscopy and DNA studies, all invaluable to extending our understanding of plants and how they grow.

You can wander around by yourself or take advantage of the Garden Guide tours and trails which enable visitors to gain a greater appreciation of the importance of plants and the role of botanic gardens. Ultimately, it is the cultivation of a unique collection of plants in a beautifully landscaped setting that makes the Royal Botanic Garden in Edinburgh such a world-famous visitor attraction.

The magnificent gardens are the result of two Edinburgh physicians establishing a physic garden in 1670. Medicine at the time relied largely upon herbs and, from the Dark Ages to the early Middle Ages, upon the work of monks. The use of plants until about the beginning of the nineteenth century was central to medicine and, until the creation and development of physic gardens in the sixteenth and seventeenth centuries, it was the monastic communities that maintained interest in herbs and their healing potential.

Physic gardens were always associated with universities where medicine was taught because medicine relied upon plant life and its study. Dr. Robert Sibbald, the first Professor of Medicine at Edinburgh University, and Dr. Robert Balfour, an eminent physician, recognizing the unsatisfactory state of medicine in the city, decided to establish a physic garden for the cultivation of medicinal and other plants.

The site the two doctors secured was just 40 feet (12m) square, a small plot of land not far from Holyrood Abbey. The

This plan of the Royal Botanic Garden pinpoints the major houses and gardens of interest. The map above locates the Garden in relation to the city centre.

Gardens came under the Commissioners of Her Majesty's Works and Public Buildings.

John Hope's period as Superintendent of the Garden was one of great activity. His two great interests were plant physiology and systematic botany and these studies and his teaching contributed greatly to the science. He encouraged his students to research in the field and it is now acknowledged that he and his pupils were the pioneer investigators of Scottish plant life, collecting not only from the mainland but from Arran, Mull, Orkney, Shetland and Skye as well. His name has been commemorated for all time in the genus of trees from South China, South-east Asia and Indonesia and Malaysia—*Hopea*.

Hope was succeeded in 1786 by Daniel Rutherford who, as a chemist, was more interested in plants as objects for his experiments in determining the chemistry of the atmosphere. Of his six principal gardeners during his 33 years as Professor and Keeper of the Royal Garden, John Tweedie was notable. Tweedie had worked at Dalkeith Palace Gardens, and later, in 1825 at the age of 50, left to explore the reported botanical splendour of South America. Tweedie introduced several species of *Verbena*, the Chilean Jasmine and a number of other exotic and colourful plants which can be seen in the herbarium at the Gardens.

Rutherford was responsible too for appointing John McKay of Edinburgh as Principal Gardener in 1800. He removed old trees, exchanged plants with the Gardens at Kew, London, and embarked on botanical excursions with a number of dedicated students. McKay died in 1802 but in 1810 Rutherford was again lucky in his gardeners; this time he appointed William McNab, a leading horticulturalist from Kew.

venture was successful, with the assistance of James Sutherland, the first Superintendent of the Garden, but they could not have dreamed that such humble beginnings would result in today's renowned Botanic Garden.

In 1676 Balfour and Sibbald realized that more land was required and they took over the garden attached to Trinity Hospital—on the site of which Waverley Station stands today. James Sutherland was responsible for both gardens and in 1695 was appointed Professor of Botany at the university and in the same year took control of part of the Royal Garden at Holyrood.

The Royal Botanic Garden was extremely fortunate both in Sutherland and, later, John Hope. Hope had originally entered the University of Edinburgh as a medical student but his interest in botany took him over. In 1763 he carried out his greatest achievement from the point of view of the garden's history. The Trinity Hospital Garden was in 1763 moved to a larger site of about five acres (2 ha) off Leith Walk, to a site where Haddington Place now stands. At the same time, Professor John Hope, the Regius Keeper, obtained a permanent income for the new garden from the Crown, from which time the

McNab showed immense enthusiasm in his task of developing the Botanic Garden. He introduced many new and rare plants and carried out the culture of aquatic plants such as Egyptian water lilies and other water-living plants from Bengal, south and east Asia, the United States and India.

McNab was the organizer for the move to Inverleith. Transporting and transplanting well-established trees and shrubs has never been easy. McNab invented a transplanting machine to allow the removal of mature trees. The operation took over two years and it is McNab who should be credited for the fact that virtually nothing died.

Up until this time specimens from abroad had been introduced in a rather haphazard way; most of the botanical excursions were concentrated on native Scottish plant life.

Naturalists had accompanied expeditions: the group of monkey puzzle trees between the Pond and the Azalea Lawn, for example, were introduced in 1795 by Archibald Menzies, a student under Professor John Hope. He had accompanied Captain Vancouver in the *Discovery* in 1790 and returned with the specimens from Chile. Later expeditions included that of Captain James Clark Ross's *Erebus* to the Antarctic in 1839. Many specimens were intro-

duced, however, by an informal system of exchange with other gardens, notably Kew.

The Universities (Scotland) Act of 1889 proposed that the Botanic Garden should be transferred to the University of Edinburgh. Balfour resisted for a number of reasons. As a result the gardens were handed over by the Treasury to the First Commissioner of Works and the gardens had to be open on Sundays. The public showed their approval: 27,000 visited over four Sundays while the Free Church Presbytery denounced the arrangement as 'a most wanton desecration'.

The following year, 1890, the Right Hon. the Lords Commissioners of HM Treasury set up an enquiry to consider the role of the Keeper and the outlay for the gardens in the future. The beginning of the Royal Botanic Garden as it is today at last began to take form.

Towards the end of the 1830s more formal transactions on a large scale were contemplated, and by 1844 the first volume of *Transactions* had been published. But the scheme was on a small scale until the period from 1905 to 1925 which was especially rich in the introduction of foreign species—in particular the collections of George Forrest from western China. Their classification by botanists on the university

and garden staffs resulted in botanical papers on Asiatic rhododendrons, primulas, gentians, lilies, conifers and other groups of plants which were to completely transform the gardens. Exchanges of seeds are now made with gardens all over the world, and trust funds, such as the Rock Plant Trust Fund, sponsor botanists on collecting trips.

In 1864 the Experimental Garden of the Royal Caledonian Horticultural Society was transferred to the Botanic Garden and in 1876 a further 30 acres (12 ha) of ground surrounding Inverleith House were added. The gardens were at this time under the supervision of Isaac Bayley Balfour, who had succeeded his father John Hutton Balfour.

New accommodation for botanical research and teaching was built, laying out of the Rock Garden started and new glasshouses were constructed —some of which survived until 1966. Edinburgh became an important centre for taxonomic research, especially on the plants of China and the Himalayas, which included the famous rhododendrons. This work owed much to the naturalists who accompanied expeditions of exploration, and in particular to the plant collector, George Forrest, who brought from China many important horticultural plants and over 46,000 dried and living specimens for scientific research.

Isaac Bayley Balfour quickly realized the need for extensive modernization and reorganization of the gardens themselves and the way in which they were controlled. Up until 1889 the Botanic Garden was under the dual control of the Treasury and the Commissioner of Works. Balfour saw that dual control led to inefficiency, more money was needed for maintenance and development and research should be furthered.

The Winter Palace in the late nineteenth century.

Today the Royal Botanic Garden is a four-garden institution. Three specialist gardens in other parts of Scotland provide additional space in different environmental conditions for cultivating plants: a mild, highland hillside at the Younger Botanic Garden, Benmore, near Dunoon, Argyll; a cool Borders glen at Dawyck Botanic Garden, near Peebles, Tweeddale; and a warm, almost subtropical oasis at Logan Botanic garden near Stranraer in Galloway.

A walk through the gardens

The Rhododendron Walk

Edinburgh's Royal Botanic Garden now contains the largest collection of rhododendrons in Britain. The most beautiful display is in the Rhododendron Walk which extends from the West Gate entrance, and many others are dotted around.

Thickets of the largest leaved of the hardy bamboos provide shade and protection for other plants, which include specimens of *Bergenia*, mainly Himalayan and Chinese, and plantain lilies.

Shrubs from New Zealand have found the protection from wind and frost and the full sun they need on the south and west facing walls of Inverleith House. These include *Sophora tetraptera*, the kowhai, with its curious golden yellow flowers that appear in June and *Hoheria sexstylosa* which flowers profusely in July and August.

To the north of Inverleith House and along one side of the *Rhododendron x praecox*

hedge is a collection of *Enkianthus* species. Their clusters of white, pink or reddish flowers appear in spring, and in autumn their foliage turns magnificent hues of orange and crimson.

Near the *Enkianthus* are several plants which would be considered delicate when grown on the east coast of Scotland: the evergreen *Desfontainea spinosa* from Chile produces yellow-lobed scarlet flowers during the summer and *Mahonia lomariifolia* blossoms yellow flowers in November.

Several plants in the Rhododendron Walk produce either fruits or flowers as late as November and, in the case of the hellebores, in December and January. The spectacular Corsican hellebore, for example, produces pale green flowers from a mass of toothed foliage well after the New Year. On the east side of Inverleith House is a collection of magnolias which, as well as producing large, attractive flowers in spring, also contribute to autumn colour.

The Arboretum

Much of the original planting in the Arboretum, south of the Rhododendron Walk, was carried out on the basis of assembling all the species of a single genus as near together as possible. The introduction of new species, especially from the Himalayas, western China and North America, and the need to plant some species to give shelter to others, has made it impossible to adhere strictly to the plan. The main collection of oaks, for example, is on the lawn to the north of Inverleith

House, but some fine specimens are found near the pond, to the east, as well.

The Arboretum, the Latin name for a botanic garden of trees, has been added to continually since its founding in 1877. The lawns include a varied sampling of trees of the rose family, such as the flowering crabs and rowans, hawthorns, and of the maple and lime families. There are also willows, poplars, silver birches and alders. The extensive collection of barberries is located principally on the lawn between the conifers and the main collection of oaks.

Pringle Chinese Collection

The Pringle Chinese Collection, on the south-facing slope of Inverleith Hill, is an extensive collection of wild-origin plants created to reflect a natural Chinese landscape in ecological plantings of four vegetation zones.

At the foot of the hill deciduous woodland gives way to coniferous woodland and rhododendron forest, and culminates with alpine and meadow plants at the top of the hill. The inclusion of large boulders and water features accurately reflects a Chinese landscape and the whole development provides colour throughout the year, particularly during the summer. Visitors are led through the Collection by a series of pathways, which cross a spectacular wild water ravine that flows down into a tranquil pool at the bottom of the hillside where a Chinese pavilion (T'ing) provides an area for relaxation and contemplation.

Spring

Summer

Autumn

Winter

The Peat Garden

It was under the direction of William Wright Smith that the Peat Garden, the first in Britain, was constructed in 1939 at the north entrance of the Woodland Garden. A series of raised borders, rich in peat, has allowed the successful cultivation of plants like dwarf rhododendrons, primulas, gentians, lilies. An immense variety of creeping shrubs and dwarf shrubs provide winter cover so that ground penetration by frost is reduced. The dwarf lilies and the terrestrial orchids, notably the North African *Dactylorhiza elata* and the Madeiran *D. maderensis* are particularly interesting. *Primula whitei* and *P. gracilipes* are two of the primulas that attract visitors in such numbers, from spring onwards, that the surrounding turf is often worn bare. Ferns, such as the native Adder's Tongue, thrive in the peaty conditions.

The Woodland Garden

The Woodland (or wild) Garden is the least formal of the sections: the illusion of remoteness is achieved by introducing large masses of evergreen shrubs which shut off the surrounding buildings, and by trees which provide partial overhead shade.

Grassy paths wind through the woodland and the area is enlivened with evergreen shrubs to provide a leafy background and masses of colour in season.

Shade and shelter for the woodland vegetation is given in part by conifers such as cypress, thuja, fir and pine. Owing to atmospheric pollution, unfortunately, none of these is really splendid but at least they help the survival of other plants.

As well as an abundance of rhododendrons, the shrubs include hydrangeas, viburnums, eucryphias, camellias, magnolias and cotoneasters—as well as many others. Shade-loving plants include the striking May lily, with its heart-shaped leaves and small, white flowers, the wood anemone, greater celandine, the North American bleeding heart or Dutchman's breeches, the plantain lily of Japan, with its beautiful foliage, and, not least, bluebells and poppies.

The Rock Garden

To the east of the conifers in the Woodland Garden, lies the Rock Garden with plants from Europe, India, China, Japan, Australia, New Zealand and the Americas.

James McNab, as principal gardener, conceived and constructed the Rock Garden in 1871. He used the well-worn steps and landing of the old School of Arts in Adam Square, carried stones from the old Bank of Scotland buildings, basalts from Giants Causeway and Staffa, and large masses of granite and quartz, black hecla or lava stones. Isaac Bayley Balfour, however, wished to make improvements and the reconstruction work, which took until 1914, produced a rock garden that is fundamentally the one you see today. Large pieces of conglomerate from the slopes of Ben Ledi in Perthshire and red sandstone from Dumfries were used.

The spaces between the rocks harbour plants from many mountainous parts of the world—which are sometimes incorrectly thought to provide all rock garden plants. High mountain, or alpine, plants are found in great numbers in the Rock Garden, together with species from the varied environments of the warm Mediterranean shores and the cold permafrost regions of the Arctic.

There is a collection of mainly Scottish alpine plants in the centre of the Rock Garden; there are saxifrages, campanulas, alliums, gentians from Europe, America, Asia Minor, the Himalayas, China, Turkestan; a variety of species from Spain, Portugal, North Africa and the Americas; and the plants with white flowers from New Zealand include the celmisias with silvery, often sword-shaped, leaves and great daisy-like flowers and *Ranunculus lyallii*, probably the most beautiful buttercup in the world.

Miniature waterfalls and pools give the area added interest as well as ensuring sufficient moisture. Much of the rock is covered by prostrate or creeping shrubs. Species of *Cotoneaster* from the Himalayas, southeast Tibet and western China, for example, carpet the rocks and provide decorative fruits as well. The cotoneasters are best seen in the autumn, while shrubby potentillas and several species of broom provide bright colour during the summer. The dwarf rhododendrons are invaluable for colour and cover and vary from the carpeting *Rhododendron forrestii* var. *repens* (named after its collector, George Forrest) and the taller species such as *R. lapponicum* which may reach 3 feet (about 1m) in height and flower profusely in May.

Apart from the many creeping shrubs and the mats of herbaceous plants, conifers such as juniper help to hide the slabs of rock with the evergreen dwarf conifers adding colour and interest during the winter.

The Heath Garden
In the southeast corner of the gardens is the Heath Garden. There are over 30 varieties of heather which flower at different times from the beginning of June until the end of October. With colours ranging through gold, dark red and mauve and the varying colours of foliage, the heath garden is attractive at any time of the year.

In the 1830s, in the time of William McNab, a spendid collection of heathers from South Africa was cultivated. By the 1930s, however, heathers had become less popular with the public and only a few of McNab's specialities remained. Heaths from all over Britain and continental Europe gradually became more popular and so in 1935 a new Heath Garden was laid with thousands of plants being propagated. Species included the many forms of the variable ling or heather *Calluna vulgaris*, and the bell-heather *Erica cinerea* from the Scottish highlands and other parts of Great Britain and Europe; the many forms of *Erica carnea* from the mountains of central and southern Europe, together with many

other species of *Erica* from southern Europe, the Mediterranean and North Africa.

Thousands of these foreign relatives of the Scottish heather were introduced and planted informally with junipers, pernettyas and brooms as well as crocuses and squills to provide colour in every month of the year.

The Pond
North of the Rock Garden, past the East Gate, is the area where the Pond is the focal point. Several hardy aquatic and marsh plants can be seen here: the yellow water lily, *Nuphar lutea*, and the American species *N. advena*; groups of reed mace, also known as bullrushes, are especially conspicuous after the appearance of their cylindrical brown fruiting heads. Emerging well above the surface of the water in summer and autumn is the marestail, *Hippuris vulgaris*; the Cape pond weed, with its curiously branched white flowers, floats all over the surface; and during the summer the water lilac, native to Scotland, can be seen.

The first glimpse of colour around the Pond in spring is the Himalayan primula and in summer the most conspicuous plant is *Gunnera manicata*. This plant is the largest leaved plant hardy in Britain and resembles giant rhubarb—in a good season its leaves will grow to more than five feet (1.5m) across. Moisture-loving plants such as primulas, irises and astilbes flower in summer and the bright scarlet flowers of species of *Lobelia* continue into the autumn. Winter colour is provided by the royal fern,

Osmunda, and the leaves and fruiting heads of reed mace.

Trees framing and overhanging the pond area include the golden weeping willow, the Austrian pine, a weeping ash and a group of Japanese maples to the west. The Pond is the main source of water for the Rock Garden and for the animal life seen in the gardens. Foxes, grey squirrels, birds and smaller creatures all inhabit the gardens.

The Azalea Lawn
Northwest of the Pond, in the centre of the gardens, is the lawn devoted to azaleas—part of the genus *Rhododendron* which start to flower in May. Azaleas are among the most popular of flowering shrubs with an astonishing variety of flower form, colour and perfume.

Azaleas and rhododendrons belong to the ericaceous family, which also includes heathers. They differ from rhododendrons in that they are often deciduous (and those described as evergreen are not true evergreens because the leaves formed on the lower parts of the shoots fall in autumn).

The Lawn includes both deciduous types from eastern Europe, the Caucasus and Belgium and evergreen types from Japan. *Rhododendron x albicans* yield an exceptional scent from their white, pale pink or pale yellow flowers. They are the last to bloom, extending the season into July.

The Lawn is dominated by beeches and there are also numerous birches which include the two North American

The many glorious trees, flowers, shrubs and plants found in the Royal Botanic Gardens are represented on the left-hand page by *Trillium sessile*, which prefers to live in the shade (**top left**); *Trillium grandiflora* in the Peat Garden (**middle left**); the 150-year old palm *Sabal blackburniana* from Bermuda (**main picture**) a mauve dwarf rhododendron (**bottom left**); and the immaculately kept pond near Inverleith House. On this page are Himalayan poppies, also found in the Peat Garden (**top left**); exotica in the Cactus and Succulent House (**top right**); the tranquillity and miniature plants of the Rock Garden (**middle left**); a hybrid orchid of the *Odontonia* genus (**middle right**); and near the Palm House, the delights of the Heath Garden where one bush or another flowers in every season.

species, the canoe birch and the river birch.

At the foot of the Lawn there are rhododendron hybrids and several beautiful examples of the rose family. The hybrid crab-apple of the family *Rosaceae*, for example, produces bronze leaves and an abundance of purplish crimson flowers.

The Glasshouse Experience

There are ten glasshouses to explore, providing a fascinating introduction to the great diversity of plant life that has evolved in the warm temperate and tropical parts of the world. Over 80% of the world's flora occurs in these warm regions, a selection from which is displayed in the houses.

A short walk through the beautifully landscaped plantings, in their computer-controlled environments, will take you from Canary Island hillsides to Australian cloud forest, from Amazonian rainforest to Madagascan desert, and from Mexican jungle to Bornean mountainside.

A tour of the Glasshouse Experience is also a celebration of nearly a century and a half of changing glasshouse design, from the Victorian elegance of the Tropical Palm House (1834) to the contemporary simplicity of the open-plan Peat and Tropical Rock Houses (1978).

The plants include groups that are the subject of current scientific research at Edinburgh and some that support education programmes. There are also a number of rare specimens being conserved against the threat of extinction in the wild.

Temperate House

This house is in the centre of the spectacular main range of glasshouses, which are remarkable for the lack of internal supports, the roof and walls being suspended by external pylons. The design maximises the light available to the plants and provides an internal area which is landscaped to recreate the atomosphere of exotic habitats and makes it possible for many of the trees in here to grow to their full height. The plants all derive from the warm temperate regions of the world, especially Australia, New Zealand and the Canary Isles. At the west end of the house is the Aqua-ium which presents not only a collection of aquatic plants with tropical and cold-water fish, but also allows you an underwater view of the pool in the Tropical Aquatic House above.

Tropical Aquatic House

Here in the tropical rainforest a pond is surrounded by luxuriant vegetation containing many important economic crop plants. Look out for the sources of rice, bananas, sugar, coffee, cocoa and rubber. In summer the pool is dominated by the huge floating leaves of the giant water lily (*Victoria amazonica*), which thrive in the high humidity and hot conditions (night minimum 18°C).

Fern House

Ferns and their allies, the horsetails, were among the first plants to invade the land, 400 million years ago. The grove of tree ferns around the cascading stream in the centre of the house echoes the montane cloud forests of temperate Australasia. Among the plants around the perimeter of the house look out for the giant horsetail rising behind the limestone pave-ment and the climbing fern *Lygodium*, whose fronds can exceed 5 metres in length.

Orchid & Cycad House

This house is dominated by the cycads, an ancient group of plants from the time of the dinosaurs. They have tough palm-like leaves and both the male and female plants bear spectacular cones. Some of them in this house are over 2,000 years old.

The orchid family (*Orchidaceae*) is one of the most numerous and diverse in the plant kingdom, characterized by highly evolved, complex and often very showy flowers. A wide range of orchids flourishes in the moderate humidity and warmth of this house. Some, referred to as terrestrial orchids, are rooted in the ground, but many others grow epiphytically—on the surfaces of other plants.

Tropical Palm House

This octagonal 'Palm Stove' was the largest of its kind in Britain when it opened in 1834. The combination of straight bare trunks rising to a canopy of large leaves in a hot and humid environment echoes the atmosphere of a rainforest. In addition to these stately trees, look out for the massive clump of bamboo and the barbed, rope-like rattan palms, flamboyant climbers that can reach over 100 metres in length.

Temperate Palm House

This glasshouse, at 70ft (21m) is the tallest in Britain. Palms are arguably the most useful group of plants on our planet. They provide a vast range of economic products, ranging from foodstuffs such as dates, coconuts and palm hearts, to oils used in cosmetics and cooking. In addition palm trunks and leaves are used as construction materials in thatching and basket-weaving.

South American Aquatic House

The plants in this house come from the moist forests of tropical America. A range of exotic climbers, many of which have extraordinary flowers, festoon the walls and railings that overlook the pool. However, the character of the vegetation here is dominated by the versatile pineapple family (Bromeliaceae). Some members of this group provide a herbaceous ground cover on the forest floor, while others are epiphytes, growing on the surface of larger plants.

Cactus House

Plants from dry lands throughout the world—from central America to southern Africa, from Arabia to Madagascar—are grouped geographically in this house. They all share a need to save water and, in a remarkable demonstration of convergent evolution, exhibit a variety of common strategies to achieve this.

Peat House

The Peat House has been landscaped to provide the acidic peaty conditions in which tender members of the heath family (Ericaceae) can thrive. Most noteworthy are the vireya rhododendrons from the mountains of New Guinea, Borneo and other parts of the Malaysian archipelago. At the entrance, two special cases display a range of insectivouous plants, as well as a collection of delicate orchids belonging to the genus Dendrobium and its allies from the mountains of south-east Asia.

Tropical Rock House

The main feature of this house is a limestone cliff in the shelter of whose rocks you can see familiar and unusual members of the African violet family (Gesneriaceae). Around the edge of the house notice the spectacular cone-like flowers of the ginger family (Zingiberaceae).

The Fossil Garden

This Garden was established in 1991. The Royal Botanic Garden has in its possession two of five fossilised Pitys trees which were uncovered in the Craigleith Quarry, Edinburgh, between 1835 and 1865. At 35ft (10.5m) long, one is Scotland's largest fossil and at 320 million years old, they are certainly the oldest specimens in the gardens. The purpose of the Fossil Garden, supported by the adjacent living fern and cycad collections, is to demonstrate the evolution of Scotland's vegetation in the context of its geological history. Plantings around the fossil trees are of species which belong to ancient groups of extant plants. These include ferns, horsetails and clubmosses, as well as living relatives of plants known from fossil records. The finest examples of such living fossils are the dawn redwoods (Metasequoia glyptostroboides), which together with the monkey puzzle trees (Araucaria araucana) are planted in the corners of the site.

The Alpine House

This House and its adjacent frames provide special protection from extremes of climate for a remarkable range of montane plants. The colourful cushion plants, bulbous species and other treasures welcome the summer shading, frost protection and controlled dry periods that can be provided here. Stone troughs, raised beds and walls around the courtyard provide a diversity of other richly planted substrates to complement the Alpine House.

The Copse

West of the Alpine House, and the other Plant Exhibition Houses, is the delightfully informal Copse, similar in style to the Woodland Garden. Here in the Copse are birches, pine and eucalyptus, which are especially striking during the winter, while the Acer palmatum 'Senkaki' provides colour in spring and autumn.

Situated on a knoll overlooking the Palm Houses, the Copse is protected by belts of holly and pines. Winding grassy paths are lined with bushes of rhododendrons, magnolia, meconopsis, lily and many others. The collection of viburnums extends beyond the Copse onto a grassy slope. Of special note is the rapid growing Japanese Magnolia obovata, whose large creamy-white flowers are conspicuous in June not only on account of their size but also because of their heavy perfume which, on a still evening, is noticeable many yards away.

Northwards from the Copse is the most magnificent herbaceous border. The planting has been carried out with the aim of a succession of flowering, so that when one end has finished flowering the other is still in full bloom, making the border a constant attraction.

Near the western end of the herbaceous border is the Monterey cypress, one of the best specimens in Britain of this species native only to California. Continuing round to the West Gate entrance, outstanding among the trees are the maples and yews.

The Herbaceous Border and Winter Garden
Sheltered beneath a massive beech hedge, the spectacular 165m long Herbaceous Border provides a riot of summer colour. By contrast the nearby Winter Garden is planted with shrubs, bulbs and other perennials that are a highlight at the opposite end of the year. In the sunken area beyond, a range of plants, many of mediterranean origin, provide silver foliage displays throughout the year.

The Demonstration Garden
The informative role of the Royal Botanic Garden is served by the Exhibition Hall and the Demonstration Garden, as 'classrooms for the public'.

The display of annual plants shows the gardener what he can grow at home. The layout is changed each year, but it may include pansies, marigolds, wallflowers and dahlias. Hedges, too, are exhibited so that the intending gardener can select with a better idea of what he or she may expect.

Species of the *Brassica* genus, such as cabbage, cauliflower and kale, are grouped to show their various relationships to one another.

Plantings include culinary and medicinal herbs, grasses including the South American pampas grass, while others illustrate aspects of plant biology.

The Cryptogamic Garden
Cryptogams is a collective name for the so-called lower plants, several unrelated groups of organisms, which include ferns and their allies, mosses, liverworts and algae as well as fungi and lichens. These groups are all vital components of our natural vegetation; indeed in some habitats such as damp woodlands and upper mountain slopes they provide the dominant ground cover. The term cryptogam literally means 'hidden sex', in contrast to the more flamboyant flowers or cones of higher plants (*Phanerogams*) with their obvious reproductive structures. The Royal Botanic Garden is an important world centre for scientific research on cryptogams and the only institute in Britain with an expert specializing in each of the major groups. Knowledge of these plants is of vital importance in biodiversity surveys, environmental monitoring and effective habitat conservation.

The Cryptogamic Garden was established during 1991 to provide a window on the world of lower plants. In the setting of regenerating woodland, affording a wide variety of microhabitats, selected species of ferns, horsetails and other woodland flora have been planted out. Progressively, as the canopy develops, mosses, liverworts, lichens and algae will colonize appropriate surfaces. Special emphasis has been placed on the fungi, which have a particularly close relationship with most higher plants. Scottish native trees, including birch, hazel and pine were transplanted with associated soil to preserve this symbiosis. Decay fungi were also imported on tree stumps, logs and other forest debris.

This is a dynamic garden which will change dramatically over the years as it matures and new colonists arrive.

The Ecological Garden
This is being developed to display elements of the native Scottish flora in zones reflecting a range of major habitats.

The habitats to be represented range from oak-birch woodland on neutral soil through ash-rowan copse to an acid grassland to the west. In the centre there will be an oak-birch association on acidic soil with adjacent mire and boggy willow carr. At the east end of the garden Scots pine wood is flanked by juniper scrub and ling-heather moor. Across the main track a meadow and area of calcareous grassland will be established.

In conjunction with the Scottish Rare Plant Trail, the Ecological Garden will afford visitors an introduction to the finest elements of Scotland's native flora. Within a few acres at Inverleith, everyone can learn about this vital component of our natural heritage.

Zoological Park

A marvellous menagerie where education and research are paramount

The deceptively narrow entrance to Edinburgh Zoo gives way to the 80 acres (30 ha) which contain some of the world's rarest and most beautiful animals in an area of natural beauty which, at its north-western tip, fades into the woodland of Corstorphine Hill.

Edinburgh Zoo is in a constant state of development with its international co-operative breeding programmes, the introduction of new species from other zoos and the continuous schedule of new buildings and enclosures on the areas acquired for development. With such activity, it is difficult for the zoo itself to keep pace with the location of each species. The map contained in their otherwise most informative booklet is therefore sometimes out of date. The map that appears on the opposite page, however, records the species to be seen in the zoo in the spring of 1998.

With so much to see in such sympathetic surroundings, it is wise to allow at least half a day, if not more, for a tour of the zoo. As you enter through the main gates, taking the path to the right, you will see the Californian sea lions on your left. There are two females and one male, one bull being on loan to London Zoo for breeding purposes. The pool was cut from natural rock in 1914 and sea lions have always been happy in it. Sea lions can move very fast in water, achieving nearly 20 miles per hour (32 km/h) by planing across the surface.

Feeding times, when the sea lions dive and leap for fish, are popular with visitors.

Flightless birds and flamingos are on the right, followed by the Brunton aviaries and the pheasants. Edinburgh Zoo has several pairs of Chilean flamingos, all of which have bred successfully. These graceful birds with rosy-pink plumage are particularly interesting to watch when they are performing courtship displays before mating: the elegant rose-peach tail feathers are raised in a fan as the male bird struts and circles. Pheasants have been hunted so extensively in the wild that the group now numbers several of the world's most endangered species. These rare and beautiful birds are high on Edinburgh Zoo's list for its commitment to breeding.

North of the aviaries is the Orchard Paddock, with its small pond and overhanging apple trees, home to a lively group of ring-tailed lemurs.

Further up the hill, to the right, you will come upon the Reptile House. Of the tortoises, turtles, snakes, lizards, crocodiles and frogs, toads, newts and salamanders in the Reptile House, the two dwarf broad-fronted crocodiles should not be missed. Great efforts have been made to establish breeding colonies. Edinburgh Zoo is the first in Europe to breed the blue poison-arrow frog which originates from southern Surinam and is now very rare. Strawberry-pink and yellow frogs can also be seen.

In the summer, some of the collection is moved outside to the Reptile Rock, where the animals can be seen in a more natural environment.

The Parrot Garden houses several species of parrot, the Australian cockatoo and the South American macaw. There are over 300 species in the family of birds known as the parrots. The demands of the pet trade and deforestation have combined to endanger many of the species. The Zoo is specializing in parrots and is liaising with other zoos to establish viable breeding pairs. Chicks of the Mexican green thick-billed parrots, for example, have been successfully reared and this is a species which could well be reintroduced to the wild if the success continues.

Look out for the free-ranging cotton-top tamarins—squirrel-sized primates who can emerge from their shelter through a series of tubes. Don't expect to pat them though, they are only sociable with each other.

You will easily find the Chimpanzee House by following the noise. A constant display of screaming, clapping, gesticulating and hurtling down the slope to their enclosure to land, full face, against the 1 1/4-inch thick (32mm) armoured glass is all part of a chimpanzee's fun. In fact, such displays indicate a continual competitiveness found in any group of chimpanzees, since their society is founded upon a dominance hierarchy.

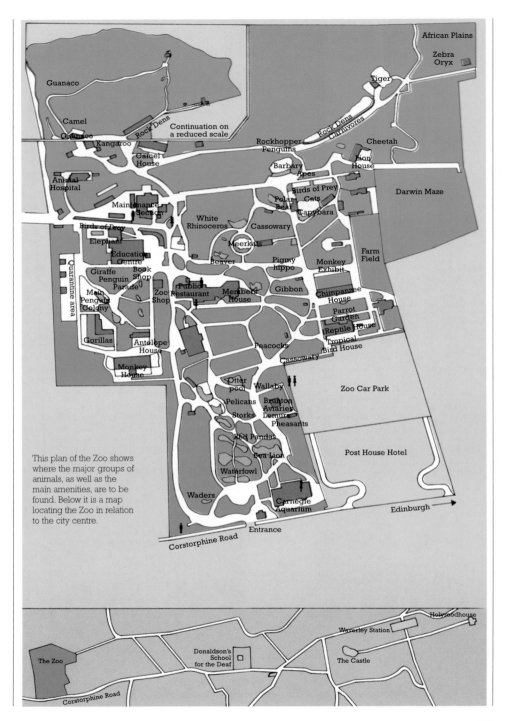

This plan of the Zoo shows where the major groups of animals, as well as the main amenities, are to be found. Below it is a map locating the Zoo in relation to the city centre.

African Plains

Zebra
Oryx

Guanaco

Tiger

Camel
Guanaco

Rock Dens

Continuation on
a reduced scale

Rockhopper
Penguins

Rock Dens
Carnivores

Cheetah

Kangaroo

Camel
House

Barbary
Apes

Lion
House

Animal
Hospital

Birds of Prey

Darwin Maze

Maintenance
Section

Polar
Bear

Cats

Capybara

Birds of Prey

White
Rhinoceros

Cassowary

Elephant

Education
Centre

Meerkats

Farm
Field

Giraffe
Penguin
Parade

Book
Shop

Beaver

Pigmy
hippo

Monkey
Exhibit

Main
Penguin
Colony

Zoo
Shop

Public
Restaurant

Members
House

Gibbon

Chimpanzee
House

Parrot
Garden

Reptile House

Gorillas

Antelope
House

Peacocks

Tropical
Bird House

Monkey
House

Cassowary

Otter
pool

Wallaby

Zoo Car Park

Pelicans

Storks

Brunton
Aviaries
Lemurs

Pheasants

Red Pandas

Post House Hotel

Sea Lion

Waterfowl

Waders

Carnegie
Aquarium

Edinburgh

Corstorphine Road

Entrance

Holyroodhouse

Waverley Station

The Zoo

Donaldson's
School
for the Deaf

The Castle

Corstorphine Road

181

After the chimps you will come to the Darwin Maze which was opened by the Princess Royal in 1995. It is made in a tortoise shape from 650 metres of yew hedges. You go in at the head and find your way to the body. The shape is significant because it was while studying tortoises in the Galapagos islands that Charles Darwin first began to formulate his ideas about evolution. Children will enjoy working out how to bypass fountains of water which react to different triggers, although it has to be said that some of them like getting wet! A picnic terrace overlooks the maze.

West of the Darwin Maze is the Zoo's only polar bear, Mercedes. The story of how she came to be in the Zoo is the stuff of fairytales. In the town of Churchill, in Manitoba, northern Canada, polar bears come down during the harsh winters to forage in rubbish tips and gardens. The first winter they come they are sedated and numbered (Mercedes is numbered 39). If, however, they come back a third time they are shot. Mercedes was fortunate. The

The ring-tailed lemurs are a lively bunch.

owners of the garden in which she looked for food had grown fond of her. They had a relative who was a member of Edinburgh Zoo and he helped fund her long journey over here. Unlike most other bears, the polar bear is mainly carnivorous, favouring seals. In its native habitat around the fringes of the Arctic icecaps its off-white colouring affords effective camouflage so that it may sneak up on its unsuspecting prey.

After the polar bear you can see the bush dogs, native to the tropical forests of Central and South America. Bush dogs socialize in packs which, it is thought, are made up of extended families. They communicate by bird-like calls and screeches.

Edinburgh Zoo is noted for its success in breeding Snowy owls, to be seen with other owls in the Birds of Prey enclosures. In the wild, the Snowy owl is a winter visitor to northern Scotland and further north still. Its feathers are basically white with brownish-black markings.

(**left**) A giraffe looks thoughtful and (**right**) a tiger sits in the sun.

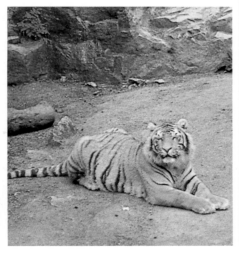

In its natural environment of snow-covered areas, it is camouflaged most effectively from a potential predator: if it were completely white, it would be far more noticeable.

The Birds of Prey enclosure leads you to the Barbary Rock which is a most impressive home for the Barbary macaques (of the monkey family). Steep layers have been hewn into the rock, which towers many feet above the path. Continuing eastwards, you will come upon the African lion, who is located in an enclosure interspersed with crags of old Midlothian farmhouse stone. It is intended to build a larger enclosure for completion in 1999.

On to the cheetah, which in the wild would be able to achieve speeds of 70 miles per hour (113 km/h) in short bursts. The cheetah's large enclosure slopes upwards into a mass of long grass and trees where the animal bounds about. On the right as you go uphill are the endangered addax from the southern Sahara. They have been bred successfully here and their names may sound familiar—they are all called after characters from *Neighbours*!

Up ahead is the area called African Plains, where the zebra can be seen. Many theories have been advanced to explain the zebra's brilliant black and white stripes: one theory suggests that the stripes distort the form of the animal from a distance so that at dusk, when the predators in the wild are hunting, they merge together to form a uniform grey. The theory seems convincing when you see the zebras in Edinburgh's zoo silhouetted on the horizon.

The uphill path past the cheetah's enclosure takes you to the tiger enclosure (there are only 150 Siberian tigers left in the wild) and the Rock Dens, which house several species of jaguar, leopard, and lynx. In the 1970s Edinburgh Zoo established a colony of rockhopper penguins, now accommodated in a special enclosure with a steep rocky backdrop, as these are cliff nesters. Again, there have been excellent breeding results with some birds being sent to establish colonies in other zoos.

Further north, in large paddocks—if you have the energy to climb!—are Pere David's deer, a species of Chinese deer which is now extinct in the wild, and the guanacos. Originating from the windswept slopes of the Andes, these wild llamas can be seen out in all weathers.

A sense of freedom is not entirely lost when you leave the fields and the kangaroo enclosures as you wind your way down to the camels. Their enclosure is surrounded by a dyke which is concealed by a slight rise in the ground. The Arabian camel or dromedary has one hump and is found only in a domesticated state. Camels can tolerate extreme heat and cold and can survive days without water. Look out for the muntjack, or barking deer, in Whitson Wood. Muntjack are not endangered— some have escaped from captivity and live wild in southern England. One of the most extraordinary-looking species in the Zoo comes next —the babirusa, a pig from Indonesia. The male has two— apparently functionless—sets of upturned tusks.

The white rhinoceroses, towards the centre of the Zoo, are fascinating to watch as they indulge in mock battles. Their agility belies their great weight, as does their name their colour. It is thought that 'white' came from the Afrikaans *wijd* meaning wide.

Next to the white rhino is the Beaver Pool, which is another excellent example of how a zoo can exhibit animals in a happy and natural environment. Beavers are aquatic mammals which use their paddle-shaped tail as a rudder. It is also beaten on the ground or on the water to indicate alarm, and is used to flatten mud when they are building dams.

One of the most popular species in the Zoo is the meerkat, a member of the mongoose family. Meerkats come from southern Africa. They are very social animals and very well organised among themselves, sharing tasks such as babysitting. They stand on their hind legs and squeak to each other if they see a bird of prey.

The pygmy hippopotamuses now come into sight. These are much rarer than the better-known common hippo and little is known of their habits in the wild. Their range is restricted to one or two rainforest areas of west Africa. That habitat has been recreated as far as possible here. There has been some success in breeding them in the Zoo—including the hand-rearing of baby Cleo in 1993 when her mother's milk dried up.

Moving towards the western zone of the Zoo you will find the giraffe, tapir, apes, monkeys, and, most important of all, penguins.

Edinburgh Zoo 's well known for its splendid collection of penguins, which is the largest in Europe. In 1992 the spectacular Penguin Exhibit was opened—the world's largest penguin enclosure, with three varieties of penguin.

The king penguins number approximately 35-40 birds. (The first king penguin ever to be born in captivity hatched in Edinburgh Zoo in 1919). There are around 80 gentoo penguins and—the latest addition— about 29 macaroni penguins.

The enclosure affords enough land space for all three species to have separate breeding colonies and there is a 3-metre deep pool where, for the first time, visitors can appreciate the amazing grace of the penguins as they 'fly' underwater behind huge glass viewing panels.

Penguins are found mainly on the islands around the Antarctic and occasionally in tropical waters—and so it is astonishing that they have bred so successfully in Edinburgh. Penguins cannot fly, but they more than compensate for this by using their wings as paddles so that they speed through the water at up to 25 miles per hour (40 km/h). They are able to emerge, bullet-like, from the sea and land on their feet on ledges or ice-floes as much as 6 feet (1.8m) above the water.

King penguins have a slate-grey back and white underside, with brilliant orange patches on the sides of the head, throat and upper part of the breast. Young birds are covered in a thick brown down. The king penguin does not make a nest but holds a single egg on its feet with a fold of its skin and the feathers of its abdomen. Both males and females help to incubate the egg, which takes about 8 weeks.

The gentoo, basically black and white, has distinctive white markings on the crown and sides of the head which resemble earphones. Gentoos lay two eggs, which in the wild would be protected in a nest of pebbles and twigs and other pieces of vegetation. In the Zoo, they are presented with nesting rings filled with pebbles on 14 February each year. Gentoo courtship involves the exchange of pebble 'gifts', as well as stealing pebble-nesting material from neighbours. By the end of March, 80 to 90 eggs will have appeared and by the end of April they will have hatched. The macaroni penguins arrived as eggs from South

King penguins in conference.

Georgia and were successfully incubated and hand-reared in the Zoo. They get their name from the time they were identified at the turn of the 20th century when their yellow head feathers, neatly parted in the middle, reminded people of the favoured hairstyle of Italian-American men who were known as 'macaronis'.

When the young penguins are about 6 to 8 weeks old they are removed to a crèche for a few months. When they are ready, they are allowed to rejoin the flock.

At 14.00 every summer afternoon just before feeding time, the penguins embark on a voluntary parade around the paths of the central area of the zoo. The spectacle of the penguin parade began in the late 1940s, quite accidentally, when a keeper left the enclosure gate open. The inquisitive penguins—and they are of a generally inquiring disposition—followed by an equally curious keeper, walked down the drive and along the pavement of the main road until the keeper judged it wise to turn them.

The penguins are fed at 14.30, after the parade.

The Monkey House, the largest of the animal buildings in the Zoo, houses ten different species of monkey. The cages are fronted with armoured glass rather than bars, as the zoo has discovered this prevents the animals from begging and showing off and it prevents the public from disrupting a carefully controlled diet by indiscriminate feeding. The Zoo currently operates a policy of 'enrichment' which is aimed at providing an environment which stimulates an animal's natural behaviour. This is seen to most dramatic effect in the Monkey House. Where previously a sterilized environment was thought to be best and the monkeys were fed from troughs, now they have branches to swing on, bark on the floor, and their food is scattered, encouraging them to forage. The monkeys have responded by being healthier and happier.

The largest primates, the gentle vegetarian gorillas, are by the Monkey House, one silver-backed male and two females. In with them are Diana monkeys whose behaviour fascinates and stimulates the gorillas, and since they eat different fruits there are no arguments at mealtimes.

The rest of the southern zone is devoted to red lechwe antelopes, pelicans, gannets (the emblem of the Royal Zoological Society of Scotland) and storks, which are all fed after the sea-lions; the shy and wary otter, an aquatic mammal that lives on fish; the raccoon, noted for its habit in captivity of washing all its food; the South American Maguari stork; and a splendid series of shrub-covered terraces with three large pools and waterfalls for the collection of ducks from all over the world, swans, and wild birds such as the waterhen. The lower duck pond has been netted over to protect it from predators. Have a look for the rare Meller's duck from Madagascar.

Flamingos and storks lend their own particular grace to the Zoo. You have to look up in the trees to see the red panda. Edinburgh Zoo has the world's largest penguin enclosure, with three groups of penguins.

Red pandas can be seen in the trees nearby. They are just as endangered as their giant cousins and almost as reluctant to breed in captivity.

The Zoological Society of Scotland was founded in 1909 as a non-profit making organization devoted to the study and conservation of wildlife. It became increasingly disenchanted with its inheritance of undersized, old-fashioned cages, which are often the trademark of an urban zoo.

The Zoo acquired royal patronage in 1948 and today the dedication and energy demanded by a far-seeing programme of acquisition of land, new buildings and enclosures is clearly demonstrated.

New species are usually acquired from other zoos on the basis of exchange—the introduction of animals from the wild is something of the past. Breed-loan schemes are in operation with zoos all over the world, so that Edinburgh, for example, may send out a male sea-lion to another zoo that has only females and receive in return one of the species it needs to continue it own breeding programmes. These coordinated schemes are based on mutual co-operation—how,

in any case, would it be possible to assess the financial worth of a male sea-lion versus a female gentoo?

Edinburgh Zoo now has red pandas, a smaller and more interesting relative of the giant panda. More than one zoologist has been heard to comment on the intrinsic dullness of the giant panda, despite its great popularity with the public and continual exposure by the media.

The Zoo's staff of 140 is supplemented by about 100 volunteers. Much of the building work has been carried out as a result of the government's Training for Work scheme. The Zoo, in this way, has been able to save thousands of pounds on labour. The Darwin Maze, for example, was built by trainees and Telford College students and funded by Lothian and Edinburgh Enterprise Ltd. (LEEL).

The Zoo is financed by admission fees, membership subscriptions and by the Animal Sponsorship Scheme. The need to adopt zoo animals resulted from the conditions of war prevailing in 1940, when food was scarce. Anyone can now adopt an animal for as little as £20 per year and for £60 a

year can have their name engraved on a plaque.

The Zoo's philosophy has always centred on the need to educate as well as to entertain. The Education Centre, which is visited by up to 50,000 schoolchildren a year, runs properly structured programmes of education as well as producing the necessary topic sheets and literature. All topics relate to the 5-14 curriculum.

About 60 students a year use the Zoo as a place to do primary research into animal behaviour. This research by observation has produced suggestions which have been implemented to help animals both in captivity and in the wild.

A large shop, Arkadia, is located in the entrance complex and you don't have to pay to go into it. There is a wide variety of goods from toys at pocket-money prices to exclusive jewellery and pottery. All profits from it go back into the Zoo.

A visit to the Zoo is something that should not be missed when you are in Edinburgh. The tranquillity and beauty of this huge park is rivalled only by its variety of animal life.

The polar bear always draws the crowds as it clambers from the water and reclines on rocky islands.

(**opposite**) The Californian sealion.

Edinburgh's Festivals

In summer and winter the festival city plays host to the world

For three weeks every year Edinburgh is besieged by the top talent of the world—yet the identity of the city remains impregnable. Seen in full Festival regalia, this Athens of the north might well have been custom built for just such an explosion of a diverse mixture of culture—for even as the Old Town lives in harmony with the New, so do the activities of the Festival merge the artistry of great names with new, young, experimental talents. Visitors of all nationalities give the city a boost of adrenalin which can be felt in the spring of each step along Princes Street, suddenly frivolous with bunting and hanging baskets of flowers. Old hands feel superior watching the awe of newcomers as yet unaccustomed to the one o'clock gun.

It was not always thus. The first year of the Festival—1947—was a grey year. Britain was still in the grip of austerity. Rationing did not end until 1952. Dior's New Look was in fashion with its nipped waistline and flowing skirts succeeding years of utility clothing and coupons. Platform shoes clumped precariously over the cobbled streets of the city and trams still clanged their cheerful way along Princes Street.

Edinburgh was not renowned for her contributions to culture at this time, although there was talent in plenty to be found in the Rose Street pubs, with writers, painters and poets vying to utter the wittiest, pithiest *bon mot* of the evening.

From a theatrical point of view, there was little beyond the occasional visiting pre-London show, pantomime at Christmas and the semi-professional resident Gateway Company Theatre. Yet it was out of this post-war malaise that Rudolf Bing, then with the Glyndebourne Festival Opera, had the courage to persist in his vision of a British festival comparable in stature to those of Salzburg and Bayreuth.

Rudolf Bing became the Festival's first director. His worldwide connections proved invaluable in contracting Bruno Walter, reunited with his Vienna Philharmonic, Sir John Barbirolli and the Hallé, Arthur Schnabel, Pierre Fournier, Joseph Szigeti, William Primrose and the Louis Jouvet Company. A spirit of alliances recreated was behind the rebirth of artistic vitality in Europe urged to life by the uphill task of creating the very first Edinburgh Festival. It was with this concept in mind that the honour of playing the opening concert was given to the Orchestre des Concerts Colonne, Paris.

The sun actually shone—for three weeks. Visitors complained of the heat. The critics were impressed. The new Festival was a success. Later, of course, there were niggles about the predominance of music at the expense of drama. Criticism was made about the proportionately small Scottish contribution, despite the participation of the

prominent Glasgow-born violist William Primrose, the Scottish Orchestra and the Scottish Singers. Over the following years the situation was to be rectified, aided by a mercuric rise in the standards of Scottish performers. This gave rise to the eventual formation of a Scottish Opera and Ballet Company, a Scottish National Orchestra, Chamber Orchestra and the Scottish Baroque Ensemble—all developed to an internationally accepted level.

It is hard to remember today that in the late 1940s Scottish television was in its infancy, there was no stereo, and the Scots were isolated from first-hand knowledge of the standards of cultural activity in other countries until the Festival brought it all to their doorstep. It was particularly thrilling in those early years to listen to orchestras from Europe or the United States and to their interpretation of the works of great composers.

The Usher Hall, in Lothian Road, is Edinburgh's main concert hall. Within its Edwardian elegance, audiences have been privileged to hear the best soloists in the world, to listen to leading orchestras performing under the contrasting influences of various distinguished conductors.

Live theatre
The Mound snakes southwards up that great castle-bearing glacial rock, both floodlit each festive night to dominate Princes Street. It is a stiff climb

to reach the Gothic-style dignity of the Assembly Hall of the Kirk of Scotland. It seems as though the Mound has had to bend to go respectfully round it, yet this was to become the unlikely home for the Scots breakthrough into their own festival with a bawdy play in 'the auld tongue' which satirized and challenged the very authority of the Church. Much to the astonishment of all, the Church authorities gave consent to Tyrone Guthrie's production of *The Thrie Estaites*, although they mildly suggested that nails should not be knocked into the Moderator's throne. No restriction was made against singing or dancing or even against the provision of a bar.

In 1948 the play had its first performance since the original seven-hour version of 1540. Robert Kemp adapted it to a more acceptable length and under Guthrie's magic touch it became a recurring feature, giving Scottish actors their vehicle in many future Festivals. Few who saw the production will forget the exquisite gyra-

A taste of the variety and personalities the main Festival has offered through the years: the Scottish National Opera's *Hermiston*; Carlo Maria Giulini and Leonard Bernstein conducting; Dietrich in cabaret and Max Wall as Buster Keaton.

tions of the late Duncan Macrae as Flatterie, the droning of James Gibson's Deceipt, the resonant power of Tom Fleming and the vigour and pageantry of this ancient satire. The supporting music was by a Scottish composer, Cedric Thorpe Davie, who later set the music

Mark Morris Dance Group in one of their sensational appearances at the Edinburgh Festival.

for another Scottish triumph, *The Jolly Beggars*.

During the three years of Rudolf Bing's directorship, he commissioned *The Cocktail Party* by T. S. Eliot. He brought to Edinburgh Trevor Howard, Bernard Miles and Patricia Burke in *The Taming of the Shrew*; Alec Guinness in a production by Ralph Richardson of *Richard II*; Margot Fonteyn, Beryl Grey and Frederick Ashton with the Royal Ballet, then known as Sadlers Wells; Leslie Caron and Jean Babilée with Les Ballets des Champs Elysées. Naturally the Glyndebourne Opera was well in evidence. Mozart's *Le Nozze di Figaro* and Verdi's *Macbeth* were presented, The late, incomparable Kathleen Ferrier sang with the Vienna Philarmonic one year and with the Hallé another. Her *Das Lied von der Erde* still haunts the Usher Hall and those fortunate enough to have been there.

Even doubting Sir Thomas Beecham was prevailed upon to conduct with his Royal Philharmonic Orchestra in 1949, Bing's final year as director.

Over the years the Festival has benefitted enormously from the widely varying influences imposed upon it by its six very different directors. Each built upon the work of his predecessors. Each had something new and individual to contribute.

Ian Hunter became the second director in 1950 for a period of seven years. He will be remembered particularly for his promotion of exhibitions—a new feature in the Festival programme. He initiated exhibitions which were acclaimed throughout the art world and which became an important aspect.

Major exhibitions are held in Edinburgh's galleries during the period of the Festival. These are organised by the galleries themselves rather than by the official administration.

Military Tattoo

A stroke of genius, in 1950, was to add the Tattoo to the ever-widening field of Festival activities. Although independent of the main administration, the Tattoo has become an inseparable part of the festivities. It starts a week earlier than the main Festival and finishes a week earlier. The performance —a highly polished, well-rehearsed military event— takes place in that time before dusk on the esplanade of Edinburgh Castle which provides a dramatic backdrop to historic tableaux, gymnastics, highland dancing, pageantry, mock battles and other popular entertainment devised by the military. It has all the attractions of the Royal Tournament, from horses to the occasional elephant. Each year

TAG Theatre Company perform *A Scots Quair.*

visiting military groups display colourful regimental costume and custom, some appearing to have come straight out of Ruritania. Perhaps most popular of all is the stirring sight and sound of the massed pipe bands.

As dusk falls, the floodlights dim and a spotlight picks out a solitary piper on the battlements. In the sudden silence of the summer evening, he pipes a farewell lament.

Music

In that same year of 1950, the Castle was the setting for an after dark, open-air performance of Handel's *Music for the Royal Fireworks*, complete with firework display and live cannon obligato from the Castle battery. The conductor was Beecham himself, a figure of rare distinction in tails and a steel helmet provided by the Quartermaster's Stores as a protection against sparks.

The current director, Brian McMaster, a former director of Wesh National Opera, has expanded the music programme and raised its standards to new heights. The critics have been loud in their praise and ticket sales have gone up.

The administration

In 1952, the Festival administrators faced up for the first time to the inherent problems of inviting an overseas opera company to perform at the King's Theatre. The exterior of the theatre, built in 1906, is undistinguished but the plush interior is a gem of gilt baroque —like an opera house in miniature. Its smallness was the main problem for the first visitors, the Hamburg Opera Company, which was accustomed to its own vast stage, For one thing, the scenery would not fit. The problem persists, but years of experience have taught ways and means of making the best of it. Another venue for drama,

opera, music, variey and dance was added in 1994 following a £24m refurbishment of the old Empire Theatre—now called the Festival Theatre—seating 1,900 and one of the best-equipped lyric theatres in the country.

Robert Ponsonby took over from Ian Hunter in 1956. It was he who encouraged and developed the late night satirical aspect of the Festival which spread on to TV screens with such success. Anna Russell was allowed to make a little fun of the hallowed Festival itself. Then, in 1959, Michael Flanders and Donald Swan appeared in *At the Drop of a Hat. Beyond the Fringe* hit the boards in 1960.

Ponsonby's interest in ballet was clearly marked by twelve new works especially commissioned for 1958. Until then the major balletic contribution had come principally from the Sadler's Wells Company, which had presented a varied classical and modern programme ranging from *Swan Lake* to early works by the talented young choreographers John Cranko and Scotland's Kenneth MacMillan. There had, of course, been other visiting companies—Ram Gopal with his Indian ballet, Les Ballets de Champs Elysées, the Yugoslav Ballet and the American Ballet Theater.

duction of Maria Callas to Edinburgh. She took the Festival by storm as Amina in *La Sonnambula* with the La Scala Company from Milan.

Lord Harewood's reign— 1961 to 1965—was both stimulating and controversial. He introduced the concept of featuring a particular composer each year, and Edinburgh was treated to twenty-

Edinburgh Festival Chorus and the basis of the Scottish Opera company.

The first appearance of Scottish Opera at a Festival came in 1967 with productions of *The Rake's Progress* and *The Soldier's Tale*. By this time, Peter Diamand had been appointed as director and was continuing the policy of featuring composers each year. It was

The colourful costumes of singers in *Don Giovanni* at the King's Theatre and a group from the Scottish National Orchestra playing in the Library of the Signet.

In 1959 and 1960 there were performances at the Royal Lyceum by the National Ballet of Finland, Les Ballets Babilée, the Little Ballet Troupe from Bombay, the Ballets Européens de Nervi, Susana y José from Madrid, the Royal Ballet and the new excitement of Jerome Robbins with his Ballet USA.

Robert Burns had his 200th anniversary at that time, an event which inspired Iain Hamilton to create his *Sinfonia for Two Orchestras*. There were intensive Burns readings and the premiere of *The Jolly Beggars* to boost Scottish morale.

The Ponsonby period was also distinguished by his intro-

four performances by Schoenberg in the first Harewood Festival. Subsequent years were saturated with Boulez, Tippett and Janácek. Some critics felt, however, that such a policy was departing somewhat from the original concept as expressed by Lord Provost Sir John Falconer in the inaugural year: '. . . the programme should be for the delight of the average listener'. But Shostakovitch played by Russian performers was exciting and vindicating. For other tastes there were thrilling appearances by Rex Harrison, Martha Graham and Marlene Dietrich; in the theatre there were new plays by Dylan Thomas, Lawrence Durrell and Nigel Dennis.

It was during this phase of the Festival's growth that conductor Alexander Gibson formed the Scottish Opera Chorus, later to become the

Schubert and Britten year in 1968, during which the new national opera company presented *Peter Grimes*. At that time a performance of Britten's *War Requiem* underlined the emotional intensity aroused by the Soviet-led invasion of Czechoslovakia which had reached its climax during the Festival. Drama was transferred to the streets in the form of pickets and demonstrations outside the Usher Hall where the State Orchestra of the USSR was playing.

During the 13 years of Peter Diamand's control the Festival had its 21st birthday. In its maturity the proportion of younger artists invited to take part was increased. The new policy demonstrated that the Festival was now sufficiently established to become a patron—perhaps too it was aimed at reducing the gap between the official events and the essentially young Fringe movement which had been developing alongside.

Among the highlights of this prolonged administration was an adaptation of Ariosto's *Orlando Furioso* by the Teatro Libero Rome, which took place in 1970 at the Haymarket Ice Rink and used the open-stage technique to bring the audience into the performance as *Technicolour Dreamcoat*, with music by Andrew Lloyd-Webber, which was playing at the Haymarket Ice Rink along with, and in striking contrast to, the Japanese Hosho Noh Theatre. These few examples reflect the care and skill with which an interesting mix of content was planned for each year's programme in the face of ever-increasing costs.

Scotland and France produced in 1985 one of the most successful festivals.

Following Frank Dunlop came Brian McMaster in 1992 and he has been credited with introducing stability to the administration and growth to the Festival programme. With the opening in 1994 of the Festival Theatre Brian McMaster says '. . . we were able

Performing for the Fringe Festival in a former municipal poorhouse overlooking Greyfriars churchyard, a company of Polish actors provoke their audience.

Guthrie had done with *The Thrie Estaites*. At the Assembly Hall the Prospect Company enlivened Shakespeare's *Much Ado About Nothing* with John Neville playing Benedict. The Royal Lyceum Company—Edinburgh's new Civic Theatre—presented *The Changeling* by Thomas Middleton, and thus established itself as a company able to hold its own.

The actors' co-operative

In 1972 came the birth of the Actors' Company, a co-operative venture in which there were no stars and '. . . all decisions were made through mutual discussion'. The cast included Moira Redmond, Ian McKellen and Frank Middlemas. The new company contributed lunch-time and evening performances and was highly praised. Londoners subsequently became familiar with *Joseph and the Amazing*

John Drummond took over in 1978 for the 1979 Festival. Formerly head of the BBC Television Music and Arts Department, he may be remembered as the director who preserved the Edinburgh International Festival through the years of world recession. At one time visiting companies had subsidised part of the cost of coming to perform, but they can no longer afford to do so. In 1947 the total cost of the Festival was just under £130,000; in 1996 it was £5.7m. But by 1996 public subsidy had decreased to just 35% of the running costs with £1.4m generated through sponsorship and donations. Ticket sales reached a record £2.15m.

In 1983 Frank Dunlop was appointed director, the first to come from the world of theatre, and under his leadership the Festival's scope was widened considerably. The celebration of the Auld Alliance between

to plan the Festival we always wanted—limited only by· our imagination.' The emphasis is on large-scale productions in a city that has a venue base second to none. Mark Morris and his dancers made their debut in Edinburgh six years before they appeared on a London stage.

The 50th anniversary of the Festival was in 1996 and the 50th birthday was celebrated in 1997 by staging new productions or performances of a few of the great works which have been particularly associated with the Festival—such as Verdi's opera *Macbeth* and T. S. Eliot's *The Cocktail Party*.

Practical workshops on music and dance and a series of lunchtime talks are now a popular addition to the Festival programme. The Fireworks Concert in Princes Street Gardens on the last Thursday of the Festival with its joyful noise and colour is perhaps symbolic of the whole three weeks of events.

It is planned to open an all-year-round Festival Centre in 1999. The Highland Tolbooth at the Castle end of the Royal Mile is being converted for this purpose. It will be an exhibition and information point for all of Edinburgh's festivals and there will be a cafe, bookshop and Festival Club.

The Film Festival

The Edinburgh International Film Festival has been an event in the capital since the Festival as a whole started in 1947.

At first it was confined to one week of documentary films, but it has grown in size and prestige to compare with the festivals at Cannes and Berlin.

The Film Festival, based at Filmhouse, 88 Lothian Road, uses all of Edinburgh'a cinemas, including the new ABC multiplex at Wester Hailes, and the GFT in Glasgow. The Festival takes place over the first two weeks of the main Festival. In 1996, when the Festival was opened by its patron Sean Connery, over 350 films were screened in front of 40,000 cinema fans. More than 1,000 industry delegates attended from all over the world alongside 650 members of the international press corps.

An august amateur body, the Edinburgh Film Guild, established the first festival with the aim of showing 'unusual films not normally seen in the ordinary cinema' such as the documentaries pioneered by Scottish-born John Grierson. By the second year, feature films had been introduced as well and the programme extended to three weeks to cover over 100 entries from 25 countries.

Film directors were soon appearing personally to explain their work to the public. Flaherty, Grierson, Michael Balcon, Vittorio de Sica, Charles Frend, Samuel Fuller, John Huston, Douglas Sirk, Joseph Losey and Peter Ustinov are a few who have appeared over the years to help clarify new trends and techniques for filmgoers.

The Film Festival has a reputation for giving the first British screenings of some of the most celebrated films— like *ET* in 1982, and *Paris, Texas* in 1984. The film to provoke the strongest reaction in 1985 was *My Beautiful Launderette*.

Recent guests have included Steve Martin, Bernardo Bertolucci, Leslie Caron, Walter Murch, Diane Ladd, Peter Greenaway, Ken Loach, Terence Davies, Bryan Singer and Thelma Schoonmaker.

The Festival is organised into a series of distinct sections: Gala (world, European or British premières); Rosebud (world or international premières of innovative drama films); Scene by Scene (illustrated lectures by filmmakers); Retrospective (filmmakers and themed events); Documentary (newly-devised section devoted to non-fiction films); Mirrorball (music videos and music-related projects); and NBX (a market place of UK productions).

Coming just before Venice in the International film Festival diary, Edinburgh is not a competitive festival, but very much one for the public.

The Edinburgh Book Festival

A successful additional element in the world's largest arts festival took place biennially until 1997, and now happens annually. Happen is the word, for this is now considered to be the biggest public book event in the world. It is held in the privately owned Charlotte Square Gardens which lie at the heart of Edinburgh's magnificent Georgian city centre. A series of impressive summer marquees, arranged in a double courtyard and linked by covered walkways, house the Festival. Visitors can eat, drink and enjoy free cabaret entertainment, meet some of the 250 authors performing at the Festival, and browse through the thousands of books on sale and display in these splendid surroundings. The Festival introduces new writers and writers of international renown at events ranging from literary discussions to readings, practical demonstrations and workshops. Story-tellings, special workshops and activity sessions are all held as part of an extensive programme of events for children, many of which are free.

Authors who have appeared in recent years include David Bellamy, Louis de Bernières, Dorothy Dunnett, Margaret Forster, Nick Hornby, Shirley Hughes, Garrison Keillor, Doris Lessing, Edna O'Brien, Ben Okri, Terry Pratchett, Ralph Steadman, Joanna Trollope and Irvine Welsh.

Edinburgh International Jazz and Blues Festival

There is a healthy traditional jazz movement in Edinburgh all year round, and a jazz festival evolved out of it which happens in the week before the main Festival, A 'Mardi Gras' in the Grassmarket starts it off on the first Saturday, followed on Sunday by 'Jazz on a Summer's Day' in Princes Street Gardens. There follows a week of performances in venues throughout the city.

The Fringe

Can 500,000 people be wrong? In 1995 they flocked to the Fringe to see over 1,000 companies from 36 nations perform 1,523 shows in 189 venues over 23 days. The Oxford Dictionary defines 'fringe' as an ornamental bordering of threads left loose—a fairly fitting description of this colourful embellishment to the official Festival. It was born 'spontaneously' in the same year as its more staid parent, by virtue of eight theatre companies which simply set out to do their own thing. The university theatre companies of Oxford and Cambridge were early on the scene, using small halls in the Old Town. By the end of the fifties the bordering had grown to some 30 groups spread all over Edinburgh, a central box office had been organized, a programme published yearly and a Fringe Club opened.

Today's printed programme has grown to an 88-page brochure. Each listing gives some idea of what the event is about. With such a wealth of choice, the bewildered visitor often turns for guidance to the review pages of *The Scotsman* or *The Herald*—a review here can make or break a Fringe show and there are several newspaper-sponsored awards in various categories which can result in sell-out shows.

As well as premières, well-tried classics, revue and dance, the Fringe acts as the platform to some of the most unusual shows ever seen. *The Warp* at the 1979 Fringe made the Guinness Book of Records as the longest play in the world, taking over 24 hours to perform. And none of its tiny audience will forget *2001—A Space Odyssey* performed in the front of a Hillman Avenger (the audience sat on the back seat) while parked outside the Fringe Office.

Visitors are often surprised at the world-wide success of the Fringe; its story is an interesting one. It was in 1960 that Jonathan Miller, Alan Bennett, Peter Cook and Dudley Moore first captured international attention with their show *Beyond the Fringe*. They were allocated four performances in the official venue of the Royal

Lyceum theatre, put new life into British humour and went on to become part of an unorthodox establishment of their own making. They also set beyond challenge the Fringe's early reputation for the quality of its late night shows.

The Oxford Theatre Group's premiere of *Rosencrantz and Guildernstern Are Dead* brought Tom Stoppard the attention he deserved and the controversial Traverse Theatre Club, with stimulating interpretations of Shakespeare, was founded in Edinburgh in 1963 as a result of Fringe events.

Joan Littlewood, already well known for her theatre in east London, was quick to see the advantage of taking her Theatre Workshop to the Fringe. *Hinge*

and Bracket, now nationally famous, first charmed Edinburgh in 1974, and a 1977 production of *Writer's Cramp* by John Byrne transferred successfully to London's West End.

The Fringe Club in the university union building, Bristo Square, provides a social meeting place for actors and audience. There are two restaurants and four bars open til late. Club membership is a modest sum for the three-week season, and is also available per day.

The Fringe supports a variety of exhibitions, many of them free. The scope is wide and varied. An annual exhibition shows 200 of the best entries in the Fringe Poster Competition, open to all Scottish schoolchildren. The open-was the Russian clown Slava Polunin's *Snowshow*, which won two major awards.

Children are well catered for on the Fringe with a wide variety of shows described in a separate programme. There is plenty of free entertainment too, whether it is watching superb circus tricks by French youngsters against the backdrop of St Giles Cathedral, or being amused by the antics of performers in the Royal Mile, anxious to entice you to come to their shows.

Cited by the *Guinness Book of Records* as the largest arts festival in the world, the Fringe, and the atmosphere it generates in Edinburgh for three weeks, has to be experienced to be believed.

Edinburgh's Hogmanay

Edinburgh's newest festival is a five-day extravaganza finishing in the first day of the new year. It is now the biggest winter festival of its kind anywhere in the world.

Among the popular events are the Torchlight Procession and Fire Festival, Hogmanay Carnival, Street Theatre Spectacular, Hogmany Food Fair and New Year's Day Triathlon. There is also a wealth of concerts and ceilidhs, both indoor and out, free and ticketed. The Street Party in the city centre on the night of the 31st consists of a spectacular combination of fireworks displays, live music and street theatre performances.

Scottish International Childrens Festival

Billed as Britain's biggest performing arts event for young people, this festival takes place annually, in Inverleith Park, during the third week of May. Aimed at 3–14 year olds, there are over 30 theatre shows and activities to choose from.

ing of the Richard Demarco Gallery in 1966 was an important event in Fringe history. In defiance perhaps of the established giants on show at the official exhibitions, this new gallery concentrated on twentieth-century art. The Demarco Gallery had its origins in the Traverse Theatre, now located in Cambridge Street.

A recent development on the Fringe has been the increasing number of multi-venues, where visitors can find a number of theatres, bar and restaurant under one roof. This is undoubtedly due to the influence of Bill Burdett-Coutts and Assembly Theatre. In 1981 the main Festival vacated the magnificent Georgian Assembly Rooms on George Street,

taking its Festival Club elsewhere, and the building was converted for the three weeks into 5 theatres for 37 different shows, plus exhibitions. Together with the Gilded Balloon in the Cowgate and The Pleasance it now houses some of the most popular names in light entertainment as well as international companies during the Fringe. Perrier's Pick of the Fringe is Britain's most prestigious comedy award. Overseas dance companies had hugely successful shows in the nineties, including Australia's Legs on the Wall which launched the first of the award ceremonies in 1996 by abseiling down in front of the Festival Theatre. For many the highlight of the Fringe that year

Scottish Products

A wealth of goods results from the blend of tradition and innovation

Scotland, and especially its capital, offers a treasure trove to the shopper. Everyone will be familiar with the country's well-known products such as smoked salmon, oatcakes, haggis and kilts. But Edinburgh's shops and workshops offer an infinite variety of handmade and manufactured goods which should not be overlooked. Bagpipes and Edinburgh rock are just two of the products still made in Edinburgh itself, while there is a thriving coterie of craftsmen producing local wares.

Arts and crafts shops are generally located in areas around the Grassmarket and the High Street

A wealth of goods results from tradition and innovation

(the Royal Mile). Look in the 'Yellow Pages' telephone directory under 'Art and Craft' for a list of shops and producers. Appointments should be made to visit most workshops, which often work on a commission basis rather than holding a large amount of stock. For further information on Scottish Crafts contact Made in Scotland, Scottish Craft Centre, Beauly, Inverness-shire IV4 7EH, tel. 01463 782578.

Edinburgh's crafts include candles, ceramics, dolls, embroidery, furniture and woodwork, glass, pottery, jewellery and silversmithing, knitwear and crochet, leatherwork, musical instruments, textiles, weaving.

Products which are still made in Edinburgh or for which a significant number of retail outlets and stockists exist in Edinburgh include kilts and all the elements of highland dress, tweeds, woollens such as cashmere and Shetland, bagpipes, whisky, Drambuie, Glayva, smoked salmon, oatcakes, kippers, haggis, cheeses and Edinburgh rock. The articles on the following pages describe their origins and processes of production.

Whether you are looking for presents or to indulge yourself there are some wonderful shops in the High Street, of which the following is just a selection, selling Scottish crafts and produce.

Starting up at the Castle end, Scottish Crafts, 328 Lawnmarket, is an Aladdin's cave of Scottish dolls and other tartan favourites. Royal Mile Whiskies, 379 High Street, sells an appetizing array of food as well as a huge range of whiskies. At 207 High Street is the Celtic Art and Travel Centre which sells prints, books, tapes, pottery and jewellery and also has on display the kilt worn by Liam Neeson in the film *Rob Roy*. Further down at 64 High Street is knitwear designer Judith Glue's shop. There you will find her Orkney Knitware Collection as well as Highland Stoneware, handmade soaps, toys, stationery and much more. At 60 High Street is the Judith Glue Interiors and Gallery Shop. Tartan tableware can be bought at Anta, 32 High Street: this distinctive stoneware is made in Ross-shire. At 299 Canongate, Simply Scotland have a range of quality Scottish crafts and designer knitwear.

Antiques

A rare Bohemian liqueur glass from about 1720 and a traditional pewter 'tappit hen'.

The Scots have always been great travellers—sometimes for pleasure, more often through necessity—and they have always sent or brought back to Scotland a most remarkable variety of antiques from all over the world. From Chinese porcelain to Peruvian pottery and American Indian and Eskimo artefacts, antiques continually make their way onto the market. But apart from such international treasures the visitor to Edinburgh is more often looking for items which are distinctively Scottish.

When antique-hunting, the conventional bagpipe and tartan image, so often fostered by the Scots themselves, must be discarded. This aspect of Scotland's past was largely confined to the Gaelic, clan-based society of the northwest, although it is true that the highland drover, with his pistols and broadsword and dressed in short kilt, was once a familiar sight in the Old Town.

The famous highland pistols with their all-steel construction and ball-shaped triggers are now largely to be seen only in museums, but good eighteenth-century broadswords can still be found.

Another nationally distinctive antique is high-quality Scottish pewter. The famous 'tappit hen', a tankard with a distinctive nobbed lid, derivative in shape from the French *pichet* used in Normandy for cider, is perhaps the best known and most sought after of all Scottish pewter objects. The Scots pint was equal to three Imperial pints and the 'hen' was made both in this size and in intermediate sizes of 'chopin' (about two pints), 'mutchkin' (just under a pint) and 'half mutchkin'. It also appeared in Imperial capacity, with and without a crest, and even in a lidless form, so its permutations are many.

As a poor country Scotland had little church plate or silver but it had a great many churches, each with its pewter flagons and chalices and alms plates. All of these are distinctively Scottish in shape and many bear attractive makers' marks or 'touches'.

Despite comparative poverty the Scots loved fine silver and it was worked in most of the royal burghs. Early Scottish silver, even the humblest of articles, is distinguished by a respect for the metal, a severity of line which is very much reflective of the national character. While fine examples from the seventeenth and early eighteenth centuries fetch very high prices, most Scottish silver from the later period is priced about the same as its London equivalent. Edinburgh silver bears the attractive hallmarks of the city, the thistle denoting the sterling quality of the metal and the castle derived from the city's coat of arms. Most Scottish silver was

The present Edinburgh assayer's mark stamped on silver

made and assayed in Edinburgh and there is no better buy for the discerning visitor today than Edinburgh silver of the late Georgian period, even if only a modest set of spoons.

Edinburgh during the eighteenth century was a centre for the production of fine quality goods of all kinds. Apart from silver, glass and pottery, much fine furniture was made, marked by a particular robustness in design which set it apart from London-made furniture, particularly during the neo-classical period. Earlier Scottish furniture—chests, coffers and chairs and tables from the seventeenth century—exists in surprising quantity. It is usually made of oak.

The eighteenth century was also a halcyon time for the Scottish clockmaker who, at least in the larger towns, often doubled up as a maker of barometers as well. Almost every village or town boasted its clockmaker and these country clocks, often with attractive painted faces and usually of the longcase or 'grandfather' variety, are much preferred to English-made clocks of the same period. Scottish clocks always have a movement of eight days' duration while the country-made English clock had a simpler movement without a second hand and had to be wound daily.

down Victoria Street and into the Grassmarket, you will find yourself in the original centre of the antiques trade in Edinburgh, for the area was in decline and property was cheap. It is worth taking time to browse. On Saturdays during the Festival a street market of antique/junk stalls gives you the opportunity to hunt for a bargain. Twenty minutes walk from the Grassmarket will take you to Bruntsfield and several interesting shops whose wares include furniture, luggage, jewellery and clocks.

On the other side of Princes Street, in the New Town, try Thistle Street, North West Circus Place and Stockbridge, particularly St Stephen Street. Jewellery, period clothing, linen goods and lamps are just some of the items which make the

rich and varied. The lack of specialized outlets make the opportunities for the buyer much less predictable, but by the same token the fun and the chance of making a real discovery are even greater.

Furniture

Over the years cabinet-making in Edinburgh grew from a rough trade to a fine art, the brilliance of which was not to be submerged until the onset of the Victorian Age. Its early history features criminal episodes quite uncharacteristic of the staid image of this craft.

Edinburgh was a centre for furniture-making by the mid-fifteenth century when the Incorporation of Wrights was formed, admitting only those who made their living working in wood. However, for almost three centuries their products were crude copies of English and French designs. The business ethics of these early craftsmen seem to have been equally crude for in the 1670s they seized and closed down the workshop of a colleague whose only crime was making superior furniture.

The renaissance of design and craftsmanship in England which followed the Restoration of Charles II in 1606 was not mirrored in Scotland. The first step towards such a boom north of the border was taken by Alexander Peter, considered by some experts to be Scotland's finest cabinetmaker. There are records showing he supplied furniture to George Dundas of Dundas Castle in 1734 and a flood of orders from other aristocratic clients followed. Among these was an order for some 150 pieces for Lord Dumfries.

He also commissioned Edinburgh's second outstanding

The Scottish capital's hallmarks, used between 1544 and 1792.

Collectors' items of Scottish type which are easily found include snuff boxes, or 'mulls', made in great variety from sheeps' horns and traditional Scottish brooches and other jewellery.

Edinburgh is a compact city and most of its antique shops tend to be within easy reach of each other.

The area around Causeway-side has a number of shops worth visiting including one which just sells chairs. Coming

shops here so intriguing. In Dean Village can be found Whytock and Reid, a large cabinet-making and antique furniture warehouse.

The large auction houses have their rooms in George Street, and in South West Thistle Street Lane, Lyon and Turnbull have their 'Lane sales' on Tuesdays, Wednesdays and Fridays.

The opportunities which exist in Edinburgh for the antique enthusiast are indeed cabinetmaker, Peter's ex-apprentice William Mathie, to make a series of carved mirrors for his castle. As Lord Dumfries had been made a Knight of the Thistle in 1752, Mathie varied his usual rococo and Chinese style of decoration to include a naturalistic thistle and the entire insignia of the Order on certain mirrors.

was a special reason for its popularity in Edinburgh. It was probably financed by Rannie, Chippendale's partner, who came from Leith. His brother was a prosperous wine and spirits merchant there and Chippendale and Rannie received many orders through this connection.

The *Director's* illustrations of

success of the Cockpen Chair. The firm also benefited from its success, and from Hamilton's cabinet-making skills. Within a few decades it had changed from a small upholstery and soft-furnishings importing business into a major furniture supplier for the burgeoning New Town and statelier homes in the area.

Tim Hardie's antique shop in Bruntsfield, one of several in the area, has a wide range of furniture.

However, fine as the work of these craftsmen was, they did not create an Edinburgh style. Indeed, among the Dumfries furniture is a side table which so meticulously copies a Chippendale design that only Peter's account for it convinces experts it is local work. The source of this design was Chippendale's book, *The Gentleman and Cabinet-Maker's Director*, first published in 1753 and subscribed to by many Edinburgh cabinetmakers including Peter. The book had tremendous impact on furniture design throughout Europe but there

Chinese-style furniture undoubtedly contributed to the thought behind the popular Cockpen Chair, so-called because several early examples stood in the Dalhousie pew at Cockpen Church. But the actual creation of this charming chair, with its lattice-work back resembling a Chinese puzzle, is now attributed to James Hamilton. He was employed by a firm called Young and Trotter founded in 1751. The first records of his activities there date from 1774 but he became a partner very soon after, probably as a result of the enormous

The rapid rise of Young, Hamilton and Trotter can partly be attributed to the even more abrupt downfall of the Brodie family's business. Francis and his son William were both Deacons of Wright and sat on the Town Council, thereby cornering the market for civic furniture and fittings. While in the mid-eighteenth century the Brodies continuously supplied furniture to the Town College, as the university was then known, tradesmen's accounts show that Young and Trotter only picked up minor work such as stripping wallpaper, and replacing it using rat-proof material in the paste.

But in 1788 a bungled raid on the Excise Office revealed that William (Dean) Brodie, libertine and gambler, but a very competent cabinetmaker, was less capable in his second-string occupation of burglar. His execution brought disgrace to the firm.

The other factor promoting the success of Young, Hamilton and Trotter was William Trotter, a descendant of John Knox who became sole proprietor of the

This perfect mahogany swing-top table with satin wood cross-banding was made c.1820 by Trotter's firm.

firm in 1809. Despite active involvement in public life, including being Master of the Merchant Company and Lord Provost of Edinburgh, he created the version of Regency furniture known as the 'Trotter' style. From his premises in Princes Street with its workshop in Waverley Market he did a roaring trade by supplying the local customers with value for money and a distinctively Scottish style.

This furniture can be recognized by its air of masculine solidity, the use of high quality materials including wood and brass inlays and most notably by the carved lion's paws which frequently replaced the Engish Regency brass feet. One of the largest collections of his work is in Paxton House where he furnished the library and picture gallery in 1815. He also supplied furniture to the university, the Assembly Rooms and the Parliament.

There are survivors from the 100 cabinet-making businesses in Edinburgh in 1812. The firm of Whytock and Reid founded in that year still flourishes in Belford Mews, Dean Village, and it supplies and restores furniture for Holyrood House. But the death of William Trotter in 1833 brought the golden era of Edinburgh cabinet-making to a sudden close. The pleasing and distinctive designs of the eighteenth century disappeared as cabinet-makers turned to producing much heavier pieces. These conformed with Victorian standards of taste but have certainly not found such favour with twentieth-century furniture connoisseurs. It is the older pieces which are sought after.

Clocks

Though clockmaking in Scotland started in Aberdeen in the 1400s, a hundred years were to pass before Edinburgh entered the stage. And it was not until the sixteenth century that a native school of craftsmen emerged in the capital. By 1600 however the art had reached a fairly advanced stage, as is evident from the work of David Ramsay, watchmaker to James VI. Originally from Dundee, he possibly worked for a while in France before coming to Edinburgh and then finally travelled to London in the wake of his royal patron as Clockmaker Extraordinary to the King. Ramsay's skill was rewarded by James, who made him Page of the Bedchamber in 1627, while in 1631 he became one of the founder members of the Clockmakers' Company of London.

Throughout the seventeenth century the development of the craft accelerated. By the middle of the 1600s there were sufficient clockmakers for them to be recognized as a distinct branch of the locksmiths' trade and thus form part of the Edinburgh Incorporation of Hammermen. The first qualified 'knokmaker' to be admitted to this august body was a George Smith, on September 6, 1649.

One of the earliest members of the Incorporation, an example of whose work has survived, was Humphrey Milne or Mills who became a freeman in 1660. He has left a very fine example of a brass lantern clock. This type of clock, so called because of its lantern-like shape, was introduced in England around 1620 and continued in popularity until the first half of the eighteenth century. Such clocks usually stood on wall brackets and normally had one hand. They were

Above Brass lantern clock by Humphrey Milne, 1660-1692.
Right Engraved silver and brass pocket watch by David Ramsay, 1600-1650.
Far right Marquetry longcase clock by Paul Roumieu Jnr, 1682-1712.

probably among the first clocks produced in Scotland to meet the demand for individual time pieces.

During the second half of the seventeenth century there began the development of what was to become the most popular type of clock in Scotland—the longcase or grandfather clock. Humphrey Milne is thought to have produced some early longcase clocks and one of his apprentices, Andrew Brown, made several very beautiful clocks of this type. By far the most famous clockmaker of the late seventeenth century was Paul Roumieu. His father, Paul

senior, arrived in Scotland from France sometime before 1677 and, after David Ramsay, is the earliest watchmaker recorded in Scotland. He passed on his skill to his son, who became a freeman of the Incorporation of Hammermen in 1682. The Roumieus' French connection is a good example of the close economic links which existed between the two countries, and no doubt both father and son introduced technical advances which originated in France. The Roumieus' shop and house is thought to have been in the Clockmakers' Land at the top of the West Bow. Dr. Chambers in his *Traditions of Edinburgh*

records that on the fourth floor of this house, which was demolished in 1835, were the remains of a curious piece of mechanism, namely a gilt ball representing the moon which was made to revolve by means of a clock.

By the middle of the eighteenth century Edinburgh clockmakers' skills could be compared favourably with those of clockmakers in any other part of Britain as the clockmakers responded to the demands accompanying economic prosperity.

By this time the craftsmen had perfected the movements of ordinary clocks and were becoming more adventurous. This manifested itself in a profusion of 'performing' clocks which could play complicated series of tunes or had ingenious automata. This development reached its climax in the production of extremely complicated astronomical clocks. One such was made by John Scott, who worked in Princes Street and East Register Street between 1779 and 1798. He was described as clockmaker to the Prince of Wales, and certainly he must have been a craftsman of the highest order.

The final phase in the development of the longcase clock began during the period of the painted or white dial clocks, which were popular from about 1790 to 1870. They were made in their thousands by clockmakers in virtually every town and large village in Scotland to satisfy the increased demand for a good quality 'knok' at a reasonable price. This was the era when the possibility of owning a clock came within the reach of the ordinary man. The earlier dials were decorated rather sparsely with much of the white enamelled underpainting showing, while the later dials tended to show much more flamboyant and picturesque painting. One of the reasons for the comparative cheapness of these clocks was that the faces came from clock face factories—firms specializing in making the painted dial plate and supplying them to the local clockmakers who fitted them to their own movements. Edinburgh was in the forefront of this trade, with several firms producing these dials, including Bell and Meundell, Russell and Clark and Dallaway and Son. Because of the numbers produced, this type of longcase clock is the one that has survived best and has become synonymous with the term grandfather clock.

Books

Edinburgh has a long tradition of books and bookselling. The city has even erected statues to the memory of some: Allan Ramsay, bookseller, wig-maker and poet, stands in Princes Street

Edinburgh has some fine bookshops. One of Scotland's largest bookshops is James Thin, 53-62 South Bridge, Edinburgh, founded in 1848 and still a family business.

Gardens, and Provost Chambers, bookseller and publisher, looks down from a pedestal in the street named for him.

The early history of the business is obscure but when James IV was encouraging the spread of the European Renaissance into Scotland, two printer-booksellers called Chepman and Myllar were setting up a little shop in the Cowgate. Their

books, which appeared around 1508, are the earliest dated works known to be printed in Scotland—only a few decades after Gutenberg's invention of moveable type.

Bookselling and publishing tended to be in the same premises right up to the beginning of the twentieth century and even now a few of Edinburgh's

secondhand booksellers have their own presses.

In the eighteenth century when Adam Smith and David Hume were revolutionizing economics and philosophy, the literati met in Edinburgh bookshops in the way they now do in pubs. Allan Ramsay had a shop, first at Netherbow, then by the Luckenbooths, where he combined bookselling and poetry with hairdressing and wig-making, He was, he said, attending to both the inside and outside of his customers' heads.

In 1777 there were 98 hairdressers and 20 bookshops in the city but by 1867 the balance had changed to 43 hairdressers and 128 booksellers. One of the best of these was run by William Creech, the first Edinburgh publisher of Burns. Creech was Lord Provost from 1811 to 1813; it was remarkable how many of those involved in bookselling won high office in the city in the nineteenth century. Bookselling was very big business indeed.

In fact, what became one of the world's largest publishing houses, Archibald Constable, started publishing the *Encyclopaedia Britannica* in a small Edinburgh close at the end of the eighteenth century. Constable, who also produced the *Edinburgh Review*, was also the publisher of Walter Scott's first novel, *The Lay of The Last Minstrel*, which sold 44,000 copies between 1805 and 1830.

Ballantyne, Adam Black, John Blackie, William Blackwood, William Collins, William and Robert Chambers, Archibald Constable, and Thomas Nelson are just some of the big names of nineteenth-century Scottish publishing and bookselling. Some, like Bartholomew the mapmakers, specialized; others leant more heavily towards bookselling, like Thins or John Menzies which began in Princes Street in 1833.

If you are a book collector, Edinburgh can still surprise with its great treasure trove of old books. The city has dozens of bookshops, spread through both the Old and New Towns, selling second-hand books by the thousand, from cramped quarters that can take hours to scour for titles.

It is still possible to spot a good bargain—perhaps a first edition Scott or Stevenson at the very best—in among the many more common volumes that line the shelves and those that are displayed with pride within the shops.

Books are very much loved in Scotland and there is a busy trade in them, so the turnover, even in some of the smaller bookshops, can be faster than you think. If you find nothing the first time around, visit again, talk with the bookseller, make your wants known, and you may well walk out with the very volume the next time you visit.

Prices vary greatly, of course, with the condition and scarcity of the book in question, but it is usually possible to strike a good bargain with a bookseller. And it is certainly worthwhile having a chat with the bookseller and showing your fascination for the subject. He or she will certainly be interested and knowledgeable about the books and may well open up for you an intriguing world of literary back-alleys.

their long history is embodied in the impressive appearance of the pipers in full highland dress in the streets of Edinburgh.

Bagpipes consist essentially of a bag of skin which is inflated under pressure from the arm to produce a stream of air to the pipes. The invention of the bag did not represent a new musical instrument but merely an addition to pipes blown by the mouth. Reed pipes were known well before the time of Christ, particularly in hill countries where shepherds and cowherds played the pipes during their long hours of solitude.

The earliest surviving examples of the reed-sounded pipe or pipes have been found in Babylonia and ancient Egypt, but it is likely that the principle was discovered independently in innumerable countries all over the world, and certainly they were known in ancient Greece and Rome. Reeds or pieces of straw when pinched

This shop has dealt in kilts and bagpipes for nearly 150 years.

Bagpipes

It is said that there is no inhabited continent where the Scottish highland bagpipe is not played, and certainly most people are familiar with its distinctive sound. Bagpipes are an essential part of Scotland's national heritage and

flat and blown with compressed lips yield a crude musical sound, and this principle was named the double reed after the two surfaces created by compression. The single reed is constructed by a cut a short way along the straw, which when played produces a musical sound.

Today's bagpipes comprise a bass drone (the longest pipe),

which is essentially the single reed type; two tenor drones (identical in appearance) both of single reed type; a blow pipe (the short pipe which narrows at the end for use as the mouthpiece); and the chanter, which with its finger holes enables a tune to be played according to the double-reed principle. The bag acts as a reservoir and

of Britain in the first century AD. The Royal Museum of Scotland possesses the Roman stone found at Bridgeness in East Lothian which has carvings of the double pipe.

The pipes of ancient Britain however are thought to have developed from the Egyptian model, the parallel pipes, as a result of the earliest Mediter-

fourteenth century that a drone was added.

James I of Scotland (1424-1437) played the pipes, and bagpipes were the national music of England during the reign of Henry V (1413-1422). James II of Scotland (1437-1460) passed an act for the suppression of the pipes in 1449, but they were restored by James III, (1460-1488) and James IV (1488-1513) had English pipers playing at the gates of Edinburgh Castle until 1507. Up until this time pipers had traditionally been associated with the English Court from the reign of Edward III (1327-1377) but by the end of the fifteenth century there were town or burgh pipers as well. The bagpipes acquired battle status in the mid-sixteenth century in Scotland, being associated with Scottish armies, and the clans employed their own pipers. The English Court dispensed with the pipers in the 1660s, from which time bagpipes in England were relegated to folk music. It was about this time that the third pipe, the base drone, also known as the great drone, was added.

After the Jacobite Rebellion of 1745, the second (and far more vicious) Disarming Act was passed. It was judged in the High Court that bagpipes were an instrument of war, being associated with armies, and, together with weapons and symbols of nationalism such as tartan, were banned.

The result for the piper was disastrous—and furthermore there was far less employment by the clans owing to their own impoverishment because of the forfeiture of their estates. In 1757, however, the new highland regiments were formed in response to troubles abroad, and they were allowed once more to play the pipes. The Disarming Act was repealed in 1782 from which time Scotland

An array of drones, chanters and reeds used in sets of pipes.

pump to supply air to the pipes. The modern version is basically the result of adding a bag to the hornpipe, the generic name for double, single and parallel pipes.

Although the double pipes existed in ancient Britain, it is known that the Romans introduced them after their invasion

ranean migrations between 2000 and 3000 BC. This theory is supported by the fact that the highlanders did not adopt the Romans' double pipes.

Up until the twelfth century the pipes comprised the hornpipe, a type of chanter fitted with a bag or skin, and the blowpipe. It was not until the enjoyed its piping tradition without interruption to the present day.

There is now a College of Piping in Glasgow, and Edinburgh, like other towns in Scotland, has its own bagpipe makers. The water reed gave way first to cane and then to hard woods such as laburnum, cocus, rosewood and, in this century, African blackwood or Canadian maple. The hardness of the wood is essential, since the harder the wood, the better the tone. If Canadian maple is used, it has to be specially treated. It 'works' better than the other woods and can be bored without the need for mounts. Square sections of about ten inches (25.4cm) in length and two inches (5.1cm) in width are turned on a lathe into pipes. Plastic, ivory or silver are used for the embellishments and so is the traditional horn. A set of pipes will cost not less than £300 and a full-mounted silver set with hand engraved family crest or runic devices may be £2000. The pipes will last for ever, except for the bag which is made of sheepskin or cowhide and needs replacing every year or two. If the pipes are not played regularly, the skin will harden within two months.

William Sinclair has been making bagpipes in Edinburgh since the 1920s and started his own business in 1963. You have to wait several months after placing an order for the authentic article. Sinclair & Son produce about 100 sets a year, mostly for professional pipers in Edinburgh. They have also exported to South Africa, Canada, the United States, Australia, France, Norway, Sweden and Finland. The United States is one of the biggest importers but the continental countries are apparently increasing their orders.

Allistair Sinclair's advice to the hopeful piper is to start learning by the age of ten and he emphasizes the importance of a good ear since you have to tune the instrument yourself.

The pipes are pitched at B flat to play with brass bands and possess just eight notes—which do not represent a true scale. The notes relate to the white notes of the piano which means there is no minor key. The instrument is tuned by rotating the two ends of the pipe, decreasing or increasing the space from end to end according to the desired sound.

The sound of the bagpipes is a uniquely haunting one which compels the ear and, with its evocation of Scotland and its history and traditions, perceptibly moves every foot.

Tartan

*O*f everything that is exclusively associated with Scotland, tartan is the most vivid and the most instantly recognizable, particularly in the form of the kilt. But the tartan has an uncertain history and the misconceptions are many.

Many writers claim that the word tartan is English, the Gaelic being *breacan*, but it now seems accepted that tartan derives from *tiretaine*, French for a coloured woollen material. Scotland has produced lengths of cloth since medieval times. The basic garment for both nobleman and peasant until the end of the sixteenth century was the *leine croich*, a linen tunic. Over this was worn a woollen mantle, which developed into a large tartan blanket, the *breacan filleadh*, or folded plaid.

The wearer would lay it flat on the ground, pleat it to reduce the width, leaving a short length at either edge unpleated. He would then lie on it, with the lower edge in line with his knees. The two unpleated ends were folded across the body, overlapping, and the whole garment held in place with a belt at the waist.

The excess of fabric above the belt was either raised and draped over the head and shoulders or draped around the torso where it was fastened on the shoulder with a brooch, button or pin.

The garment was obviously an encumbrance, and towards the end of the sixteenth century the forerunner of today's kilt emerged: the lower section of the plaid had pleats stitched in place and the upper half was cut away. This became the length of plaid that today is worn over the left shoulder and fastened with a decorative brooch.

Claims that the clansmen adhered rigidly to one particular tartan so that they would not kill their own clansmen in disputes and retaliations are clearly insupportable: you would be unlikely to cross someone else's territory wearing an outfit that marked you as a target for assassination.

Some experts on the subject say that it was an Englishman, Thomas Rawlinson, manager of a Glengarry ironworks, who invented the little kilt, as it was then known. He felt his workers were too restricted in the belted plaid and so, in about 1727 he dispensed with the plaid, had pleats sewn in the lower part of the garment and hence the kilt was born.

But there are references and engravings well before 1727 which show the little kilt, and so the story of Rawlinson's invention must have been embroidered.

The tartan chosen for the kilt depended largely upon where the wearer hailed from and was not necessarily related to his clan. Since chemical dyes did not exist, vegetable dyes were used in the making of the cloth: so it was a matter of personal preference combined with the plants available that would determine the colours of the kilt. And if a great many Macdonalds, for example, existed in one area, then no doubt many of them wore kilts of the same or similar colours.

Although there was no rigid organisation concerning a party to information known to no one else.

Their astonishing publication (weighing 22 pounds and requiring 6 square feet in which to read it) was a response to the revival in popularity of Scotland in general and tartan in particular due to George IV's visit to Scotland in 1822 and his

Shops such as Kinloch Anderson in Leith will then be able to advise you on the selection of a tartan. If you know which area either you or your ancestors are associated with, Kinloch Anderson will be able to arrange the design of a new tartan according to the predominant colours of the plant

The tartan marks the clan of each child here but not until the 1840s, when the Sobieski Stuart brothers published their disputed works on the classification of tartans, did each clan adhere to one pattern.

clan's tartan, there were personal preferences and tartan had become a symbol of the highlander.

After the Jacobite Rebellion of 1745, all such symbols were banned under the Disarming Act of 1747. Tartan was not worn, legally at least, until 1782 when the Act was repealed.

Fragments of the old tartans that exist today, and these include some in the Royal Museum of Scotland, show that the later tartans conceived in the nineteenth century bear little or no relation to those worn before 1745 and must have been the product either of misguided historians or imaginative entrepreneurs.

Two such entrepreneurs, the Brothers Allan, also known as the Sobieski Stuart brothers, produced The Costumes of the Clans in 1842. The brothers claimed to be grandsons of Bonnie Prince Charlie and thus

fascination for it—rivalled only by Queen Victoria's interest and affection.

By the 1850s and 1860s, the tartan industry was thoroughly established and the vogue for Scotland and its symbols was at its peak.

There are now over 500 clan tartans and it is accepted that if you have links with a particular clan, then you may assume its tartan—and, if not, you should not really wear any tartan.

If you wish to establish your crest or any other heraldic device, the Lord Lyon office in Edinburgh can advise. If you wish to establish whether you are descended from a particular clan, you should contact the Scots Ancestry Research Society in Edinburgh. The terms are a £50 (plus VAT) non-returnable registration fee and an authorization for research to be carried out for a fee of £100 to £150.

life in that area.

Men normally wear the kilt, while women wear kilted skirts. The women's version usually takes about six to seven yards (5.4 to 6.4m) of cloth, while the kilt proper requires eight to nine yards (7.3 to 8.2m).

Visit the Scottish Tartans Museum within The Scotch House shop in Princes Street, and at the Edinburgh Old Town Weaving Co. at the Castle end of the Royal Mile you can watch tartan being made 'from sheep to shop'.

Tweed

*E*dinburgh is one of the best market places you can find for tweed and Harris tweed.

Tweed comes in an infinite variety of colours, weights and in herringbone or check.

The weight is selected according to the garment the tweed is destined for and the use it will receive. Men's suits, women's suits, coats, jackets, skirts and trousers can all be made up in Edinburgh once you have selected the preferred colour from the roll, or you can buy ready-mades.

Tweed was made in southern Scotland from about the 1840s and the main centres of production, in a textile industry that was otherwise depressed, included Galashiels, Jedburgh and Hawick in the Tweed river basin. The Border towns found a ready market for the tweeds in the south. Demand increased with Queen Victoria's affection for Scotland and all things Scottish.

It was the English who unwittingly gave tweed its name, rather than the river of the same name. *Tweel*, the Scottish version of the French word for cloth, *toile*, was misread—and so tweed was born.

The best quality tweed is Harris tweed, a 100 per cent wool cloth, which is handwoven on the islands of the Outer Hebrides, notably the isles of Harris and Lewis. It is usually a heavyweight cloth, and it is legally protected from imitation.

The traditional cloths come in subtle shades of browns and greens. Its internationally recognized standard of durability makes tweed an attractive investment.

Cashmere

ashmere is sheer magic. With its uniquely soft and velvety touch, it has become a supreme symbol of luxury and opulence. The hard-wearing quality, colour retention and classic design of Scottish produced cashmere garments have given it an undisputed lead in the world's knitwear

markets. Some of the world's top designers will work only with cashmere produced in Scotland.

Expensive—of course! Just 1 kilogram of top quality cashmere is worth around £90, even before any garment is produced. The reason for its high cost lies partly in the difficulty of obtaining the raw material.

Raw cashmere fibre comes from the underfleece of cashmere goats. The word cashmere is an anglicization of Kashmir, the province of India where cashmere goats were first discovered. Nowadays, however, the best quality raw fibre comes from goats reared in Inner Mongolia, in China. Other cashmere producing areas include Iran, Afghanistan and the former Soviet Union. Great expense is involved not only because the goats are reared in isloated areas of mountainous regions, but also because much time and skill is involved in the manufacturing process.

The development and availability of cashmere can be traced most recently to Dawson International PLC, the Scottish-based international textile and apparel group. In the late 1800s the Yorkshire mill owner, Joseph Dawson, was visiting his daughter in India, where he came across cashmere and watched local women separate by hand the coarse hair of the outer coat of cashmere goats from the fine hair of the underfleece, making it suitable for spinning. Subsequently, in 1901, Dawson developed a machine which would carry out this process mechanically. As a result, Joseph Dawson has today developed into the world's foremost cashmere dehairers.

Although Joseph Dawson started producing dehaired cashmere in the early 1900s, it was not until the 1950s that cashmere earned the luxury

status it has today. Towards the end of the 1940s, a mixed textile company named Todd & Duncan started making lambswool yarn and subsequently, cashmere yarn. By 1960, Todd & Duncan were using 70 per cent of Joseph Dawson's dehaired cashmere production. Joseph Dawson, by then a public company, joined forces with Todd & Duncan and formed the foundations of what was to become Dawson International. One year later, the spinning strength of the company increased through the acquisition of Laidlaw & Fairgrieve, the firm which had pioneered in Shetland yarns in the 1950s. Dawson International subsequently added to its portfolio a number of quality Scottish knitwear manufacturers, now known by the famous names of Pringle of Scotland, Ballantyne Cashmere and Barrie Knitwear, all of whom knit with the top quality cashmere and wool produced by Dawson's yarn spinners.

Of great importance to these companies' pre-eminent position in cashmere is Dawson International's majority shareholding in a new cashmere procurement and dehairing operation in Baotou, Inner Mongolia. This investment provides Dawson International's spinners and knitters with guaranteed supplies of the world's top quality white cashmere fibre.

Dawson International's Scottish Knitwear brands supply all kinds of knitted cashmere outer garments to the retail market, both at home and abroad: coats and shawls; hats, scarves and gloves; jumpers, skirts, trousers and dresses. A more recent development being pioneered by Todd & Duncan is the development of woven cashmere for suiting material. A plain cashmere jumper from Ballantyne Cashmere will today retail at around £250, while a hand-knitted intarsia will cost, on average, £650. Intarsia design and production is one of the most intricate features of Dawson International's cashmere production. The word has been borrowed from the woodworking craft of marquetry. Of the many intarsia designs, the original Argyll remains popular, while flowers, birds, butterflies and other animals are much in demand, especially in the Japanese and Italian markets. Ballantyne Cashmere's intarsia knitters are based at Ballantyne's headquarters in Innerleithen, just outside Edinburgh. Their training takes two years, after which time they can produce a diamond pattern jersey front on a single bed machine in about three and a half hours—the more complex designs may take many hours longer.

Assembly of the fronts with the backs and sleeves produced in Innerleithen is carried out here as well. The stitch length selected on the different machines ensures that the hand-knitted intarsia front exactly matches the machine knitted sleeves and back. The matching and seaming carried out during assembly is a skilled process, subject to several quality checks at each stage. Assembly training takes about one to one and a half years. Batch numbers are attached to the collars and other trims so that each whole garment is produced from the same batch of wool. When the garment has been assembled, it goes to the milling house with its corresponding trims. The garments and trims are thoroughly scoured in special detergent to remove the oil which has been left on to ease the knitting process. The fibre is then broken down in a milling process to produce the characteristic softness. The millman estimates just how long each batch requires in the machine. The time factor is crucial, as the machine may contain thousands of pounds worth of garments at any one time. The garments are then spun and dried, boarded (pulled over steel frames and set to size by steaming and vacuuming) and then sent out for hand-finishing. Necks are cut out for V-necks and collars: buttons, pockets, trimming, binding and braiding constitute the next stages. A series of examinations determines whether the garment can be passed for pressing, when it is again checked for quality.

The quality, colours and designs of cashmere garments produced in Scotland ensure that they retain a supreme position in the world's knitwear markets. Although much of the total production goes for export, Edinburgh nevertheless offers, in its concentrated shopping area, many shops specialising in Scottish cashmere, woollens and tweeds, most notably along the Royal Mile and Princes Street.

Alongside cashmere you will find lambswool, botany wool, Shetlands from the Shetland Isles and Fair Isles which originated from the sparsely populated Fair Isle off the coast of northern Scotland. Fair Isle colours and designs are said to be Moorish and are traceable to survivors of the Spanish Armada in 1588.

Whisky

𝒟o not ask for whisky, do not request a Scotch—you are in a land where brands and blends can be as individual as the wines of France. If you apply yourself diligently to the task, you can soon become a true Scot and pick out the particular glass of golden liquor to suit your mood. It will probably be one of the scores of 'single malts', the pure and crowning glory of Scottish distilling. But it might be one of hundreds of blends, which are made from a mixture of malt and grain whiskies and account for 98 per cent of all whisky sold.

Whether the choice is a light and delicate blend or the dark, smokey tang of an island malt, what you are sampling is the Gaelic 'water of life'. That is the meaning of the word *uisge-beagh*, from which whisky got its name.

The malts are a pure product made from malted barley in a series of processes known as malting, mashing, fermentation and distillation in pot stills. The barley is steeped in water so that the germination process is triggered and rootlets start to sprout. A grain of barley is in fact a small store of starch which is insoluble. After about seven days, the conversion of the starch will have taken place and the maltster then dries it in a kiln fired by peat.

The distiller grinds the soluble starch and adds water during the process known as mashing. A sugary liquid, maltose, is extracted and fermented with yeast. During the course of about 40 hours, the sugar is converted into a crude alcohol of about 12 per cent strength, known as wash.

The final product requires two distillations in large copper pot stills. The first distillation separates the alcohol from the fermented liquid and the resulting distillate, known as low wines, is then passed to another still where it is distilled a second time. The first runnings from the second distillation, the foreshots, are very strong and are set aside. Towards the end of the distillation, the strength and quality of the spirit is reduced and these runnings, known as feints, are drawn off and, together with the foreshots, are redistilled in the next distillation of low wines.

It is the mixture of the three elements, the low wines, the

The Magic of Malt Whisky

1 Silo containing dry ripened barley

2 Barley soaks in water for up to 70 hours

3 Drained barley germinates to become green malt

4 Green malt in the kiln

5 Grain crushed to give malt grist

6 Grist plus water produces wort

7 Yeast added

8 Distillation produces 120° proof spirit

9 Dilution with pure water to 110° proof

10 Casked whisky matures

The exacting task of producing the true malt is part of a centuries-old tradition.

foreshots and the feints, that is largely responsible for the character of the whisky. The middle cut, the runnings that are taken off between the foreshots and the feints, are pumped into casks and left to mature for a minimum of three years. It is often left for considerably longer—The Glen-livet, for example, is not bottled until 12 years later. About $1\frac{1}{2}$ percent a year is lost in evaporation, but the process of maturation is an important one since it results in a smoother and more mature whisky. After about 15 years or so, the whisky becomes progressively smoother and less recogniz-able for what it is. One might guess that it is a cognac which is being offered. After maturation, the whisky is coloured with an infinitesimal quantity of caramelized sugar, if the casks have not already imparted sufficient colour. Once bottled, the whisky does not then change in state or flavour—so you can drink it straightaway.

Malt whisky comes from four distinct regions, the Highlands, the Lowlands, Islay and Campbeltown on the Mull of Kintyre, which together represent Scotland's total 130 distilleries, of which 116 are malt distilleries.

three areas: those around the Livet valley, which include The Glenlivet, Glen Grant, Glenfarclas, Tormore, Cardhu, Longmorn, Linkwood, Glen Rothes and Glengoyne; around Dufftown and Keith, the group including Glenfiddich, very much responsible for promot-

Lowlanders are much lighter and are most often used in the production of blended whiskies. The Islay distilleries make a characteristic heavy, peaty, pungent, almost medicinal style of malt for which an acquired taste is needed. The single malts

The history of whisky is brought to life at the Scotch Whisky Heritage Centre beside the Castle.

Although generalizations can be made about the malt whiskies to come from these geographical areas, it is worth remembering that each still produces a whisky that to someone in the trade is as individual as a fingerprint. Glenfiddich and Balvenie, for example, which are literally across the road from each other and use the same water and the same barley, make noticeably different products.

The Highlanders, the largest group, can be subdivided into

ing the single malt in recent years, Strathisla, the oldest distillery, founded in 1786, Balvenie, Dufftown-Glenlivet and Mortlach; and, thirdly, north of the Spey from Inverness almost to John O'Groats, a group including Glenmorangie, Old Pulteney, Dalmore and Clynelish.

The Highland malts have traditionally been regarded as the best, with the Speyside products, from around the River Spey, being regarded in the trade as excellent malts. The

from Islay include Bowmore, Laphroaig, Lagavulin and Bruichladdich.

A blender or broker can appreciate the difference between the malts sufficiently to enable him to identify its age and area of origin and to pinpoint it to one of three or four. An Edinburgh broker, with many years in the trade, has said that of all the malts, those that commanded high prices included Aultinore, Glen Grant, Longmorn, The Glenlivet, and Mortlach, all of them Highland Malts. He added that Glenmorangie, one of the best sellers, is a very fine malt—but, naturally, no one in the trade will commit themselves to naming the best.

Your own tasting is probably best carried out with a selection of miniatures. Try William Cadenhead Ltd., 172 Canongate and the Whisky Shop of Edinburgh, Waverley Shopping Centre. Cadenhead's specialize in old and rare malts, and also have their own export service as well as mail order. The Whisky Shop's stock includes about 400 malts. It has a web site and export service and also sells Scottish food and gifts.

Whereas the malt whiskies are made purely from barley, the grains are made from a mixture of malted barley with unmalted cereals such as maize. The process, which is far less costly, is a continuous one, with the distillation carried out in a Patent or Coffey still, rather than a pot still, and the spirit is collected at a much higher strength. Since the whisky can be run at a much higher strength, and continuously, the Coffey stills can produce as much as 14,000 gallons per hour. Grain whisky is not influenced by geographical factors and it has a less pronounced aroma and flavour than the malts.

The well-known brands of blended whisky, exported all over the world, make up 98 percent of Scotland's total whisky, and so it is to the manufacture of the blends that much of the malt and grain production goes. A blend may contain between 15 and 50 different whiskies, the process of blending being known as vatting. Blending is an art, in which the malts and grains are selected to complement their respective flavours, so that the best qualities of each are brought out. Once mixed in a blending vat,

after a battery of testing, they are returned to the cask to 'marry' for several months before bottling. Some are vatted separately and only combined during bottling.

Blending was pioneered by Andrew Usher in Edinburgh in the early 1860s. It was only when this practice became common that a taste for Scotch whisky spread first to England and then throughout the world. Pot still malt whisky, although its popularity has increased

Window-shopping—a parade of Scotland's matchless whiskies.

greatly in the last 20 years, is inclined to be rather strongly flavoured, particularly for those in warmer climates and sedentary occupations.

To the Scotsman of the cold, rugged hills in centuries past, however, the pure malt must have been more than welcome. It is thought that distilling started in the East many centuries ago; the fact that eastern civilizations had bamboo tubes which would have been good for conducting vapour when the West had only crude implements seems to support this assumption. From the Far East the practice seems to have spread through India and the Middle East with the Crusaders to the monastic houses of Europe in the Middle Ages. The

centres of learning were keeping the practice alive by distilling medicinal preparations of herbs and perhaps by making something akin to whisky for their own consumption, a practice which spread to Ireland and then to the west of Scotland. A fifth-century Welsh song refers to 'strong liquor', while the first recorded reference in Scotland is an entry in the Exchequer Rolls of 1494: 'eight bolls of malt to Friar John Cor wherewith to make aquavitae'—eight boils is well over 2645 pounds (1200 kg), so it is clear that Friar John Cor was involved in the distillation of rather more than would be required for one monastery.

It seems that the monasteries constituted a cottage industry, and the crofters in the highlands, too, would have been producing their own fire-water. After centuries of illegal distillation, 1823 saw the imposing of a £10 tax on stills of over 40 gallons' capacity. Although illicit distillation continued, the industry was eventually brought under control.

Scotch whisky can only be made in Scotland. It is not, by law, Scotch whisky otherwise. The words whiskey and whisky used to be confused, but whiskey is now confined to Irish whiskey, which is subjected to three distillations and uses a wider range of cereals.

Before the product can claim to be called whisky, it has to mature in wooden casks for a minimum of three years. The casks used were traditionally, and until recently, the sherry casks that are imported from Spain. These would impart a certain flavour and colour to the whisky depending on which type of sherry the cask had been used for. Other factors are involved, however, in the production of a drink that has not been repeated successfully anywhere in the world. (Much whisky is now matured in bourbon casks from the United States.)

The natural elements of water, peat (which is introduced in the malting process) and the climate, affecting the crop as well as the final product during maturation, all influence flavour of the malt whiskies. The distilling process is crucial, too. The amount of secondary constituents retained in the spirit depends upon the shape of the still, the way in which it is operated and on the strength at which the spirit is drawn off.

The history of whisky is brought to life at The Scotch Whisky Heritage Centre, 358 Castlehill. Travelling through time on an electric car you will experience Scotland's turbulent past and learn of the ancient traditions that surround the making of whisky.

When you are in Edinburgh, you should not miss the chance of sampling the range of one of Scotland's oldest and most revered products.

Drambuie

Drambuie owes its origins to a royal debt. Disguised as a serving maid, Bonnie Prince Charlie, head of the Stuarts, fled to Skye towards the end of the 1745 rebellion after suffering a crushing defeat at the hands of the English. MacKinnon of Straithard, ancestor of today's chairman and managing director of the Drambuie Liqueur Company, sheltered the exhausted Prince and, at the end of the Jacobite Rebellion, engineered his escape from the English.

Charles Edward Louis John Sylvester Maria Casimir Stuart, before leading his faithful followers into battle, had travelled the courts of Europe, where he had achieved fluency in four languages and a considerable knowledge of food and wines.

It is said that Drambuie was the Prince's favourite drink and in grateful recognition that he owed his life to MacKinnon of Straithard presented him with the recipe.

For over 150 years the recipe was handed from father to eldest son, small quantities being made for members of the MacKinnon clan. It was not until the beginning of this century that Malcolm MacKinnon decided to experiment with the treasured recipe on a commercial basis. In the first year of production, 1906, only 12 cases were sold in Edinburgh. Edwardian conservatism gradually weakened, however, and in 1916 the cellarman of the House of Lords gave it the seal of his personal approbation. Malcolm's son Norman single-handedly established Drambuie in the postwar period as the leading imported brand of liqueur in the United States. Still independently owned by the MacKinnon family, the company is led today by a management team selected by brothers Calum and Duncan MacKinnon, who direct the day-to-day production, marketing, worldwide sales and distribution of Drambuie to more than 160 countries.

Drambuie is blended in the ancient way with the same care and quality as a 15-18 year old malt whisky. Its unique flavour comes from the careful combination of up to 18 separate aged malt whiskies, a magical blend of herbs and a hint of heather honey.

Traditionally, the recipe for the secret essence is handed down the female line of the MacKinnon family. The continuing importance of this role is recognised through the honorary post of lifetime Chairman of Drambuie Limited, which is held by Calum and Duncan's mother, while the secret of the essential essence is currently held by Calum's wife. The only written copy is lodged with an Edinburgh bank.

Different ways of drinking Drambuie and recipes for its use in cooking abound, but the purists recommend that it is drunk on its own after dinner. It can be drunk at any time, as an aperitif for example, and like whisky can be drunk over ice. A Rusty Nail is said to be excellent: a good measure of Drambuie is mixed in equal proportions with a good Scotch whisky, stirred gently and served in a chilled glass.

Cheese

Scotland has a long and largely unsung tradition of cheese-making which has recently undergone something of a renaissance. Edinburgh sells the full variety of Scottish cheeses and you should not miss the opportunity of sampling them. The quality is assured by the richness and fertility of the soil which provides lush pastures for the cattle.

Caboc has been made in the highlands since the fifteenth century and is made purely from cream, shaped like a thick sausage and rolled in coarse oatmeal. As it is comparatively bland, it is best accompanied by oatcakes or cheese biscuits and sprinkled with freshly milled black pepper.

Crowdie is a soft cottage cheese which is best when made with fresh milk. It is regarded as the traditional cheese of the highlands.

Dunlop is one of Scotland's traditional cheeses, having been made first towards the end of the seventeenth century. Not unlike Cheddar, it is somewhat softer and more mellow.

Lanark Blue is an aromatic, slightly sweet, Roquefort-style cheese, made from ewe's milk, and matured for three months, in the Clyde Valley.

Orkney cheese is fairly similar to Dunlop and it can be white or red and is sometimes available smoked. Orkney was originally a farmhouse cheese produced in the Orkney Islands.

Bonchester is a Camembert-style cheese made from the milk of Jersey cows. This gives it a rich yellow colour and a smooth velvety feel.

Other cheeses to look out for include *Cairnsmore*, another ewe's milk cheese, which is made on a farm in Galloway and has a sweet nutty taste, *Loch Arthur*, *St Andrews*, *Arran*, *Gigha* and, not least, *Scottish Cheddar*.

Try Ian Mellis' cheese shops at 30a Victoria Street (0131 226 6215, he also does mail order), and 205 Bruntsfield Place, or for stockists call the British Cheese Awards on (0171) 371 6466.

Glayva

*G*layva means 'very good' and this was the name Ronald Morrison and his partner, George Petrie, a chemist, thought the most apt christen-ing for the liqueur they first produced in Leith, the port town of Edinburgh, in the 1940s. The company was taken over by Whyte & Mackay in the late 1980s.

Glayva is made from malt and grain whiskies which are blended with herbal oils, heather honey and sugar.

Only three people know the exact recipe for Glayva. In accordance with the mystique of the drink trade, they are not prepared to divulge the formula.

Ronald Morrison's family were in the whisky business and he subsequently spent several years in Spain, learning the sherry trade. Before his death, Ronald Morrison passed on the secrets of the recipe to his two sons.

It is, of course, a matter of personal taste which of the Scottish liqueurs one elects to drink. Glayva is less sweet than Drambuie, for example, and it has a lower alcohol content.

Of the 70 countries importing, the largest consumers are those where Scots have settled —Canada, Australia and New Zealand.

Glayva is said to mix well in cocktails, particularly with soft drinks such as orange, lemon and lime, and is frequently used in cooking.

Haggis

*H*aggis is probably the most traditional and certainly the best known of all Scottish dishes. It is sometimes maligned by the foreigner, but its undistinguished ingredients amount to a flavoursome, nutritious and satisfying delicacy.

In her book *the haggis, a little history*, Clarissa Dixon Wright offers an explanation on the origin of the word along with many other interesting facts about Scotland's most famous—but most mysterious—delicacy. Haggis in different forms has been known since the early Greek and Roman civilizations. The first known English cookery book, written in 1390 by a cook to Richard II, contains a recipe for *Afronche-moyle* which is in effect a haggis.

Haggis has ever since been consumed in large and regular quantities both by local Scotsmen and Scots abroad. It is significant that Macsween of Edinburgh, established in 1953, sell haggis for consumption abroad. Such is the fame of haggis that it has been immortalized many times in literature, approved of by Queen Victoria and paid tribute to by Robert Burns, Scotland's revered poet, in his eight-verse ode *To a Haggis*:

... O what a glorious sight, warm-reekin', rich!

Haggis comprises essentially the sheep's 'pluck', the windpipe, lung, heart and liver. The windpipe is removed and the rest is boiled for 3 hours with beef fat. The fat is then skimmed off and the liver, heart and lungs minced. Oatmeal, onion, seasoning (usually pepper, salt and spices) and gravy from the boiling are then mixed into the mince.

The basic recipe has never changed, although the casing has. A number of different casings are used today and these even include plastic. Since the casing is not eaten some people maintain it is of no significance but most Scotsmen prefer their national dish properly prepared in the traditional way.

The correct casing, if only a matter of aesthetics, is the sheep's paunch, or stomach, which is filled with the mixture and then blanket-stitched with cotton thread. A sheep's stomach will take anything from 6 to 20 pounds (2.7

Traditional fare—haggis with bashed neeps and tatties.

to 9 kg) of the prepared mixture and, when it is boiled, shrinks to fit. Smaller haggises are encased in a length of caecum, known as a bung, from the ox or sheep. The caecum, part of the large intestine, is about 3 to 4 feet (1 to 1.3m) long in an ox and it is therefore cut to size and fastened with string or clips.

When the sheep's stomach or bung has been filled it is replaced in the boiler for a short time. It is then simmered wrapped in foil, at home, for 1 to 1¹/₂ hours and served steaming hot with mashed potatoes and turnips, or swedes as they are called in England. 'Bashed neeps and champit tatties' are the only acceptable accompaniment to be served with haggis, according to the traditionalists.

The haggis is served as hot as possible, slit lengthways and the mixture scooped out.

There is virtually no limit to the variations in size of the haggis. Three to four people will require about 1 to 1¹/₂ pounds (0.4 to 0.6 kg) but miniatures are available.

Natural Scottish thriftiness and perhaps an element of barbarism is well demonstrated by the success and long history of the haggis. Use of ingredients which alone would not be particularly desirable ensures that very little of the animal is wasted. Plenty of Scotsmen eat haggis once a week, it is served for school lunches and, more prestigiously, features on Taste of Scotland menus. These menus include other Scottish specialities such as smoked salmon, mussels and venison. To obtain copies of *The Taste of Scotland Guide* (produced annually) write to Amanda Clark, 33 Melville Street, Edinburgh EH3 7JF (0131 220 1900).

John Macsween, son of the founder, supplies not only the people of Edinburgh but the English, who he says are large consumers of haggis, and the Americans. (You should check with Customs beforehand if you wish to take haggis out of Britain for regulations relating to meat import into other countries.)

Macsween's sell haggis all the year round up to the 3 or 4 pound (1.3 or 1.8 kg) size and, on receipt of an order the day before, will supply any of the larger sizes. They produce about 270 tons (486,000 kg) of haggis each year, of which 15 percent is a vegetarian version. The company also sell haggis boxed in presentation packs, which show Burns' poem *To a Haggis* and serving instructions.

During the Gulf War a ton of haggis was shipped out to Scottish troops in the desert.

Demand otherwise fluctuates according to the time of year, since haggis is traditionally a winter dish, but it is January when consumption is at its highest. Burns Night, Robert Burns' anniversary, is on January 25 and this is marked by banquets and dinners where it is customary to serve haggis and to drink a glass of neat whisky with it. The haggis is piped in by a highlander in full regalia, and the haggis is slit with a dirk (the dagger worn with highland dress). Apart from Burns Night, other festivals and occasions where haggis is *de rigueur* include Hogmanay on December 31, and St. Andrew's Day on November 30.

Kippers

Kippers were once regarded as food just for the masses, but the tasty smoked herring have long graced the tables of rich and poor alike. Few foods can beat that special breakfast flavour, a fact recognized by the perceptive French who have made a habit of importing kippers from Scot-land to add to their own distinctive cuisine. One important tip—don't boil them in water as so many English people do. Let them cook gently in the oil that emerges when they are heated.

Until 1977 the kipper bought in Edinburgh would be the result of smoking home-caught herring, which has always been considered superior both in size and texture. Since then, only very limited quantities of fresh herring have been available from the Clyde fishery and Edinburgh's remaining two kipper producers have had to rely upon importing frozen herrings from Ireland, Iceland and Canada for fear of decimating Britain's stock.

It has been recorded that herring was smoked in England in 1349, but it was not until the 1890s that Eyemouth on the east coast became a principal centre of Scotland's herring industry. Other important centres included the Clyde in the South Minch, Mallaig and Ullapool in the Minch, Peterhead, Fraserburgh, Aberdeen and North Shields.

Robert Croan & Sons Ltd, one of the last two companies

be passed on racks by one man to another perched high up in the kiln who would hang each one up on hooks. The smoking process took 8 hours and kilns varied in capability from 140 pounds (63.5 kg) of herrings to 14,000 pounds (6350 kg). Today's Torry kiln developed by the Torry Research Station at Aberdeen, takes 1680 pounds (76.2 kg) (420 pounds on each rack) and can perform three cycles a day.

Croans sell all their produce within the United Kingdom, half going to England and the re-

salmon has been netted or rod-caught, rather than farmed, the fins will be properly formed and the flesh will be firm to the touch. The flesh will also be coarser grained than the farmed fish with a richer colour and flavour.

Salmon are netted from the sea around the northwest of Scotland, the Moray Firth areas of the northeast or from the east coast rivers, the Tay and the Tweed. The sale of netted fish is permitted from the last week in January until September 15 or until late October for rod-

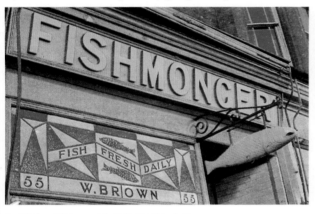

An Edinburgh fishmonger's distinctive shop-front.

Campbell's shop smoke your own salmon.

producing kippers in Edinburgh, started business in 1882 in the Holyrood district and still smoke herrings in the traditional way.

The fish are split and rubbed with salt. When they have been brined, they are placed on racks in a kiln and smoked over a mixture of oak chips and sawdust at 85°F (29.4°C) for about 4 to 5 hours. The temperature has to be strictly maintained because if it is too high the fish will be cooked and if too low the 'kippers' will be wet and soggy. After removal from the kiln, the kippers are left to cool and then boxed.

Before modern electric kilns were available, the fish had to

mainder being sold in Scotland. The company believe that Loch Fyne kippers are the very best, since the fish come from inland lochs where there is a mixture of fresh water and salt which seems to produce a particularly succulent, tasty herring.

Salmon

*S*cotland's smoked salmon is world famous. Although the process of smoking has been refined by chefs from London and Paris, the taste of the product remains unique and distinctive.

Either fresh or smoked, if the

caught fish. The quality of the fish deteriorates at about the end of August, with the body becoming thinner and the head larger.

Farmed fish is heavy bellied with unformed fins, and the flesh will be fine-grained with an oily texture and bland flavour.

Salmon is still smoked by the traditional cold-kiln method, whereby the fish are placed in the kiln at a low temperature for three consecutive 6-hour periods. First, however, the head and tail are removed, the fish is gutted and the backbone removed. The body is split into two and placed in pickle for 12 to 24 hours, depending on its size. The average size for salmon is 8 pounds (3.6 kg) but they may be as large as 35 pounds (16.3 kg).

The pickle varies according to local taste but the traditional Scottish recipe requires demerera sugar and salt and pepper. The mixture is smoothed over the two sides of the fish and within 1 hour they are quite wet, the sugar and salt drawing the liquid. The salmon is left in the mixture overnight and the surplus is then washed off. The fish is removed to the smokehouse to drain and dry so that no surplus moisture remains before it is placed in the kiln. The fire is lit and another lit once it has gone out. The fish is smoked over three consecutive fires, each for a period of 6 hours at very low temperature.

The salmon is left to 'set' after removal from the kiln and, once cool, is sliced by hand. After an initial period of about two months, a fishmonger can slice a 12 pound (5.4 kg) salmon into fine slices in 10 minutes, a 12-pounder (5.4 kg) will yield about 5³/₄ pounds (2.6 kg) of smoked salmon.

Of the many fishmongers in Edinburgh where smoked salmon is available, Robert Croan & Sons Ltd and George Campbell & Sons Ltd, both of West Harbour Road, will smoke your own fresh salmon for you.

Porridge & Oatcakes

Oatmeal, from which both porridge and oatcakes are made, has been a food staple for many hundreds of years, The grain was processed in local mills and dried out in a kiln. The old-fashioned mills provided a variation in the flavour of the meal. which is still appreciated by Scots today. It seems to be a matter of personal taste, however, whether fine, medium or coarse oatmeal is used. Today's processes of mass milling and mechanical drying are said to detract from the flavour of the meal and to reduce the nutritional qualities.

Oatmeal should be closely packed and kept airtight. It was traditionally stored in an oak chest in a dry place. If it is well packed, it may keep for over a year, and it is said to improve in sweetness and digestibility.

Of the many Scottish dishes requiring oatmeal, the best known is probably a fresh herring dusted in coarse oatmeal and served with a piquant mustard sauce and, of course, porridge and oatcakes. The list includes white (or mealie) puddings and black puddings. Oatmeal is a popular ingredient in many recipes from soup to biscuits.

Porridge

Sir Walter Scott (1771-1832) wrote to his son-in-law J. G. Lockhart: 'What meal does Johnnie want for his porridge? I will send it up from Abbotsford. I think it will agree with him better than the southern food of horses.' Scott evidently believed passionately not only in the orgin of the oatmeal but in the importance of local mills.

The sole ingredients of porridge are oatmeal, salt and water. The traditional bowl was made of a local hardwood such as birch. Horn spoons were used, and it was the custom to eat the preparation standing up, General Sir Ian Hamilton in When I Was a Boy wrote that 'the small nursery critics formed their most private opinions of guests a great deal on the porridge ceremonial. The worst and most deplorable giveaway was when the lady or gentleman took sugar.'

Each person should be allowed one cup of water, a handful (about 1¹/₄ ounces or 35 g) of oatmeal and a good pinch of salt. The oatmeal is added to boiling water in a steady rain from one hand, stirring briskly with the other. When the mixture is boiling, it should be taken off the heat, the lid put on and then allowed to simmer for 20 to 30 minutes. The salt is added after about 10 minutes. The porridge is served very hot with cream, milk or buttermilk.

Oatcakes

In the days when oatcakes were served with every meal, each community traditionally had its own mill, grinding oats from the surrounding crofts to supply oatmeal.

Jean Froissart (1337-1404), French chronicler and poet, wrote that the Scottish soldier's equipment included a flat plate at his saddle and a wallet of meal at his back. When he had tired of meat, Froissart reported, the soldier would moisten some meal in water and lay it on the heated plate, and 'hence it is no marvel that the Scots should be able to make longer marches'.

Oatcakes are now eaten as an accompaniment to herrings, sardines, cheeses or with marmalade, honey or jams. The original oatcake was made of oatmeal and water, but it is now customary to add fat or dripping, baking soda and salt as well. Time and patience are required to make the authentic oatcake, but there are a good variety of manufactured oatcakes to choose from.

Shortbread

Shortbread owes its origins to Yule-bread, a thin bannock (circle) of oatmeal baked during Christmas and Hogmanay, and divided into farls (quarters). The ancient

Yule-bannock, from the early days of sun worship, was notched, by pinching with finger and thumb around the edge, to symbolize the sun's rays, just as shortbread is today.

The increasing popularity of white flour eventually ousted the ancient Yule-bannock and led to the development of the familiar rich, crisp shortbread of today.

Shortbread is eaten throughout the year now but it is still associated particularly with Christmas and Hogmanay. It is

Sun symbols in a range of shortbread.

traditionally offered to the 'first-footers'—those who call upon house after house in the early hours of New Year's Day.

You can choose from the several makes of shortbread on the market when you are in Edinburgh or make your own, since it is a quick and easy recipe. Cream 4 ounces (113 g) of butter and 2 ounces (57 g) of caster sugar together and then add a mixture of 4 ounces (113 g) of plain flour and 2 ounces (57 g) of rice flour, sieved. The resulting dough is pressed out by hand and laid on two ungreased sandwich tins. The rounds are cut into quarters or eighths with a knife, notched around the edges, pricked lightly all over and then baked at gas mark 4 (350°F/175°C) for 30 minutes.

Edinburgh Rock

*E*dinburgh rock is said to owe its origins to Alex Ferguson who travelled from Doune in Perthshire to Stirling in 1822 where he tossed a coin to decide whether to set up in Edinburgh or Glasgow. Ferguson started his business in the Bow, a steep twisting street between the Grassmarket and the Lawnmarket beneath Edinburgh Castle.

Sugar, water and colouring is boiled in pans at a temperature of over 300°F (131°C), flavour is added in some cases, and the mixture is then poured onto a metal slab and partially cooled with a fan. It is then folded over, moved to a stone slab (ideally Caithness flagstone), cooled, folded and pulled out.

The pulling-out process is basically one of extrusion whereby the huge, unmanageable, sticky mass is spun on a device of moving arms to inject it with air. The unwieldly skeins are then laid over six horizontal rotating rollers where the mass cools further and changes shape from plump oblong to tubular. The 'tube' is then passed through a half-inch (12.7 mm) space on to a slab where it is rolled by hand. A wooden measure marks off where each cut should be made, the cuts being made by tapping gently with the open blades of a pair of scissors. If it were actually cut through, it would splinter.

The long-established company, Ross, make 'Edinburgh Castle Rock'. Ross's was established in 1880 and now produce their rock in a range of flavours, in ever-increasing quantities, in a variety of gift boxes, prepacks and jars—an ideal souvenir of your holiday in Edinburgh.

Ross's explain that the difference between Edinburgh rock and letter rock (associated with Blackpool and Brighton) rests with the fact that Edinburgh rock is practically 100 percent sugar whereas letter rock is a mixture of sugar and glucose. In both appearance and taste it is completely different from the conventional variety. Edinburgh rock has a soft melting texture.

Scots are notorious for their sweet tooth and Ross's produce a number of other confections which are typically Scottish. Puff candy and tablet are top sellers and you can also buy their pan drops, lettered rock, Clyde toffymints, Berwick cockles, soor plums, butternuts and oddfellows.

A traditional Scottish sweet.

Useful Information

Every effort has been made to ensure accuracy at the time of going to press, but the publishers are not responsible for any consequences that may arise from errors or omissions.

Section I: General

Capital Information Service
Capinfo is the City of Edinburgh Council's free touchscreen information system, available in over 50 sites throughout Edinburgh, ranging from libraries to The Gyle shopping centre. It provides information on such subjects as leisure, environmental services, road closures and doctors. As part of the service in libraries a free telephone and fax service to council departments is also available.

Children
Edinburgh City Council run a 'Child Friendly Edinburgh' campaign among shops, restaurants etc.—look out for the window stickers. *Edinburgh for Under Fives* is a useful book which is updated every two years. Written by parents for parents, it covers such areas as shopping, eating out, toilet stops, activities, places to visit, and playgrounds. Much of the information is relevant to older children. Copies are available from bookshops or by mail order (write first for a leaflet giving the current price):
Edinburgh for Under Fives
PO Box 012345,
Edinburgh EH9 2YB
Or ask in bookshops for *Spook's Edinburgh: a Child's Guide*, written by Judy Paterson and illustrated by Aileen Paterson, which is a book and a map designed to appeal to children.

Embassies and Consulates
See 'Yellow Pages' for a complete list.

American Consulate
3 Regent Terrace
Phone: (0131) 556 8315

Italian Consulate
32 Melville Street
Phone: (0131) 226 3631

French Consulate
11 Randolph Crescent
Phone: (0131) 225 7954

Federal Republic of Germany Consulate
16 Eglinton Crescent
Phone:(0131) 337 2323

Spanish Consulate
63 North Castle Street
Phone: (0131) 220 1843

Disabled
Facilities are improving for the disabled in Edinburgh with an increasing number of lifts, ramps and toilets, but the nature of some of the older buildings means that the provision of these is impossible. A guidebook called *Access in Lothian* is available (free, but postage is charged).
Contact:

Lothian Coalition of Disabled People
8 Lochend Road,
Edinburgh EH6 8BR
Phone: (0131) 555 2151

Gay and Lesbian
Gay Switchboard
PO Box 169,
Edinburgh EH1
Phone:(0131) 556 4049
Every day 19.30-22.00

Lesbian Line
PO Box 169,
Edinburgh EH1
Phone: (0131) 557 0751
Monday, Thursday 19.30-22.00
Pride Scotland is an annual march and festival, held in June, in Glasgow and Edinburgh alternately (Glasgow in 1998). For further information ring Pride Scotland: (0131) 556 8822.
Gay Scotland magazine is a monthly publication which can be bought in some newsagents and in pubs and clubs.

Newsagents
The following newsagents sell foreign newspapers:
Bauermeister's
19 George IV Bridge

International Newsagents
351 High Street

Health
Medical Emergencies
In an emergency find the nearest telephone, dial 999 (no money is required) and ask for an ambulance.
In the event of an accident or acute illness go directly to the nearest hospital with an Accident and Emergency (A & E) Department. The following hospitals have 24-hour casualty services:

The Royal Infirmary of Edinburgh
Lauriston Place
Phone: (0131) 229 2477
A & E—first gate East Drive.

St John's Hospital
Howden Road West,
Livingston, West Lothian
Phone: (01506) 419666
One entrance, A & E marked.

Royal Hospital for Sick Children
Sciennes Road
Phone: (0131) 536 0000
A & E, Argyle Place entrance

Western General Hospital
Crewe Road South
Phone: (0131) 537 1000
Has a Minor Injuries Unit which is open from 9.00-19.00 every day.

All patients receive emergency treatment free of charge

Visiting a Doctor

For less serious problems make an appointment to see a doctor at his surgery. Local police stations have lists of doctors and Health Centres. Information can also be obtained from:

The Health Board

Primary Care Section
Phone: (0131) 537 8450
They can also give you a list of chemists with extended opening hours for emergency medicines. The most centrally situated chemist for this is:

Boots the Chemist

48 Shandwick Place
Phone:(0131) 225 6757
In addition, most hotels will have addresses of doctors.

Lost Property

If you lose a personal possession while in Edinburgh, try ringing one of the city's Lost Property Offices, who may well be able to help.

Police Lost Property Office

Fettes Avenue
Phone: (0131) 311 3141
Open: Monday to Friday, 9.00-17.00

Railway Lost Property

Waverley Station
Phone: (0131) 556 2477
(One telephone number for all rail companies but note they have different Lost Property times—see below.)
Scotrail
Monday to Friday, 19.00-17.00
Great North Eastern Railways (GNER)
7 days a week, 24 hours a day
Railtrack Scotland
Monday to Friday, 7.00-19.30

LRT Lost Property (maroon buses)

1-4 Shrub Place,
Leith Walk

Phone: (0131) 554 4494
Open: Monday to Friday, 10.00-13.30

SMT (green buses)

14-16 Eskbank Road,
Dalkeith
Phone: (0131) 663 1945
Open Monday to Friday 9.00-17.00

Police

In an emergency, find the nearest telephone, dial 999 (no money is required) and ask for the police.
In Scotland, policemen wear black uniforms and flat black caps with a black and white chequered band around the brim. They are based at the following principal Police Stations:

Lothian & Borders Police Headquarters

Fettes Avenue
(opposite Inverleith Park)
Phone: (0131) 311 3131

South Edinburgh

St. Leonard's Police Station,
St. Leonard's Street
Phone: (0131) 662 5000

North Edinburgh

Gayfield Square Police Station,
Gayfield Square
(near top of Leith Walk)
Phone: (0131) 556 9270

West Edinburgh

West End Police Station,
Torphichen Place
(near Haymarket)
Phone: (0131) 229 2323

East Edinburgh

31 Queen Charlotte Street
Phone: (0131) 554 9350

The police have the power to tow away a car if a serious parking offence has been committed. It can be retrieved after payment of a maximum fine of £105.00 (plus payment of any parking tickets). Phone: (0131) 311 3418 and ask for Traffic Link.

Post Offices

Edinburgh's main post offices are listed below, together with the extra services they offer.

40 Frederick Street

Bureau de change, passport services, first day covers, photo booth, phone booth

7 Hope Street

Bureau de change, passport services, first day covers, photo booth

265 Morningside Road

Bureau de change, passport services, photo booth, post shop (philatelic items and stationery)

4 South Clerk Street

Passport services, first day covers

8/10 St James Centre

Bureau de change, passport services, photo booth, philatelic outlet

Religious Services

See Saturday's *Scotsman* for details.

Sightseeing Tours

There are several companies which give guided walking tours, often with a theme. Ring to check times, meeting place and costs.

Auld Alliance Tours

Guided walks through historic Edinburgh. French language tours a speciality. Dutch and German also spoken.
Phone: (0131) 447 3810

Auld Reekie Underground City Tour

This includes a genuine pagan temple and a haunted vault.
Phone: (0131) 557 4700

Mercat Tours

Five day and evening tours: Hidden Underground Vaults, Ghosts and Ghouls, the Ghost Hunter Trail, the Royal Mile

Walk and Mary King's Close Tour.
Phone: (0131) 661 4541

The Original Edinburgh Literary Pub Tour

Three hundred years of Scottish literary history brought to life by professional actors.
Phone (0131) 554 0777

Robin's Tours

Four day and evening tours: Grand Tour, Royal Mile, Ghosts and Witches and Dr Jekyll's Ghosts
Phone: (0131) 661 0125 / 7722
Fax (0131) 661 0125

The Witchery Tours

Two tours: Ghosts and Gore and Murder and Mystery.
Phone: (0131) 225 6745
Fax: (0131) 220 2086
E-mail: lyal@witcherytours.
demon.co.uk

Tourist Information
Information Office, Accommodation Service and Bureau de Change

Waverley Market
Princes Street
Open all year round. May and June: Monday to Saturday, 9.00-19.00, Sunday 10.00-19.00; July and August: Monday to Saturday, 9.00-20.00, Sunday 10.00-20.00; September: Monday to Saturday, 9.00-19.00, Sunday 10.00-19.00; October to April: Monday to Saturday, 9.00-18.00, Sunday 10.00-18.00
Tourist Accommodation Service
Phone: (0131) 557 9655
Tourist Information Service
Phone: (0131) 557 1700

Scottish Tourist Board

Ravelston Terrace
Phone: (0131) 332 2433
For information and guides about Edinburgh and Scotland.

Transport:
Air Travel
Edinburgh Airport

A8, 4 miles west of Edinburgh
Phone: (0131) 333 1000

Rail Travel
Waverley Station

East end of Princes Street
Since privatisation several companies now operate trains in Scotland. Information can be obtained on all services by phoning (0345) 484950. Haymarket, in the west of the city, is Edinburgh's second station. The once defunct suburban line has been revived to a certain extent with stations at Dalmeny, South Gyle, Curriehill, Wester Hailes, Kingsknowe, Slateford, Musselburgh and Wallyford.

Bus Travel

The majority of bus services in and around Edinburgh are provided by two companies, Lothian Region Transport (maroon and white buses) and SMT (green buses). For Lothian Region buses you need the correct fare, no change is given. The Council operates an information service at: 2 Cockburn Street (corner of Market Street). It provides information on all bus services in Edinburgh and the Lothians and further afield, including tour information. A City of Edinburgh bus route map is available and can be sent to you.
Phone: (0131) 225 3858
Monday to Friday, 8.30-16.00 (but phone lines are open until 20.00)

Lothian Region Transport (LRT)

Phone: (0131) 555 6363

SMT

Phone: (0131) 663 9233 / 557 5061

Sightseeing Tours
LRT have two open-topped-bus city tours—Edinburgh

Classic Tour or the Holyrood Park and Arthur's Seat Tour—or you can go further with a Sea, City and Hills Tour (open-top if weather is suitable). All tours leave from Waverley Bridge.
Phone: (0131) 554 4494
Guide Friday run The Edinburgh Tour which leaves from Waverley Bridge. Their office is at Platform 1, Waverley Station.
Phone: (0131) 556 2244

Taxis

Edinburgh city taxis are black. See 'Yellow Pages' for a comprehensive list. Try:
Central Radio Taxis
Phone: (0131) 229 2468

Capital Castle Taxis
Phone: (0131) 228 2555

City Cabs
Phone: (0131) 228 1211

For information on taxis to and from the airport:
Phone: (0131) 344 3153

Car Hire

It is best to book in advance if possible. See 'Yellow Pages' or try:
Alamo Rent a Car
Edinburgh Airport
Phone: (0131) 331 5100

Arnold Clark Hire Drive
Lochrin Place, Tollcross
Phone: (0131) 228 4747

Hertz Rent-a-Car
10 Picardy Place
Phone: (0131) 556 8311
also at airport:
Phone: (0131)333 1019
and at Waverley Station:
Phone: (0131) 557 5272

Cycling

Edinburgh has recently improved its facilities for cyclists. For a city cycle map (also available from book and bike shops), free leaflets and further information contact:

Spokes
St Martin's Church
232 Dairy Road
Phone: (0131) 313 2114

To hire bicycles try:

Bike Trax Cycle Hire
13 Lochrin Place
Phone and fax: (0131) 228 6333/
228 6633
E-mail: biketrax@btinternet.com

Edinburgh Cycle Hire
29 Blackfriars Street
(Off Royal Mile)
Phone and fax: (0131) 556 5560

Recycling
31-33 Iona Street
Phone: (0131) 553 1130

Whistle Stop Cycle Tours
1 Kirkhill Road
Phone: (0131) 667 4936
Bicycles provided. See unspoilt historic landmarks off the beaten track.

Section II: Art Galleries, Historic Buildings, Museums, Stately Homes and Town Houses

This section of the directory gives details of various places of interest in Edinburgh and the surrounding area. The lists are not intended to be complete, but to point out the major sights.

At the time of writing Edinburgh's art galleries and museums are free, with the exception of the Royal Museum of Scotland and some special exhibitions.

Please note that not all the pictures mentioned in the Art Galleries section in the main body of the text are on permanent display.

Art Galleries
City Art Centre
1-4 Market Street
Phone: (0131) 529 3993
Temporary exhibitions, often with a very broad appeal, and Scottish artwork.
Open: June to September: Monday to Saturday, 10.00-18.00; October to May: Monday to Saturday, 10.00-17.00. During the Festival: Sunday, 14,.00-17.00

The Fruitmarket Gallery
29 Market Street
Phone: (0131) 225 2383
A large gallery with a varied exhibition programme, including both Scottish and international artists.
Open: Monday to Saturday, 10.00-18.00; Sunday, 12.00-17.00. During Festival: Monday to Saturday, 10.00-19.00; Sunday, 12.00-19.00.

National Gallery of Modern Art
Belford Road
Phone: (0131) 556 8921 or
(0131) 332 2266
The national collection of 20th-century art includes works by Picasso, Magritte, Hockney and the Scottish Colourists. (For further details see the Art Galleries article in the main body of this book.)
Open: Monday to Saturday, 10.00-17.00: Sunday, 14.00-17.00

The National Gallery of Scotland
2 The Mound
Phone: (0131) 556 8921
This is one of the best of the smaller galleries in Europe. Includes works by Raphael, Titian, El Greco, Rembrandt, Monet and Van Gogh. (For further details, see the Art Galleries article in the main body of this book.)
Open: Monday to Saturday, 10.00-17.00; Sunday, 14.00-17.00

National Portrait Gallery
2 Queen Street
Phone: (0131) 556 8921
(See the Art Galleries section in the main body of this book.)
Open: Monday to Saturday, 10.00-17.00; Sunday, 14.00-17.00. During the Festival: open until 18.00, and from 11.00 on Sundays.

The Netherbow
High Street
Phone: (0131) 586 9579
The Netherbow is incorporated with John Knox House into a cultural and community centre for the Old Town. Exhibitions tend towards work by lesser-known living Scottish artists. See also The Netherbow under Section III, Culture and Entertainment.
Open: Monday to Saturday, 10.00-16.00, plus evening theatre performances. During the Festival: late opening 18.30-22.30

The Printmakers Workshop
23 Union Street
Phone: (0131) 557 2479
The only gallery with continuous exhibitions of contemporary original prints. The work of modern Scottish printmakers is shown alongside those of printmakers from around the world. Prints from the workshop are also on sale.
Open: Tuesday to Saturday, 10.00-18.30

The Royal Scottish Academy
The Mound
Phone: (0131) 225 6671
From March to July the galleries of the Academy house the RSA's own Annual Exhibition for which 500 works are selected from those submitted by members and non-members of the Academy. During the Festival exhibitions of well-known artists are held.

Open: Monday to Saturday, 10.00-21.00 during Annual Exhibitions; Sunday, 14.00-17.00. For other exhibitions check local press.

Stills Gallery

23 Cockburn Street
Phone: (0131) 622 6200
A gallery which hosts national and international exhibitions of photography and related media.
Open: Tuesday to Saturday, 10.00-18.00. During Festival: 10.00-20.00

Talbot Rice Art Centre

Old College, South Bridge
Phone: (0131) 650 2211
The Centre has two main exhibition spaces: one houses the University of Edinburgh's permanent collection, the other being given over to temporary exhibitions of which there are approximately seven a year. The permanent collection includes examples of 17th-century Dutch painting and a number of 16th- and 17th-century bronzes. The major exhibitions are based on an interesting three-point policy of promoting Scottish artists in one-man shows, housing major touring exhibitions, and presenting occasional historical exhibitions (again with a Scottish emphasis).
Open: Tuesday to Saturday, 10.00-17.00.

Historic Buildings
Edinburgh Castle

Castle Hill
Phone: (0131) 225 9846
There has been a fortress on this site since about the 7th century. The oldest part of the present castle is the chapel built by David I and dedicated to Malcolm's queen, Margaret, in the 12th century. The Scottish crown, sceptre and sword are also kept here.
Open: 1 April to 30 September: Monday to Sunday, 9.30-

17.15*; 1 October to 31 March: Monday to Sunday, 9.30-16.15*. *The last ticket is sold at these times. The Castle closes 45 minutes later.

Parliament Hall and Buildings

11 Parliament Square
(See Old Town section of this book for further information.) Overlooking West Parliament Square.
Open Mondays to Fridays, 10.00-16.00. Closed on Public Holidays.

St Giles Cathedral

High Street
Phone: (0131) 225 4363
(See Old Town section of this book for further information.) Check press for service times.
Open April-September: Monday to Saturday, 9.00-19.00, Sunday, 7.30-21.00; October-March: Monday to Saturday, 9.00-17.00, Sunday, 7.30-21.00

Museums

The ancient city of Edinburgh is rich in historical and especially literary associations. The following is a selection of museums which should cater for most tastes, from the teddy-bear fanatic to the bibliophile. Opening times tend to change according to the season, so telephone before making your visit.

Agricultural Museum

Show Ground, Ingliston
Phone: (0131) 333 2674
The collection includes machinery and implements from footspades and flauchters (for peat-cutting) to tattie diggers and tractors.
Open: 10.00-17.00. Free, except during Royal Highland Show time in June.

Bank of Scotland Museum

The Mound
Phone: (0131) 243 5467
The Bank of Scotland was

founded in 1695. Visit the Museum to see coins, bank notes and forgeries.
Open early June-late September: Monday to Friday, 10.00-16.30 (other times by appointment). No admission charge.

Brass Rubbing Centre

Trinity Apse, Chalmer's Close, High Street
Phone: (0131) 556 4364
Children and adults can enjoy making rubbings of various subjects and sizes. A charge is made for each rubbing, materials are provided.
Open: Monday to Saturday, 10.00-17.00; Sunday, 12.00-17.00 during Festival. No admission charge.

The Edinburgh Canal Society's Scottish Wooden Dayboat Collection

The Boathouse,
100 Ashley Terrace
Phone: (0131) 556 4503
Restored dinghies and launches may be seen and rowed on the Union Canal every Sunday. The Society also runs wooden boat repair classes and organises trips to historic waterway sites. Ring for details of these.
Open all year. Sunday, 14.30-18.00. Other times by arrangement. Admission charge.

Huntly House

142 Canongate
Phone: (0131) 529 4143
Huntly House is a good example of a restored 16th-century town house. A number of the rooms have been decorated to show the changing life-style at various periods in the history of the house. The 17th-century room, for example, shows the elegance of a fairly well-off merchant, and the late 19th-century is recreated with a 'working-class kitchen'. There

is a collection of Edinburgh silver and glass dating from the 17th century onwards, Scottish pottery excavated from the Roman fort at Cramond and two rooms displaying relics of the World War I Field Marshal Earl Haig.
Open June to September: Monday to Saturday, 10.00-18.00; rest of the year: Monday to Saturday, 10.00-17.00; during the Festival: Sundays, 14.00-17.00

Mr Purves' Lighting Emporium & Museum
59 St Stephen Street
Phone: (0131) 556 4503
Part of a lighting shop selling lamps and spare parts is dedicated to the exhibition of the proprietor's collection of early domestic, transport and marine lamps from the past.
Open: Saturday, 13.00-18.00
No admission charge.

Museum of Childhood
42 High Street
Phone: (0131) 529 4142
A storehouse of memories of childhood—games, dolls, Hornby trains, clockwork mice, costumes and books. A treat for children and a nostalgic experience for their parents. Includes a few working models such as a nickelodeon. One of the galleries has scenes from the past—a 1930s schoolroom, a nursery and a Victorian street. Different temporary exhibitions throughout the year, e.g. teddies, dolls, Chalet School books.
Open June to September: Monday to Saturday, 10.00-18.00; October to May: Monday to Saturday, 10.00-17.00. During the Festival: Sunday, 14.00-17.00
No admission charge.

Museum of Flight
East Fortune Airfield
North Berwick
Phone: (01620) 880 308

Twenty miles (32 km) east of the city, the Royal Scottish Museum's collection of aircraft includes aero-engines and rockets.
For details of special excursions and open days, phone: *(0131) 225 7534*
Open: April to end September 10.30-17.00

Museum of the Royal College of Surgeons of Edinrugh
18 Nicholson Street
Phone: (0131) 527 1600
A specialist museum with exhibits of surgical, dental, pathological and historical material.
Open: Appointments only

Museum of Scotland
Chambers Street
This will be the first museum to tell the story of Scotland and its people from the time the landscape was formed to the present day. (For further details see the Museum section of this book.)
Open: scheduled to open November 1998

Myreton Motor Museum
Aberlady, East Lothian
Phone: (01875) 870288
Large collection of cars, motor cycles, commercial vehicles and World War Two vehicles. Also period advertising, posters and enamel signs.
Open: every day except Christmas and New Year's Day. 10.00-18.00 in summer, 10.00-17.00 in winter

National Library of Scotland
George IV Bridge
Phone: (0131) 226 4531
This was formerly the Advocates Library, founded in the late 17th century. It obtained the right of copyright deposit in 1710, and as a consequence obtained the best works of continental scholarship. In 1925

the Faculty of Advocates presented their library to the nation. The library has about 4° million printed items, and its collection of Scottish books and manuscripts is unrivalled. There is a map collection, a music collection dating from the early 19th century, the Haxton collection of Bibles, and material relating to the Celtic language, ships and shipping, and labour history as well.
Reading rooms: Monday, Tuesday, Thursday, Friday, 9.30-20.30; Wednesday, 10.00-20.30. Exhibition Room: Monday to Saturday, 9.30-17.00; Festival Sundays, 14.00-17.00.
Science and Map Libraries
(33 Salisbury Place, phone number as above)
Science: Monday, Tuesday, Thursday, Friday, 9.30-17.00; Wednesday, 10.00-18.30. Closed Saturday.
Map: Monday, Tuesday, Thursday, Friday, 9.30-17.00; Wednesday, 10.00-17.30; Saturday, 9.30-13.00

Newhaven Heritage Museum
Pier Place, Newhaven
Phone: (0131) 551 4165
The story of the community of Newhaven is told through reconstructed sets of fishwives and fishermen, displays of objects and photographs and written and spoken accounts.
Open: Monday to Sunday, 12.00-17.00. No admission charge.

New Town Conservation Centre
13a Dundas Street
Phone: (0131) 557 5222
The centre holds a permanent display of the conservation work in progress on the Georgian New Town. There is a conservation reference library and usually an exhibition on some aspect of architecture.
Open: Monday to Friday, 9.00-13.00, 14.00-17.00

North Berwick Museum

School Road, North Berwick, East Lothian
Phone: (01620) 895457
See the old town stocks, stroke a gannet, score an 'eagle' in the golf room, see the holiday resort of North Berwick over the years—and much more.
Open: Monday to Sunday, end March to end October, 11.00-17.00. No admission charge.

The People's Story

Canongate Tolbooth
Phone: (0131) 529 4057
Tells of the lives, work and pastimes of ordinary people in the Scottish capital from the late-18th century to the present day.
Open October to May: Monday to Saturday, 10.00-17.00; June to September: Monday to Saturday, 10.00-18.00; During the Festival: Sundays, 14.00-17.00

Prestongrange Industrial Heritage Museum

Morison's Haven, Prestonpans, East Lothian
Phone: (0131) 653 2904
Tells the story—past and present—of local industries and the lives of the people who worked in them.
Open: Monday to Sunday, end March to end October, 11.00-16.00.
No admission charge.

The Royal Museum of Scotland

Chambers Street
Phone: (0131) 225 7534
Scotland's national museum is housed in an imposing mid-Victorian building and displays range from primitive art to space-age technology. (For further details see the Museums article in the main body of this book.)
Open: Monday to Saturday,

10.00-17.00; Sunday, 14.00-17.00.
Admission charge. Season tickets available which also allow for free or discounted admission to other museums.

St Cecilia's Hall

Cowgate
Phone: (0131) 650 2806
The University of Edinburgh's Russell collection of harpsichords and clavichords is on display in this elegant Georgian hall built by Robert Milne in 1762 as the concert hall for the Edinburgh Music Society. There are 36 keyboard instruments including virginals, regals and spinets. The room also contains period tapestries and textiles, and paintings by Giovanni Pannini and Jacob van Ruysdael.
Open: Wednesday and Saturday, 14.00-17.00. During the Festival: Monday to Saturday, 10.00-12.30. Admission charge.

The Scotch Whisky Heritage Centre

Castlehill, Royal Mile
Phone: (0131) 220 0441
Travel on an electric car and learn the ancient traditions that surround the making of whisky in Scotland.
Open: Monday to Sunday, 10.00-17.30 (extended hours in the summer). Admission charge.

Scottish United Services Museum

Edinburgh Castle
Phone: (0131) 225 7534
A military museum illustrating the history of the armed forces of Scotland. There are displays of uniforms, arms and equipment, decorations, portraits and a library. There is also a comprehensive collection of prints depicting the uniforms on display.
Open 1 April to 30 September: Monday to Sunday, 9.30-17.15*; 1 October to 31 March:

Monday to Sunday, 9.30-16.15*.
* The last ticket is sold at these times. The Castle closes 45 minutes later.

Scottish Mining Museum

Lady Victoria Colliery Newtongrange, Midlothian
Phone: (0131) 663 7519
A tour of the coalfield brings to life the sights, sounds and smells of the colliery and pit village. See also the largest steam engine in Scotland—the Grant-Ritchie winding engine—in action.
Open 1 March to 31 October: 10.00-16.00. Admission charge

Scottish Reformation Society

41 Cowgate
Phone: (0131) 220 1450
This is the mid-16th century Magdalen chapel which has wonderful stained glass windows. (See the Old Town section of this book for further details.)
Open: Monday to Friday 9.30-16.30. No admission charge.

Scottish Tartans Museum

The Scotch House
39/41 Princes Street
Seven hundred tartans on display plus kilts, paintings and books.
Open: Monday to Saturday 9.00-17.30. Thursday 9.00-18.00. Last admission 30 minutes before closing. Admission charge.

The Writers' Museum, Lady Stair's House

Lady Stair's Close, Lawnmarket
Phone: (0131) 529 4901
This solid 17th-century town house contains relics of Robert Burns, Sir Walter Scott and Robert Louis Stevenson. These include the original manuscript of Burns's *Scots Wha ha'e*, locks of hair,

knives, quill pens, snuff boxes and umbrellas. The most interesting exhibits are the portraits, including one of Stevenson by Girolamo Nerli.
Open June to September: Monday to Saturday, 10.00-18.00; rest of the year, 10.00-17.00; during Festival: Sundays, 14.00-17.00

Stately Homes and Town Houses

Edinburgh's status as the capital city of Scotland and seat of the Scottish monarch and court accounts for the numerous grand mansions and stately homes in the surrounding area. This section lists those which are well worth a visit, along with a selection of town houses which are of architectural or historical interest. It is wise to telephone before setting out as opening times are variable.

Abbotsford

Melrose
Phone: (01896) 752043
Once a small farmhouse on the banks of the Tweed, Sir Walter Scott's home is now a museum to one of Scotland's favourite writers. The interior has been kept much as it was, and features, as well as paintings by Raeburn and Landseer, Scott's writing materials, his books and relics of Scottish history.
Open third Monday in March to end October: Monday to Saturday, 10.00-17.00. Sundays, June, July, August, September:10.00-17.00; March, April, May, October: 14.00-17.00

Bowhill

Selkirk
Phone: (01780) 22204
Bowhill is the border home of the Duke of Buccleuch and Queensberry. The house contains the Duke's famous art collection, which includes some Elizabethan miniature paintings. There are also

nature trails, a gift shop and tea room.
Open (Country Park) 30 April to 31 August: every day 12.00-17.00. House open (July only) every day 13.00-16.30, or by appointment.
Admission charge.

Craigmillar Castle

2m SE of Edinburgh off the A68
Phone: (0131) 661 4445
Mary Queen of Scots fled here after the murder of Rizzio. The castle was featured in the BBC production of *Ivanhoe*.
Open all year (except Thursday afternoons and Fridays in the winter).

Dalmeny House

South Queensferry
Phone: (0131) 331 1888
Only seven miles (11 km) from Edinburgh, Dalmeny House is situated on the shores of the Firth of Forth, with walks through parks and woodland. It contains two fine collections: the Rosebery art collection gathered by the 3rd, 4th and 5th Earls, and the Mentmore collection of fabulous 18th-century furniture, tapestries, porcelain and paintings.
Open 1 July to end August: Sunday, 13.00-16.45; Monday and Tuesday, 12.00-16.45

Floors Castle

Kelso
Phone: (01573) 23333
Home of the Duke of Roxburghe, and the site of the murder of James II of Scotland in 1460. William Adam helped to build this fine example of 18th-century architecture. The castle contains some porcelain, superb French and English furniture and paintings, and even some Gobelin tapestry. The collection of Battersea enamelled boxes is particularly worth seeing. There is also a walled garden, garden centre, gift shop and tea room.
Open: Monday to Sunday, Easter to end September:

10.00-16.30 (last admission 16.00); October: Sunday and Wednesday only, 10.00-14.30 (last admission 15.30). Admission charge. Garden centre and coffee shop open daily throughout the year 9.00-17.00

The Georgian House

7 Charlotte Square
Phone: (0131) 225 2160
The National Trust for Scotland has restored this magnificent piece of Georgian architecture in amazingly authentic detail. There are furnishings in the style of Chippendale, Sheraton and Hepplewhite, porcelain by Derby and Wedgwood, and paintings and engravings by Morland, Ramsay and Nasmyth. (For further details see the New Town article in the main body of this book.)
Open April to October: Monday to Saturday, 10.00-17.00; Sunday, 14.00-17.00
Last admissions 30 minutes before closing time.

Gladstone's Land

Lawnmarket
Phone: (0131) 226 5856
Situated on the Royal Mile, this 17th-century house provides a contrast with the Georgian House in the New Town. Built by Thomas Gledstanes in 1620, the house was originally intended as a tenement with a separate flat on each floor. As it is now, it gives a valuable glimpse of living conditions in a medieval city.
Open April to October: Monday to Saturday 10.00-17.00; Sunday 14.00-17.00. Closed for winter.

Palace of Holyroodhouse

Royal Mile
Phone: (0131) 556 1096
Once a guest house, Holyroodhouse was turned into a royal palace by James IV in 1488. It is now the official residence of the Queen in the city. (For further details see the Palace of Holyroodhouse article in the main body of this book.)

Open all year apart from when the Queen is in residence (a week in July), ten days in October and some public holidays (ring to check if you want to visit at these times). Monday to Sunday, 9.30-18.00. Gardens until 18.30. Last tickets sold at 17.15. No guided tours in summer. Admission charge.

Hopetoun House

South Queensferry
Phone: (0131) 331 2451
The magnificent home of the Marquis of Linlithgow, originally designed by Sir William Bruce, but completed by William Adam and his sons, Robert and John, the latter two being principally responsible for the interior decoration. The surrounding 100 acres (40.4 ha.) contain deer, peacocks, St Kilda sheep, a nature trail and picnic areas.
Open from Easter to third Monday in September: daily 10.00-17.30. Last admission 16.30. Admission charge.

John Knox House

45 High Street
Phone: (0131) 556 9579/2647
John Knox, the leader of the Protestant Reformation in Scotland, is said to have lived here in one of the most ancient dwelling houses in the city. On display are a number of pictures and lithographs of Knox, usually in the act of pulpit-thumping. There are also letters, documents and early editions of his tracts and sermons, including the famous pamphlet *The First Blast of the Trumpet against the Monstrous Regiment of Women*.
Open: Monday to Saturday 10.00-16.30.

Lauriston Castle

Cramond Road South
Phone: (0131) 336 2060
A fine mansion with beautiful grounds overlooking the Firth of Forth, this was once the home of William Robert Reid, a

cabinet-maker and collector of objets d'art. A late 16th-century tower house has been incorporated in a Jacobean-style house built in the early 19th century. Decorated by Reid in the early years of this century, it presents a prosperous Edwardian interior with mostly 18th-century English and European furniture, including a set of Chippendale dining chairs. Among the objets d'art are Reid's collection of ornaments in Derbyshire fluorspar, wool mosaic pictures, and tapestries.
Open April to October: every day except Friday. Tours 11.20, 12.20, 14.20, 15.20 and 16.20; November to March: Saturday and Sunday only. Tours 14.20, 15.20. Admission charge.

Manderston

Duns,
Berwickshire
Phone: (01361) 883450
A fine Edwardian country house surrounded by formal gardens and woodland park. As well as period furnishings in luxurious surroundings there is a marble dairy, stables and a lake. Gift shop and cream teas available.
Open mid-May to mid-September: Thursday and Sunday, 14.00-17.30. Admission charge.

Mellerstain House

Gordon,
Berwickshire
Phone: (01573) 410 225
One of the most beautiful Georgian houses in Scotland, designed and built by William and Robert Adam. The interior is decorated with their fine plasterwork and pastel colours. There are paintings by Old Masters (Gainsborough, Van Dyck, Ramsay and Raeburn), an outstanding collection of 18th-century furniture, and a library with its original decoration. Other attractions include the terraced gardens,

lake, gift shop and tea rooms.
Open: Easter weekend, May to September, Monday to Sunday, (except Saturdays), 12.30-17.00. Admission charge.

Traquair House

Innerleithen,
Peeblesshire
Phone: (01896) 830 323
Twenty-eight miles (45 km) south of the city, Traquair is the oldest inhabited house in Scotland, dating back to *circa* AD950. The Stuart family has lived there since 1491 and entertained many tragic figures including Mary, Queen of Scots and Bonnie Prince Charlie. There is a working brewery, craft workshops, a nature trail and a chapel.
Open daily from 29 March to 30 September. Fridays and Sundays in October. House 12.30-17.30 except in June, July and August, 10.30-17.30. Last admission 17.00. Grounds open daily 10.30-17.30 from Easter until end of September; October: Fridays and Sundays, 14.00-17.00

Other Places of Interest
Butterfly and Insect World

Dobbie's Garden Centre on A7 just outside Dalkeith
Phone: (0131) 663 4932
Europe's largest butterfly farm. Large heated greenhouse in landscape of tropical plants with waterfalls and pools which contain fish and terrapins.
Open every day. Opening times vary with the changing of the clocks. Late March to late October: 10.00-17.30; rest of the year: 10.00-17.00.

The Camera Obscura and Outlook Tower

Castle Hill
Phone: (0131) 226 379
Installed in the 1850s in the Outlook Tower on Castle Hill, the camera obscura throws a

clear image of Edinburgh onto a white, concave table top. Other floors have exhibitions of holography, pin-hole photography and space photography.
Open April to September: Monday to Saturday, 9.30-17.30; Sunday, 10.00-18.00; October to March: Monday to Saturday, 9.30-16.00; Sunday, 10.00-16.00. Admission charge.

Deep-Sea World
North Queensferry
Phone: (01383) 411411
Europe's largest collection of sand tiger sharks and an Amazonian riverbank with piranhas are just two of the attractions in the world's largest underwater safari. Phone to ask for details of special bus service from Waverley Bridge. Admission charge.

Edinburgh Crystal Visitor Centre
Penicuik
Phone: (01968) 675128
Guided factory tour showing glassblowing, cutting and engraving. Exhibition, factory shop, gift shop and tea room. Free minibus from Waverley Bridge (outside Shenanigans Cafe Bar) every hour from 10.00, April to September.
Open: Monday to Saturday, 9.00-17.00; Sunday, 11.00-17.00. Tours all year, Monday to Friday, 9.00-15.30, plus Saturday and Sunday, April to September, 11.00-14.30. Admission charge.

Edinburgh Old Town Weaving Co.
Castlehill, Royal Mile
Phone: (0131) 226 1555
Fax: (0131) 556 0615
A real working mill on the site of the old Castlehill reservoir where you can see the production of tartan cloth 'from sheep to shop', a water wheel working an old loom, and try your hand at weaving.

There is a Clan & Tartan Information Bureau, a shop and a restaurant. At night a Scottish entertainment, 'Prince Charlie's Extravaganza', is held.

Edinburgh Zoological Park
134 Corstorphine Road
Phone: (0131) 334 9171
Dogs are not admitted. You will need at least half a day to see around the 80 acres (32 ha.) of woodland and parkland at the Scottish National Zoological Park, Edinburgh. (For further details see the Edinburgh Zoological Park article in the main body of this book.)
Open: every day of the year. Monday to Saturday, 9.00-18.00 or dusk; Sunday, 9.30-18.00 or dusk. Admission charge.

Royal Botanic Garden
Inverleith Row
Phone: (0131) 552 7171
Established as a Physic Garden in 1670. Invalid chairs are available. Dogs not admitted. (For further details see the Royal Botanic Garden article in the main body of this book.)
Open 7 days all year except 1 January and 25 December. May to August:10.00-20.00; September and October: 10.00-18.00; November to February: 10.00-16.00; April and May: 10.00-18.00. Contact the Regius Keeper for access to the Herbarium and Library. No admission charge, but donations welcome, especially for the Glasshouse Experience.

Gorgie City Farm
51 Gorgie Road
Phone: (0131) 337 4202
Child-friendly farm in the city. Organised tours and workshops.
Open: Monday to Sunday, 9.30-16.30 (16.00 in winter). No admission charge.

Section III: Culture and Entertainment

Edinburgh's Festivals
The Edinburgh International Festival is held for three weeks in August/September. (For further details, see the Edinburgh's Festivals article in the main body of this book.)

Edinburgh Book Festival
(First two weeks of International Festival)
Scottish Book Centre
137 Dundee Street
Phone: (0131) 228 5444
Fax: (0131) 228 4333
E-mail: admin@edbookfest.co.uk

Edinburgh International Film Festival
(First two weeks of International Festival)
The Filmhouse,
88 Lothian Road
Phone: (0131) 228 4051
Fax:(0131) 229 5501
E-mail: info@edfilmfest.org.uk

Edinburgh International Festival Society
21 Market Street
Phone: (0131) 473 2001
Box office: (0131) 473 2000
Text phone (for people with hearing difficulties): (0131) 473 298
Box office fax:(0131) 473 2003
E-mail: eif@ed.ac.uk
The office is open for information Monday to Friday, 9.30-17.30 throughout the year. Details about the Festival are available from April onwards. Box office times are as follows: 5 May to 27 June: Monday to Friday, 10.00-16.30; 28 June to 19 July: Monday to Friday, 10.00-16.30, Saturday 12 noon-15.00; 20 July to 1 August: Monday to Friday, 10.00-18.00, Saturday, 12 noon-15.00; 2-30 August: Monday to Saturday,

9.00-19.00, Sunday 10.00-17.00

Edinburgh Fringe Festival Society

180 High Street
Phone: (0131) 226 5287/5259
Fax: (0131) 220 4205
E-mail: admin@edfringe.com
Open: Monday to Friday, 10.00-18.00 throughout the year. August, 7 days 10.00-19.00.
Programme available from mid-June each year. To obtain by post, send 3 first-class stamps (programme quite bulky)

Edinburgh's Hogmanay

This is organised by Unique Events Ltd.
Phone: (0131) 557 3990
Fax: (0131) 557 8566

Edinburgh Military Tattoo

22 Market Street
Phone: (0131) 225 1188
Fax: (0131) 225 8627
Web site: www.edintattoo.co.uk/
Open: Monday to Friday, 10.00-16.30, Saturday, 10.00-12.30.
On performance days the sales office remains open until the start of the performance. Postal bookings accepted from January, counter sales from end of June.

Scottish International Children's Festival

Held in Inverleith Park in May. Write to:
Scottish International Children's Festival, 22 Laurie Street, Edinburgh EH6 7AB

Concert Halls and Theatres

The visitor to Edinburgh can normally rely on finding an opera, concert, ballet or play that is to his or her taste. During the hectic August weeks of the Edinburgh Festival the range of choices is overwhelming, but throughout the year there is an ever-changing cultural programme on offer at the concert halls and theatres listed below. Contact individual box offices at the venues; check the advertisements in the *Scotsman, Evening News* and *The List* or ask at your hotel for details of the current pro-gramme.

Assembly Rooms

54 George Street
Phone: (0131) 220 4348

Bedlam Theatre

2 Forrest Road
Phone: (0131) 225 9873

Brunton Theatre

High Street, Musselburgh
Phone: (0131) 665 2240

Churchill Theatre

33a Morningside Road
Phone (0131) 447 7597

Edinburgh Festival Theatre

13-29 Nicolson Street
Phone: (0131) 529 6000 or (0131) 662 1112

French Institute

13 Randolph Crescent
Phone: (0131) 225 5366

George Square Theatre

South side of George Square
Phone: (0131) 667 1971 ext. 2006

King's Theatre

Leven Street, Tollcross
Phone: (0131) 229 1201

Nelson Hall

2-8 McDonald Road
Phone: (0131) 529 5636

The Netherbow

John Knox House, High Street
Phone: (0131) 556 0179

Playhouse Theatre

20 Greenside Place
Phone: (0131) 557 2590

The Pleasance Theatre Festival

60 the Pleasance
Phone: (0131) 556 6550 or (0131) 5561513

Queen's Hall

89 Clerk Street
Phone (0131) 668 2019

Reid Concert Hall

McEwan Hall
Teviot Row, off Teviot Place
Phone: (0131) 650 2423

Royal Lyceum Theatre

off Lothian Road next to Usher Hall, Grindlay Street
Phone: (0131) 229 9697.

St Cecilia's Hall

Cowgate
Phone: (0131) 650 2423

St Mary's Episcopal Church

Palmerston Place
Phone (0131) 225 6293
Events: The cathedral choir gives concerts throughout the year, as do visiting choirs.

Theatre Workshop

34 Hamilton Place
Phone: (0131) 226 5425

Traverse Theatre

10 Cambridge Street
Phone: (0131) 228 1404

Usher Hall

Lothian Road
Phone: (0131) 228 1155

Miscellaneous
Royal Highland Show

Royal Highland Show Ground Ingliston (7 miles/1 km from city centre on main road to Glasgow)
Phone: (0131) 333 2444
Agricultural Show takes place in June each year

Scottish Evenings

These entertainments, which usually include dinner and a 'Scots Cabaret', are designed for those visitors to Edinburgh who do not have friends or relations in the city to show them a more authentic Scottish night out. They represent the popular image of a Scottish evening rather than the actuality—nevertheless, many find them thoroughly enjoyable. It is necessary to book well ahead.

Hail Caledonia Scottish Evening

Carlton Highland Hotel,
North Bridge
Phone: (0131) 556 7277
May to September, 7pm

Jamie's Scottish Evening

King James Thistle Hotel,
107 Leith Street
Phone: (0131) 556 0111
End April to end October, 7pm

Prince Charlie's Extravaganza

Edinburgh Old Town Weaving Co.,
Castlehill, Royal Mile
Phone: (0131) 226 1555
Fax: (0131) 556 0615

Scottish Evening

George Hotel,
19-21 George Street
Phone: (0131) 225 1251
Every evening except Tuesday and Saturday, 7pm

A Taste of Scotland

Round Stables, Prestonfield
House, Priestfield Road
Phone: (0131) 668 3346
April to October, Sunday to Friday, 7pm

Section IV: Sport and Leisure

Look under Sports Clubs in 'Yellow Pages' for a complete listing.

Athletics
Meadowbank Stadium

London Road
Phone: (0131) 661 5351

Football

Edinburgh's two leading

football teams are:

Heart of Midlothian (Hearts)

Tynecastle Park, Gorgie Road
Phone: (0131) 337 6132

Hibernian (Hibs)

Easter Road Park
Phone: (0131) 661 2159

Golf

Most of Edinburgh's private golf clubs welcome visitors. Look in 'Yellow Pages' and ring first to check.
The municipal courses below are generally open every day except Christmas Day.

Braid Hills

Braid Hills Road
Phone: (0131) 447 6666

Carrick Knowe

Balgreen Road
Phone: (0131) 337 196

Craigentinny

Craigentinny Avenue
Phone: (0131) 554 7501

Portobello

Stanley Street
Phone: (0131) 669 4361

Silverknowes

Silverknowes Parkway
Phone: (0131) 336 3843

Rugby Internationals

Murrayfield Stadium.
Phone: (0131) 337 8993

Sport and Leisure Centres

Ring to check on facilities and opening times.

Ainslie Park Leisure Centre

92 Pilton Drive
Phone: (0131) 551 2400

Bonnyrigg Leisure Centre

King George IV Park
Phone: (0131) 663 7579

Craiglockhart Sports Centre

177 Colinton Road
Phone: (0131) 443 0101

Forecourt Leisure

Ashley Place,
Newhaven Road
Phone: (0131) 555 4533

Jack Kane Sports Centre

208 Niddrie Mains Road
Phone: (0131) 669 0404

Marco's Leisure Centre

51-95 Grove Street
Phone: (0131) 228 3141

Meadowbank Sports Centre

London Road
Phone: (0131) 661 5351

Swimming
Ainslie Park

92 Pilton Drive
Phone: (0131) 551 2400

Leith Waterworld

377 Easter Road
Phone: (0131) 555 6000

Royal Commonwealth Pool

Dalkeith Road
Phone: (0131) 667 7211

Warrender Swim Centre

Thirlstane Road
Phone: (0131) 447 0052

Winter Sports

Hillend, Biggar Road
Phone: (0131) 445 4433
Largest artificial ski slope in Europe.

Murrayfield Ice Rink and Indoor Arena

Riversdale Crescent
Phone: (0131) 337 6933